MARKET IMPERFECTIONS AND MACROECONOMIC DYNAMICS

MARKET IMPERFECTIONS AND MACROECONOMIC DYNAMICS

edited by

Jean-Olivier Hairault ***and*** **Hubert Kempf**
The University of Paris

Kluwer Academic Publishers
Boston/Dordrecht/London

Distributors for North, Central and South America:
Kluwer Academic Publishers
101 Philip Drive
Assinippi Park
Norwell, Massachusetts 02061 USA
Telephone (781) 871-6600
Fax (781) 871-6528
E-Mail <kluwer@wkap.com>

Distributors for all other countries:
Kluwer Academic Publishers Group
Post Office Box 322
3300 AH Dordrecht, THE NETHERLANDS
Telephone 31 786 576 000
Fax 31 786 576 254
E-mail <services@wkap.nl>

Electronic Services <http://www.wkap.nl>

Library of Congress Cataloging-in-Publication Data
Market imperfections and macroeconomic dynamics / edited by Jean-Olivier Hairault and Hubert Kempf.
p.cm.
Includes bibliographical references.
ISBN 0-7923-7404-5
1. Macroeconomics. 2. Statics and dynamics (Social sciences) 3. Economic development. 4. Monetary policy. I. Hairault, Jean-Olivier. II. Kempf, Hubert, agrégé de science économique.

HB172.5.M3636 2002
339--dc21 2002016017

Printed on acid-free paper.

Printed in the United States of America

Contents

Bruno Amable, Stéphane Auray, Jean-Paul Barinci, Arnaud Chéron, Fabrice Collard, Patrick Fève, Paul De Grauwe, Michael Gail, Donatella Gatti, Burkhard Heer, INGENUE Team, Aude Pommeret, Laurence Rioux, Andreas Schabert, Frauke Skudelny, Thierry Verdier

Part I Globalization, Competition and Macroeconomic Performances

Chapter 1: Is Perfection Optimal? Employment and Product Market Competition. 3
Bruno Amable, Donatella Gatti
1 Introduction 3
2 The model 6
3 Macroeconomic equilibrium 12
4 Labor market performance with less imperfect product markets 15
5 Conclusion 19

Chapter 2: Human Capital, Local Labor Markets and Regional Integration. 23
Laurence Rioux, Thierry Verdier
1 Introduction 23
2 The model 26
3 Integration between two identical regions 31
4 Integration between two asymmetric regions 39
5 Conclusion 44
Appendix 46

Chapter 3: A Long–Term Model for the World Economy. 51
INGENUE Team
1 Introduction 51
2 A computable, general-equilibrium, multi-regional overlapping generations model 53
3 Programming and calibration 57
4 Baseline scenario: a projection of the world economy for the 21st century 60
5 Catching-up and world capital flows: technological scenarios 66
6 Public pension reforms: some institutional scenarios 67
7 Concluding remarks 68
Appendix 71

Part II Money, Inflation and Macrodynamics

Chapter 4: Inflation and Productivity Differentials in EMU. 77
Paul De Grauwe, Frauke Skudelny
1 Introduction 77
2 Theoretical foundation of the productivity hypothesis 79
3 Previous empirical studies 82
4 Empirical analysis 87
5 Concluding remarks 97
Appendix 101

Chapter 5: Open Market Shocks in a Business Cycle Model with Financial Intermediation. 105
Burkhard Heer, Andreas Schabert
1 Introduction 105
2 The model 108
3 Propagation of monetary policy shocks 113
4 Conclusion 124
Appendix 125

Chapter 6: Optimal Monetary Policy with Sticky Prices. 131
Michael Gail
1 Introduction 131
2 The model 133
3 The policy problem 141
4 Optimal monetary policy 145
5 Conclusion 151
Appendix 152

Part III Indeterminacy and Irreversibility

Chapter 7: Real Indeterminacy in a Cash–In–Advance Economy. 163
Stéphane Auray, Fabrice Collard, Patrick Fève
1 Introduction 163
2 A simple monetary economy 165
3 Four tales for real indeterminacy 167
4 Quantitative implications of real indeterminacy 171
5 Concluding remarks 175
Appendix 176

Chapter 8: Borrowing Constraint and Indeterminacy. 179
Jean-Paul Barinci, Arnaud Chéron
1 Introduction 179
2 The model 181
3 Empirical plausibility of indeterminacy 184
4 Sunspots and the business cycle 187
5 Conclusion 189

Chapter 9: Irreversible Investment Under Uncertainty. 191
Aude Pommeret
1 Introduction 191
2 Presentation of the model 193
3 Value of the program when there is no investment 195
4 Determination of the optimal capital stock 197
5 The effect of uncertainty on the optimal capital stock 202
6 Illustration of the economy evolution 206
7 Conclusion 206
Appendix 209

Contributing authors

Bruno Amable
Université de Lille II & CEPREMAP, France

Stéphane Auray
LEN–C3E, Université de Nantes & GREMAQ, Université de Toulouse I, France

Jean-Paul Barinci
EPEE, Université d'Evry - Val d'Essonne & EUREQua, Université de Paris I, France

Arnaud Chéron
GAINS, Université du Maine & EUREQua, Université de Paris I, France

Fabrice Collard
GREMAQ, Université de Toulouse I & CNRS, France

Patrick Fève
GREMAQ, Université de Toulouse I & IDEI, France

Paul De Grauwe
Centre of Economic Studies, University of Leuven, Belgium & CEPR

Michael Gail
Universität Siegen, Germany

Donatella Gatti
Wissenschaftszentrum für Sozialforschung Berlin (WZB), Germany

Burkhard Heer
Department of Public Economics, University of Innsbruck, Austria & CESifo, Germany

INGENUE Team
Michel Aglietta, Rabah Arezki, Regis Breton, Jean Chateau, Jacky Fayolle, Michel Juillard, Cyrille Lacu, Jacques Le Cacheux, Bronka Rzepkowski and Vincent Touzé
CEPII, CEPREMAP, MINI-FORUM, OFCE, TEAM, Université de Paris I, Université de Paris X, France

Aude Pommeret
IRES, Université Catholique de Louvain, Belgium & EUREQua, Université de Paris I, France

Laurence Rioux
INSEE & CREST, France

Andreas Schabert
Department of Economics, University of Cologne, Germany

Frauke Skudelny
Centre of Economic Studies, University of Leuven, Belgium

Thierry Verdier
DELTA, France & CEPR

Foreword

Macroeconomic theory has enlarged both its scope and spectrum of tools in the last two decades. After the rather controversial tones of the seventies and early eighties, a more quiet stance has been adopted. The New Classical Macroeconomics did not only generate hotly disputed claims on monetary policy and the sources of business cycles, it also introduced a more rigorous perspective on macroeconomics. Nobody nowadays argues against the need of firmer microeconomic foundations for macroeconomic reasoning; the techniques used by macroeconomists, both in theory and in empirical works, are more and more complex, refined and potent. Macroeconomists borrow heavily from optimisation theory, game theory, time series or panel data developments, information theory. The refinement of techniques necessary to back any claim made by macroeconomists in turn has led macroeconomists to be more cautious about the extent of validity of their claim, if not more humble. This is not to say that a broad consensus has emerged, shared by almost all macroeconomists. Even though a new Neo-classical Synthesis is said to have appeared in recent years, still many discussions and disputes are currently developing. Macroeconomics remains as rich in debates as ever, on the sources of growth or dynamics, on the workings of markets, on the role of governments. But this combines with evident progress in the tools used to develop a point. This maturing of macroeconomics is beyond doubt a good news.

The present volume is a clear testimony of this trend toward the alliance of rigour and ideas which is taking place in macroeconomics. It is formed of a selection of contributions presented at the 5th *Theory and Methods in Macroeconomics* (T2M) Meeting which took place in Nanterre, near Paris, hosted by the University of Paris – Nanterre in May 2000. Some 130 contributions were presented during the meeting. The annual T2M Meeting, partly funded by France's Centre National de la Recherche Scientifique, aims to be a convening place for macroeconomists from all over the world. It offers a place where recent advances in macroeconomics may be exposed and discussed among specialists. The present volume both exemplifies what was presented at the 2000 meeting and the desire of the organizers of T2M meetings to significantly contribute to the development of the discipline.

The nine contributions selected for this volume have been organised in three parts. The first part is on "Globalisation, competition and macroeconomic performances". It is hardly necessary to stress the current importance for macroeconomics of the opening of world markets and the ever increasing competition that this entails. Throughout the world this phenomenon is taking place, shattering the structures of economies and altering the behaviour of millions of individuals. Hence an understanding of the functioning of markets, in conjunction with the ever-mounting integration, remains a primary objective for macroeconomists. Amable and Gatti, in the opening contribution, focus on the interaction between the labour and the good markets, when both are characterized by imperfect competition. It is customary to consider that an increase in competition should lead to a reduction in employment fluctuations: in more competitive markets, as the price mechanism should play a higher role in answering to shocks, the role played by quantity adjustments, and in particular by employment in the labour market, should decrease. They prove that statement to be wrong, by setting up a model of imperfect competition à la Cournot on the good market with an efficiency wage mechanism at work on the labour market. The critical element in their paper is the endogenization of the separation rate on the labour market. It happens that the separation rate is then increasing in the degree of competition on the good market. This generates an adverse effect on workers' incentives and may lead to a higher response of unemployment to an external shock. On the whole, an increase in the degree of competition on the good market may lead to a higher variability in (un)employment.

Tax competition is a major concern when economies and societies dismantle previously erected barriers A well-known result is that tax competition among governmental entities generates a "race to bottom", leading to zero tax rates in the case of full factor mobility. The second contribution by Rioux and Verdier deals with this proposition. The authors ask under which conditions a "race to top" can take place. They single out the other side of the picture, that is the public good financed through taxes: the provision of public goods may have a counter-effect to tax competition and even reverts the outcome of the opening of societies. In the present contribution, Rioux and Verdier concentrate on education and the formation of human capital and distinguish between "general" human capital, that is a capital that may be used independently of the worker's initial location, and "specific" human capital which can be mobilized only where it is formed. General human capital has then two effects: a direct "productivity effect" and a "flexibility effect", as it encourages labour mobility by reducing the cost of acquiring new specific human capital. These two effects work in opposition and may result in either "race to bottom" or "race to top" tax competition.

The contribution by the INGENUE team (consisting of 10 researchers from various French institutions) summarises the first results obtained from an ambitious project, namely the setting-up of a general equilibrium model covering the world economy. Based on a complex overlapping generations structure and taking into account the structural differences between the various "regions" which compose the world economy, this model aims to investigate the dynamic effects of these differences, under different sets of assumptions with respect to individual behaviours and the functioning of markets. In the present contribution, the INGENUE team concentrates on the interplay between demographic differences, pay-as-you-go pension systems and international capital flows over a future period extending to 2050. Various scenarios are explored which together prove the importance of the opening of capital markets for the financing of regional borrowing needs. This provides a clear illustration of the importance of globalisation nowadays.

The second part of the volume focuses on monetary matters and consists in three contributions. The first contribution by de Grauwe and Skudelny deals with the Balassa-Samuelson effect, which may play a crucial role in explaining inflation differentials among countries belonging to the Euro zone. The presence or not of such an effect is obviously a major concern with respect to monetary policy in the EMU. This explains why it recently drew attention from many researchers and policy-makers. In their contribution, de Grauwe and Skudelny innovate on several accounts: they use data on prices of traded and non-traded goods, they reason on bilateral equations involving two European countries and not multilateral equations, and finally they use panel data techniques. They conclude that it is necessary to distinguish between the traded goods sector and non-traded goods sector: the traded goods productivity differentials do not have a significant impact on inflation, but this reverts when non-traded goods productivity differentials are considered.

A number of important recent contributions have attempted to adapt the RBC methodology, that is the development and use for simulation purposes of dynamic stochastic general equilibrium models, to New Keynesian features such as imperfect competition and sticky prices. Heer and Schabert in their contribution aim at understanding the role of monetary policy when financial intermediation is taken into account. They innovate in their proposed measure of monetary policy instrument. Instead of using money supply innovations as is customary, they consider that the monetary policy-makers control the ratio of short-run public bonds to commercial banks' reserves, as monetary policy works through open-market operations. Developing a dynamic general equilibrium with sticky prices and assuming money enters the individual utility function, they prove that this model generates impulse responses to monetary innovations consistent with empirical evidence. In particular, real and nominal interest rates increase in response to monetary tightening, whereas output and factor prices decline. Even though the analysis of contemporaneous correlations entails mixed results, the proposed measure for monetary policy proves to be a promising alternative to traditional measures.

Beyond the analysis of the positive effects of macroeconomic policy, recent developments studied its normative dimension. Heavily borrowing from public finance theory and the distorsive effects of taxation, this approach aims at defining the optimal macroeconomic policy. Gail contributes to this literature by looking at monetary policy in such an extended general equilibrium model and incorporating a more general utility function than the one recently used by King and Wolman. He assumes the standard CRRA utility function, which generates substitution effects between labour and consumption, contrary to what is assumed in King and Wolman's formulation. Considering then that the goal of monetary policy is price stabilisation, Gail proves that the monetary policy-maker cannot achieve complete price stabilisation, contrary to what is claimed by King and Wolman.

The third and final part of the volume is devoted to the issues of indeterminacy and irreversibility. Though appearing as rather abstruse and technical issues, they are crucial to the understanding of the dynamics of a macroeconomic system. Indeterminacy refers to the existence of multiple equilibria or trajectories corresponding to the solution of a given system. Many macroeconomists consider this as a relevant way to assess economic fluctuations. Irreversibility refers to the fact that some economic decisions are taken forever and cannot be reversed in the future. In the first contribution in this part, Auray, Collard and Fève claim that models where money is taken into account by means of a cash-in-advance constraint, are prone to exhibit such an indeterminacy in the real variables once too simple or restrictive specifications for preferences or technology are relaxed. Monetary models with slightly more complex specifications of the utility function such as internal or external habit persistence will indeed be characterized by such indeterminacy. It happens that these alternative specifications lower intertemporal substitution, which suffices to generate real indeterminacy. However they also prove that real indeterminacy per se is not sufficient to make monetary policy significantly non neutral: beliefs then play a crucial role. In order to obtain a positive and persistent response of output to money innovations, beliefs have to be positively correlated with these innovations.

The contribution by Barinci and Chéron is a clear example of the possibility for models exhibiting indeterminacy to generate outcomes in accordance with relevant empirical features, in contrast to other more conventional models. Far from being a simple abstract curiosity, models with indeterminacy compete with other types of macromodels for the understanding of the dynamics of actual economies. In the present case, Barinci and Chéron develop a model with two categories of agents: capitalists and workers. It happens that workers are financially constrainted: they only hold money for future consumption. They first prove that this model improves upon earlier models insofar as it is able to generate indeterminacy with returns to scale parameters consistent with empirical evidence. Then they prove that the dynamics generated by their model is able to feature procyclical movements of aggregate consumption, contrary to endogenous business cycle models.

Pommeret's contribution tackles the difficult issue of irreversibility and its relationship with uncertainty. This link has been studied under partial equilibrium only. Pommeret embeds it within a general equilibrium framework. She proves that uncertainty affects the optimal decision over investment through two different channels: in addition to the standard irreversibility channel, the agents' preferences are to be taken into account. In this perspective, the standard result of a negative relationship between uncertainty and investment need not necessarily hold, since uncertainty affects investment through these two different channels. The intertemporal susbtitution elasticity matters and makes the sign of the relationship ambiguous. This exemplifies the appeal of adopting a general equilibrium perspective in macroeconomics.

This volume does not provide a comprehensive coverage neither of fields nor methods currently investigated or employed by macroeconomists. No contribution deals with growth matters, none exploit game theory, none deal with political economy issues, even though these various topics rank high in macroeconomics. And of course the list of non covered or explored topics is by no means complete. We can only hope that a future volume composed of contributions presented at future *Theories and Methods in Macroeconomics* meetings will cover these domains and prove the vitality of macroeconomic research in these field also.

More than a year has passed since the 5th T2M Meeting took place. This rather long delay comes from the fact that all submitted contributions were subject to a careful screening process and the selected ones were refereed according to standard procedures. We are grateful to the many colleagues who took part in this refereing process and hence contributed to the quality of this entire volume. We are also grateful to

Martial Dupaigne who arranged and organised the final texts so as to make them ready for publication. Our final thanks go to our editor Allard Winterink who looked after this project from the start and gave us his complete support. His efficiency in dealing with the various stages of the project and his ability to make it happen within a rather short timespan has been of crucial importance for keeping the necessary momentum.

Jean-Olivier Hairault Hubert Kempf

I

Globalization, Competition and Macroeconomic Performances

Chapter 1: Is Perfection Optimal? Employment and Product Market Competition.

Bruno Amable
Université de Lille II & CEPREMAP, France

Donatella Gatti
Wissenschaftszentrum für Sozialforschung Berlin (WZB), Germany

Abstract This paper proposes a model of efficiency wage with endogenous workers flows in interaction with imperfect competition on the product markets. Subject to economy-wide shocks, firms hire and fire workers thus generating a certain turnover. We show that the intensity of this turnover negatively affects workers' incentives and induces higher efficiency wage premia. Increased competition pushes real wages up but effort incentive requirements prevent large wage adjustments. Hence, adjustments are made with quantities: both the separation and hiring rates increase with competition, increasing the wage premium and contributing to lower employment. As a consequence, an employment-maximising level of competition may exist.

1. Introduction

The detrimental influence of labor market imperfections on employment performance has long been emphasized in the literature[1] and it has led to a large set of policy recommendations in favor of labor market reforms. A recent literature has more specifically focused on the interactions between imperfections in the labor and the product markets.[2] The basic idea is that imperfections in one market combine with those of the other markets to make matters worse in each of them. As a consequence for economic policy, labor market reforms should be accompanied by reforms on the product markets, the latter being expected to alleviate the burden of adjustments on the labor market. International

[1] See for instance Layard *et al.*, 1991, Nickell, 1997, Siebert, 1997.
[2] Boeri *et al.*, 2000, Nickell, 1999, Nicolletti *et al.*, 2000, Gersbach, 1999 and 2000.

organizations such as the OECD have advocated the implementation of structural reforms both in the labor and the product markets, towards more flexibility regarding wages and employment protection on the one hand, and the promotion of competition on the product markets by regulatory reform on the other side.[3] The elimination of imperfections in one market will facilitate the necessary adjustments in other markets.

This argument can also be stated in terms of employment fluctuations and unemployment persistence. Less imperfect competition would increase price and wage elasticities and would reduce the impact of shocks on (un)employment. This argument is also found in the so-called 'administered pricing' thesis[4] for which concentrated industries should be characterized by more rigid prices than competitive ones. Exogenous demand or cost shocks would therefore lead to wider quantity adjustments; thus for a given adverse shock, employment should decrease more in more concentrated industries.

This assertion is indeed in contrast with recent empirical findings as documented in particular by Weiss, 1998 where it is shown that both the long run level and the rate of adjustment of industry employment decrease with concentration. The latter result, in particular, shows that more competitive industries are characterized by a faster adjustment of employment to shocks, and display stronger fluctuations in employment compared to imperfectly competitive industries. In other words, imperfectly competitive industries are shown to use their market power in such a way as to smooth employment fluctuations. Although Weiss does not provide a clear theoretical explanation to his findings,[5] the empirical result has straightforward implications. This states that it is indeed problematic to assume that increased competition would unambiguously reduce employment adjustments in response to shocks.

Hence, the real nature of the interplay between product market and labor market imperfections is still unclear.[6] One general idea is that market power on the product market generate rents that may be captured by employees through higher wages. The impact of product markets competition on the operation of the labor market depends on the wage setting mechanism which complements the model. Nicoletti *et al.*,

[3]OECD, 1994, Nicoletti *et al.*, 2000, OECD, 2000.

[4]See Lebow, 1992 and references in Weiss, 1998 for instance.

[5]Weiss, 1998 proposes a theoretical model of employment and adjustment costs. Additional justifications for a negative relationship between unemployment and concentration are also given. A conjecture found in Scherer, 1980 is mentioned according to which concentrated industries making extra-profits could accept disguised unemployment when demand is low, thus avoiding the costs of rehiring when the demand level increases again.

[6]The first attempt to systematically evaluate the impact of product market competition on employment at the aggregate level is done by Boeri *et al.*, 2000 and Nicoletti at al., 2000.

2000 and Nickell, 1999 consider mainly that wages are fixed according to a wage bargaining model. One can show that the bargained wage is generally decreasing in the elasticity of labor demand;[7] then, increased competition leads to a lower bargained real wage. Hence, the authors conclude that single unionized firms which face increased competition will benefit from a higher labor demand elasticity and a lower bargained real wage.

This conclusion that increased product markets competition will improve labor market's efficiency needs not hold under different assumptions concerning the wage setting mechanism, particularly if one considers a model of efficiency wages. The link between efficiency wage and market power is not well explored in the literature. As Nicoletti *et al.* mention it, the determinants of the efficiency wage level are in general 'exogenous' elements: "*in none of these cases does there appear to be any obvious mechanism by which the market power of the firm can enter the story*" (p. 28). This paper will show that a mechanism indeed exists which links up the market power of firms to the determination of the efficiency wage by endogenizing labor market separation following demand or productivity shocks. In fact, one of the exogenous determinants of the efficiency wage level is the separation rate, which is understood at the individual worker level as the probability of losing one's job even when one provides the correct level of effort. *Ceteris paribus* this exogenous element contributes to increasing the level of the efficiency wage. This usually exogenous important determinant of the efficiency wage is made endogenous in this paper.

This paper proposes a model of imperfect competition *à la* Cournot with an endogenous determination of workers flows in and out of unemployment, where wages are determined according to an efficiency wage mechanism. More precisely, we assume that the economy moves across two different states of technology: Good and Bad. When moving, firms respectively hire or fire workers thus generating a certain turnover over time on the labor market. Under the assumption of imperfect monitoring within companies, labor force turnover negatively affects workers' incentives. We show that increased competition on the product market increases workers' separation rate and translates into a higher efficiency wage premium. Hence, our model clearly shows how wage formation can be negatively affected by the (endogenous) change in the size of the separation rate which is generated by increased product markets competition. The basic intuition behind the working of the model is the

[7]See Layard, Nickell and Jackman, 1991.

following. The combination of imperfect competition and efficiency wage contributes to smoothing employment differentials across the two states of the economy; this reduces the separation of workers as a response to demand and/or productivity shocks and contains wage pressure. However, because of relative real wage rigidities determined by the wage setting mechanism, an increase in competition leads to larger employment differentials across states, that is to a stronger turnover on the labor market. As a consequence, an adverse effect on workers' incentives is in place which ultimately generates – at the equilibrium – wage pressure, larger separations, and may under certain conditions lead to a higher level of unemployment.

The paper is organized as follows. Section 2 below presents the basic model of efficiency wage and imperfect competition on the product markets. Section 3 presents the macroeconomic equilibrium, which is shown to be unique in certain conditions. Section 4 establishes the result that an increase in product market competition may lead to a lower performance in terms of employment. A brief conclusion is proposed in the final section.

2. The model

This section sets out the model of imperfect competition on the product market and efficiency wage on the labor market. We first derive the labor demand curve and the 'price setting' real wage resulting from the decisions taken by imperfectly competitive firms subject to aggregate shocks.

2.1 Labor demand

We assume the existence of a multi-sector economy with a single final good used for consumption and a continuum of intermediate goods indexed over $[0,1]$. The final good is produced according to a constant returns to scale technology using all the intermediate goods:

$$\tilde{Y}_t = \left(\int_0^1 Y_t(s)^{\frac{\eta-1}{\eta}} ds \right)^{\frac{\eta}{\eta-1}} \tag{1}$$

$\eta > 1$ is the absolute value of the elasticity of substitution between intermediates. The final good is produced competitively, but there is imperfect competition in each of the intermediate sectors. More specifically, it is assumed that there are n firms in each intermediate sector engaged in Cournot-type competition. Each firm is small compared to the economy but has a certain market power within its sector. Such a specification leads to a derived demand addressed to sector s equal to:

$$Y_s = \left(\frac{P_s}{P}\right)^{-\eta} \cdot \tilde{Y} \tag{2}$$

where P_s is the price of intermediate s and P is the final good's price. One further has:

$$P = \left(\int_0^1 P_s^{1-\eta} ds\right)^{\frac{1}{1-\eta}} \tag{3}$$

Each firm j in every sector s has an identical production function which uses labor as its sole input:

$$y_{jt} = \alpha_{jt} \cdot l_{jt}^{\gamma} \tag{4}$$

$0 < \gamma \leq 1$, l_j is the input of effective labor, *i.e.* l_j workers providing the expected effort level. We will later pay special attention to the case where $\gamma = 1$, *i.e.* the case of constant returns to scale in the intermediate goods production.

Intermediate firms are subject to common aggregate shocks which affect their productivity. One may think of these shocks as either 'demand' shocks resulting from changes in demand or alternatively as 'supply' shocks stemming from fluctuations in factors other than labor or from a varying technological efficiency. We adopt the same shock specification as Bertola 1990, Bertola and Ichino, 1995 or Bertola and Rogerson, 1997. The shock's realizations are denoted α_t at time t. More specifically, the αs follow a two-state Markov chain with symmetric transition probability p:

$$\alpha_{t+1} = \begin{cases} \alpha_G \begin{array}{llll} \text{with probability} & p & \text{if} & \alpha_t = \alpha_B \quad \text{and} \\ \text{with probability} & 1-p & \text{if} & \alpha_t = \alpha_G \end{array} \\ \\ \alpha_B \begin{array}{llll} \text{with probability} & 1-p & \text{if} & \alpha_t = \alpha_B \quad \text{and} \\ \text{with probability} & p & \text{if} & \alpha_t = \alpha_G \end{array} \end{cases} \tag{5}$$

and $\alpha_G > \alpha_B > 0$. We further assume some degree of 'persistence' in the shocks' realization: $p < 1/2$.

There are thus two states for the technology and the economy, a 'good' state denoted G with a high labor productivity, and a 'bad' state denoted B characterized by a low value for labor productivity. The long-run probability for the economy to be in either a good or a bad state is 0.5. This specification generates aggregate fluctuations in output and employment.

Firms' hiring decisions are identical across sectors. Only spot markets for labor are open and all intermediate firms know the realization of the shock before taking their employment decisions. Profit maximization for firm j in any intermediate sector gives:

$$P_s \cdot \left(1 + \frac{\partial P_s}{\partial y_j} \cdot \frac{y_j}{P_s}\right) = W^j \cdot \frac{\partial l_j}{\partial y_j} = \frac{1}{\gamma} \cdot W^j \cdot \alpha_j^{-\frac{1}{\gamma}} \cdot y_j^{\frac{1}{\gamma}-1} \tag{6}$$

W_j is the nominal wage paid by firm j.

Each sector has the same structure, therefore the price of each intermediate is the same, which implies because of (3) that $P_s = P$ for all s. Therefore, the real wage for the firm (W_j/P_s) will be identical to the real wage for the worker (W_j/P). In what follows, we can drop the subscript s without risk of confusion. We denote: $Y_B = n \cdot y_B$ as the total output of intermediate firms when the economy is in a bad state and $Y_G = n \cdot y_G$ the total output of intermediate firms when the economy is in a good state. Likewise, l_G (l_B) is employment of a representative firm in a good (bad) state. W_G and W_B are nominal wages for a worker employed when the economy is in a good state and a bad state respectively. Following this, (6) can be expressed as:

$$P = \frac{1}{\left[1 - \frac{\varepsilon}{n}\right]} \cdot \frac{W^j}{\frac{\alpha_j}{\gamma} \cdot l_j^{\gamma-1}} \tag{7}$$

$j = G, B$. $\varepsilon \equiv \frac{1}{\eta}$ is the inverse of the elasticity of substitution between intermediates, $\left(1 - \frac{\varepsilon}{n}\right)$ is the inverse of the mark-up applied to marginal costs by imperfectly competitive firms. As is standard in Cournot competition, the mark-up decreases when the number of competing firms n increases. Besides, the mark-up is small when ε is small i.e. when there is a high degree of substitutability among the intermediate goods. ε (η) and n are indicators of the degree of imperfection in competition. Since ε (η) comes from the production function for the final good, we can suppose that it is largely invariant to policy changes designed to promote a more intense competition in the product market. It is essentially a 'technological' parameter in our setting. n on the other hand may be thought of as potentially subject to the influence of competition policy such as the removal of administrative barriers to entry, the opening the economy akin to the completion of the Single European Market or other measures that make entry into an industry easier. This is why we will concentrate in what follows on the effects of a change in the number of competitors n.

(7) gives an expression for the 'price setting' real wages for firms in either states:

$$\frac{\alpha_j}{\gamma} \cdot l_j^{\gamma-1} \cdot \left(1 - \frac{\varepsilon}{n}\right) = w^j \tag{8}$$

with $w_j \equiv \frac{W_j}{P}$. 'Price setting' real wages are influenced by the marginal productivity of labor (the $\frac{\alpha_j}{\gamma} \cdot l_j^{\gamma-1}$ term) and by firms' mark-up behavior (the term between squared brackets). This is standard in the presence of imperfect competition, real wages are lower than the marginal productivity of labor because of the mark-up. This distortion increases with the degree of imperfection of competition (a high ε and a low n).

Having determined the price-setting relative real wage, we can now turn to the 'wage-setting' side of the economy where the levels for the real wages in both a good or a bad state will be determined.

2.2 Wage setting

The economy is populated with a fixed number N of agents who supply labor inelastically within each intermediate sector. Each sector has thus an immobile labor force equal to N. Following the symmetry assumptions used throughout, the sectorial employment rate L/N is equal to the aggregate rate. Each individual worker is characterized by an identical utility function, where instantaneous utility depends on the real wage[8] and on the effort provided on the job:

$$u_t = w_t^j - e_t \tag{9}$$

$j = G, B$; e_t, the effort level, can take two values, 0, which means that the worker is 'shirking' and e, which means that the worker provides the expected work effort. The contribution of a shirker to effective labor is nil, whereas an individual working with the expected effort level e contributes for one unit to effective labor. w_t^j is the real wage. This simple specification will allow us to consider an efficiency wage model in the spirit of Solow, 1979, Shapiro and Stiglitz, 1984, Akerlof and Yellen, 1990 or Saint-Paul, 1996. The basic principle of these models is that a firm may not wish to lower wages even in the presence of unemployment for fear of reducing the incentives to provide the correct level of effort on the job. Each firm has a monitoring device whose inefficiency is measured by the parameter x_t: A worker is caught shirking with probability $1 - x_t$ and, when caught, loses his job at the end of period t.

But, as is common in efficiency wage models, shirking is not the only way to lose one's job. Every model of efficiency wage takes into account

[8] *i.e.* the consumption level of the final good.

an independent and exogenous probability of job loss. In our setting, this probability is made endogenous: firms shed labor when they are hit by an adverse shock which forces them to downward adjust their labor force. We denote q_t the probability of losing one's job following an adverse shock, then:

$$q_t = \frac{l_{Gt} - l_{Bt}}{l_{Gt}} = \left(1 - \frac{1}{l_t}\right) \tag{10}$$

Workers are concerned by this type of job loss only when the economy is in a good state, since in that case firms are likely to be hit by an adverse shock. The situation in a bad state can only improve or at worst stay the same. Assume that the economy is in a good state. Then at each subsequent period, with a given probability the economy is hit by an adverse shock and firms have to shed labor. Workers having lost their job become unemployed for at least one period and get the (real) unemployment allowance $\overline{w}_t$,[9] they may find another job when firms hire again. The reverse occurs when the economy is in a bad state. The flow probability out of unemployment is a_t, which is the probability for an unemployed of finding a job.

Workers have an infinite horizon and discount future at the rate $\beta \leq 1$. We can now compute the discounted utilities associated with the various possible positions for an individual: being employed when the economy is in a good state or in a bad state, and shirking or not shirking, or being unemployed. The discounted utility of a worker who shirks at time t when the economy is in a good state is V^G_{St}, and V^G_{NSt} when he does not shirk. The utilities associated to working when the economy is in a bad state are likewise V^B_{St} (shirking) and V^B_{NSt} (not shirking). The utility of being unemployed in either state is U^B_t and U^G_t. We then have:

$$\begin{aligned} &V^G_{St} = \\ &w^G_t + \beta \cdot \Big\{ x_t \cdot (1-p)\, V^G_{t+1} + (1-x_t) \cdot \left[(1-p) \cdot U^G_{t+1} + p \cdot U^B_{t+1}\right] \\ &+ x_t \cdot p \cdot \left[(1-q_t) \cdot V^B_{t+1} + q_t \cdot U^B_{t+1}\right] \Big\} \end{aligned} \tag{11}$$

$$\begin{aligned} &V^G_{NSt} = \\ &w^G_t - e_t + \beta \cdot \left\{(1-p)\, V^G_{t+1} + p \cdot \left[(1-q_t) \cdot V^B_{t+1} + q_t \cdot U^B_{t+1}\right]\right\} \end{aligned} \tag{12}$$

[9]The financing of this unemployment allowance is not explicitly taken into account. One may think of it as financed by a non distortionary lump-sum tax or alternatively as coming from a 'subsistence' activity undertaken by individuals.

$$V_{St}^{B} = w_t^B + \beta \cdot \Big\{ x_t \cdot (1-p) \cdot V_{t+1}^{B} + x_t \cdot p \cdot V_{t+1}^{G} + (1-x_t) \cdot \left[(1-p) \cdot U_{t+1}^{B} + p \cdot U_{t+1}^{G} \right] \Big\} \tag{13}$$

$$V_{NSt}^{B} = w_t^B - e_t + \beta \cdot \left[(1-p) \cdot V_{t+1}^{B} + p \cdot V_{t+1}^{G} \right] \tag{14}$$

$$U_t^B = \overline{w}_t + \beta \cdot \left\{ (1-p) \cdot U_{t+1}^{B} + p \cdot \left[(1-a_t) \cdot U_{t+1}^{G} + a_t \cdot V_{t+1}^{E} \right] \right\} \tag{15}$$

$$U_t^G = \overline{w}_t + \beta \cdot \left[(1-p) \cdot U_{t+1}^{G} + p \cdot U_{t+1}^{B} \right] \tag{16}$$

V_{t+1}^{E} is the utility of being employed in a firm hiring at time $t+1$. In equilibrium, only firms hit by a positive shock will hire so that V_{t+1}^{E} will be the utility associated with working in a good state.

The level of real wage in each firm must be set at a level such that workers have an incentive not to shirk. These no-shirking conditions are:

$$V_{NSt}^{j} \geq V_{St}^{j} \tag{17}$$

The conditions $V_{NSt}^{j} = V_{St}^{j} = V_t^j$, $j = G, B$ give the two limit wage levels $w_{it}^{G}\left(w_{it}^{B}\right), w_{it}^{B}\left(w_{it}^{G}\right)$ under which the optimal behavior for the worker is to shirk. Since we are dealing with constant values for all variables at the steady-state equilibrium, we may dispense with the time subscripts from now on. Both $w_i^G\left(w_i^B\right)$ and $w_t^B\left(w_i^G\right)$ are affine functions.

From these conditions, one may deduce the levels of the real wages paid in either state of the economy. This is shown in the proposition below.

Proposition 1 *The incentive-compatible equilibrium wages levels for both type firms are such that:*

$$w_B^* = \overline{w} + e \cdot \left(\frac{1-\beta-p\cdot[2\cdot(1-\beta)-\beta\cdot(a\cdot(1-2\cdot p)-(1-a)\cdot p\cdot q)]}{\beta\cdot(1-x)\cdot[1-p\cdot(2-p\cdot q)]} + 1 \right)$$
$$w_G^* = \overline{w} + e \cdot \left(\frac{1-\beta-p\cdot[2\cdot(1-\beta)-(1-\beta\cdot p)\cdot q]}{\beta\cdot(1-x)\cdot[1-p\cdot(2-p\cdot q)]} + 1 \right)$$

Proof. The no-shirking conditions (17) can be expressed as:

$$\begin{aligned} w_G &\geq w_i^G\left(w_B\right) \\ w_B &\geq w_i^B\left(w_G\right) \end{aligned} \tag{18}$$

Both $w_i^G(w_B)$ and $w_i^B(w_G)$ are affine functions. In the general case, they define an area in the (w_B, w_G) plane where both incentive constraints are fulfilled. The equilibrium real wage rates must be such that both constraints are simultaneously satisfied since wages in either state depend on the wages paid in the other state. Firms pay the lowest wages compatible with both constraints. The intersection of the two schedules $w_i^G(w_B)$ and $w_i^{B-1}(w_G)$ defines the equilibrium levels of real wages rates for good and bad states: $w_i^G(w_B^*) = w_i^{B-1}(w_G^*)$.

□

The efficiency wage paid by firms in a bad state is higher the higher the hiring rate and the lower the separation rate, while in a good state the efficiency wage is higher the higher the separation rate. The justification for these results is simple.

When the hiring rate increases, shirkers caught (and fired) while the economy is in a bad state will have a higher probability of finding new employment if the economy shifts back to a good state. Therefore, a shirker's utility increases and a compensation in the form of a higher wage in a bad state is required in order to enforce the no-shirking condition.

Firms in a good state can be hit by a bad shock and have to shed labor. Workers can then be fired regardless of their effort. This possibility is all the more plausible that the separation rate is high; thus a higher separation rate reduces the discounted utility associated to a no-shirking strategy, which calls for a higher efficiency wage in a good state.

The separation rate affects also workers in a bad state. In fact, there is always a possibility for firms to be hit by a good shock and shift back to a good state. A higher separation rate, because it pushes real wage up in a good state, also increases the wage prospect for workers who are currently employed (in a bad state) and allows for a decrease of the efficiency wage paid by firms in a bad state.

3. Macroeconomic equilibrium

This section endogenizes the separation and hiring rates, which have been shown to play an important role in the definition of the wages rates. Wages are set by firms in either state of the economy at the minimum level which respects the effort-incentive constraint and the no-arbitrage condition for workers. Every worker provides the necessary effort so that effective and employed labor are equal. At the beginning of each period, with a probability p, the state of the economy changes. If the economy goes from a good state to a bad state, firms have to shed labor in order to adjust their labor force to its optimal value, while if the economy goes from a bad state to a good state, firms need to make the opposite adjustment. In the former case, laid-off workers join the ranks of the unemployed while, in the latter situation, some unemployed workers find new employment. Recalling that a is the flow probability out of unemployment, and defining: $\tilde{N} = N/n$, one has:

$$a \cdot \left[\tilde{N} - l_B\right] = q \cdot l_G \tag{19}$$

Equation (8) defines the price setting real wage for firms in either states:

$$w_{ps}^{j} = \frac{\alpha_j}{\gamma} \cdot l_j^{\gamma-1} \cdot \left(1 - \frac{\varepsilon}{n}\right) \tag{20}$$

and the efficiency wages are:

$$w_{ws}^{B} = \overline{w} + e \cdot \left\{1 + \frac{1-\beta-p\cdot[2\cdot(1-\beta)-\beta\cdot(a\cdot(1-2\cdot p)-(1-a)\cdot p\cdot q)]}{\beta\cdot(1-x)\cdot[1-p\cdot(2-p\cdot q)]}\right\} \tag{21}$$

$$w_{ws}^{G} = \overline{w} + e \cdot \left\{1 + \frac{1-\beta-p\cdot[2\cdot(1-\beta)-(1-\beta\cdot p)\cdot q]}{\beta\cdot(1-x)\cdot[1-p\cdot(2-p\cdot q)]}\right\} \tag{22}$$

Production can be expressed as the output of firms in either states:

$$Y_j = n \cdot \alpha_j \cdot l_j^{\gamma} \tag{23}$$

Equation (10) for the steady-state is:

$$q = \frac{l_G - l_B}{l_G} = \left(1 - \frac{1}{l}\right) \tag{24}$$

with $l \equiv \frac{l_B}{l_G}$.

Equations (19), (20), (23), (24), (21), and (22) constitute the reduced form of the model, with w_B, w_G, l_B, l_G, a and q as the endogenous variables. No loss of generality is incurred if we state $e = 1$.

We will simplify matters regarding solving the full model by considering the constant returns to scale case: $\gamma = 1$. Call $\tilde{\alpha} = (1-p)\cdot\alpha_B + p\cdot\alpha_G$. We can then establish the following result.

Proposition 2 *If* $\frac{1-(1-p)\cdot x\cdot\beta}{(1-p)\cdot(1-x)\cdot\beta} + \overline{w} > \alpha_G$, $\tilde{\alpha} > 2\cdot\frac{(1-x\cdot\beta)+(1-x)\cdot\beta\cdot\overline{w}}{(1-x)\cdot(2-\varepsilon)\cdot\beta}$, $\overline{w} < \frac{x}{1-x} - \frac{2-p\cdot(4-\varepsilon)}{(1-p)\cdot(1-x)\cdot\beta\cdot(2-p\cdot(2-\varepsilon))}$ *and* $\beta > \frac{2-p\cdot(4-\varepsilon)}{(1-p)\cdot x\cdot(2-p\cdot(2-\varepsilon))}$, *then a unique* *equilibrium exists characterized by a probability of losing one's job when being employed in a good state given by:*

$q^* = \frac{(1-2\cdot p)\cdot[n\cdot(x\cdot\beta+\beta\cdot(1-x)\cdot(\alpha_G-\overline{w})-1)-\beta\cdot(1-x)\cdot\alpha_G\cdot\varepsilon]}{p\cdot[n\cdot(1-x\cdot\beta\cdot p-\beta\cdot p\cdot(1-x)\cdot(\alpha_G-\overline{w}))+p\cdot\beta\cdot(1-x)\cdot\alpha_G\cdot\varepsilon]}$,

The corresponding value of the hiring rate applying the bad state is given by:

$a^* = \frac{n[\beta\cdot(x+(1-x)\cdot(\tilde{\alpha}-\overline{w}))-1]-\beta\cdot(1-x)\cdot\tilde{\alpha}\cdot\varepsilon}{(1-p)\cdot p\cdot\beta^2\cdot[n\cdot(x+(1-x)\cdot(\alpha_G-\overline{w}))-(1-x)\cdot\alpha_G\cdot\varepsilon]}$.

Proof. Consider wage determination in a good state. Equation (22) and (20) must be equalized *ex post* which reads: $\alpha_G\cdot\left[1-\frac{\varepsilon}{n}\right]=\overline{w}+1+\frac{1-\beta\cdot-p\cdot[2\cdot(1-\beta)-(1-\beta\cdot p)\cdot q]}{\beta\cdot(1-x)\cdot[1-p\cdot(2-p\cdot q)]}$. Since w_{ws}^G is uniformly increasing in q, the equality allows the derivation of the equilibrium value of the separation rate $q^*(n)$.

To ensure that a positive equilibrium always exists, we impose restrictions on parameters such as to enforce $w_{ws}^G < w_{ps}^G$ when $q=0$ and $n=2$, and $w_{ws}^G > w_{ps}^G$ when $q=1$ and $n\to\infty$. This corresponds to $\alpha_G\cdot\left[1-\frac{\varepsilon}{2}\right]>\overline{w}+1+\frac{1-\beta\cdot-p\cdot 2\cdot(1-\beta)}{\beta\cdot(1-x)\cdot[1-p\cdot 2]}$ and $\alpha_G<\overline{w}+1+\frac{1-\beta\cdot-p\cdot[2\cdot(1-\beta)-(1-\beta\cdot p)]}{\beta\cdot(1-x)\cdot[1-p\cdot(2-p)]}$. We retain the former condition here which fixes a minimum value for α_G.

As for the latter condition, we apply the same kind of reasoning to a^* which leads us to define a condition on $\tilde{\alpha}$ which is similar but more restrictive than the corresponding condition on α_G. Hence, we select to retain the condition on $\tilde{\alpha}$. To ensure the compatibility of the two conditions on $\tilde{\alpha}$ and α_G, we need to impose the restriction on $\overline{w}$ reported in the text of proposition 2; this only makes sense under the condition on β stated in the proposition.

As for the bad state, since w_{ws}^B is decreasing in q and increasing in a, wage determination in a bad state defines a hiring schedule $a(q;n)$ with a positive slope. If we now substitute $q^*(n)$ into equation (21) and hold $w_{ws}^B = w_{ps}^B$ we finally obtain the equilibrium value of the hiring rate $a^*(n)$. One can check the equilibrium value of a is always positive under the conditions given above.

□

Hence, we have by now established sufficient conditions for the existence of a unique equilibrium to which is associated a certain level for real wage rates and the rate of unemployment. This result has been derived given a certain degree of imperfection in product market competition, i.e. a certain degree of concentration or more precisely a certain number of competing firms n. Building on this, we can now move on to the analysis of the macroeconomic consequences of an increase in competition on the product market.

4. Labor market performance with less imperfect product markets

This section investigates the consequences of an increase in the number of competing firms within each industry. The number of competitors in a given industry is a straightforward measure of imperfection in Cournot-type models of imperfect competition. In such models the mark-up on marginal costs decreases when the number of firms increases, and imperfections in competition vanish when this number goes to infinity. More than the price elasticity of demand, which is technologically derived in our model, the number of competitors in an industry may be considered, if not as a policy variable, at least as influenced by competition policy measures. In most countries, entry in some industries is *de facto* if not *de jure* restricted, making market structures oligopolistic. Some of these restrictions are the consequences of international differences in regulations, norms or other administrative matters that make cross-border competition more difficult that competition between domestic firms. The elimination of such barriers to competition was the aim of the Single European Market completion for instance. As mentioned before, one expects an improved economic performance from the implementation of competition policies.

In this model, the effects of an increase in product market competition cannot just be read off the shift in the labor demand curve. The consequences in terms of wage-setting behavior have to be taken into account too. When the number n of firms increases, the price setting wage in either states of the economy increases, which calls for an adjustment on the labor market to re-equilibrate the levels of the efficiency and price setting wages. Due to real wage rigidities, this adjustment is mainly done through a modification of the separation and hiring rates. The subsequent result in terms of job turnover on the labor market is established in the following proposition.

Proposition 3 *An increase in product market competition characterized by a higher number of competing firms (a higher n) brings about an increase in the separation rate q and the hiring rate a.*

Proof. One simply needs to calculate the total derivatives of q^* and a^* given in the preceding proposition with respect to n. This gives the following results:

$$\frac{\partial q}{\partial n} = \frac{(1-p)\cdot(1-2\cdot p)\cdot(1-x)\cdot\alpha_G\cdot\beta\cdot\varepsilon}{p\cdot\{n\cdot[1-p\cdot\beta\cdot(x+(1-x)\cdot(\alpha_G-\overline{w}))]+p\cdot\beta\cdot(1-x)\cdot\varepsilon\cdot\alpha_G\}^2} > 0,$$

$$\frac{\partial a}{\partial n} = \frac{(1-x)\cdot\varepsilon\cdot[\alpha_G\cdot(1-x\cdot\beta)+\tilde{\alpha}\cdot x\cdot\beta+(1-x)\cdot\beta\cdot\overline{w}\cdot(\alpha_G-\tilde{\alpha})]}{(1-p)\cdot p\cdot\beta^2\cdot\{n\cdot[x+(1-x)\cdot(\alpha_G-\overline{w})]-(1-x)\cdot\varepsilon\cdot\alpha_G\}^2} > 0.$$

□

Therefore, proposition 3 establishes that an increase in product market competition leads to an increase in job turnover. The rationale of this results is straightforward. When the number n of firms increases, the price setting wage in a good state increases, which calls for an increase in the separation rate to re-equilibrate price setting and efficiency wage rates. The same mechanism applies to wage determination in a bad state and explains why the hiring schedule $a(q)$ shifts upward when n increases. The consequences of this conclusion, as far as employment variation across the two states is concerned, are spelled out in the following corollary.

Corollary 1 *Less imperfect product markets lead to larger adjustments of employment on the labor market for any given size of shocks.*

Proof. One can easily derive the expression for employments differentials across the two states of the economy. This is given by : $\Delta L = L_G - L_B = \frac{a \cdot q \cdot N}{a + q \cdot (1-a)}$. One can further show that $\frac{\partial(\Delta L)}{\partial a} = \frac{q^2 \cdot N}{[a + q \cdot (1-a)]^2} > 0$, $\frac{\partial(\Delta L)}{\partial q} = \frac{a^2 \cdot N}{[a + q \cdot (1-a)]^2} > 0$. □

Hence, more competitive product markets are associated with more *de facto* flexible labor markets; for a given size of shocks, the adjustments in the level of employment are larger when product markets competition is stronger. This runs contrary to the 'administered prices' theory referred to in the introduction. What distinguishes our result from the more standard view that associates a higher degree of product market competition to smaller quantity adjustments is the wage-setting process. Efficiency wage requirements prevent large real wages adjustments, which would not respect the incentive compatibility constraint for workers. As a result, the adjustment is made with quantities. On the basis of these mechanisms, one should therefore expect larger fluctuations in employment to be associated with stronger product markets competition.

The consequence of the above results in terms of the average level of the unemployment rate is not unambiguous. One may take as a measure of average employment $L = \frac{L_G + L_B}{2}$, where L_G and L_B are employment when the economy is in a good state and a bad state respectively. This makes sense because over a long period, the economy is likely to be in a good state (bad state) half of the time. Increased competition will affect differently employment in either state of the economy. The final impact of increased competition on unemployment clearly depends on the overall combination of the effects on the hiring and separation rates. This can be more formally stated as in the following proposition.

Proposition 4 *Average employment always increases with n for small values of n. Further increases in the number of firms may either increase or decrease employment depending on the parameter values.*

Proof. Average employment is equal to $L = \frac{(2-q)\cdot a\cdot N}{2\cdot(a+q-a\cdot q)}$ and we define $\alpha = \frac{\alpha_G}{\alpha_B}$. Solving for equilibrium values for q and a gives:

$$L(n) = \frac{a_1 \cdot n^2 + b_1 \cdot n + c_1}{a_2 \cdot n^2 + b_2 \cdot n + c_2} \cdot \frac{N}{2\cdot(1-p)}$$

with:

$$a_1 = \left\{\beta \cdot \left[x + (1-x)\cdot(\alpha - \overline{w})\right] - 1\right\} \cdot$$
$$\left\{1 - \left[1 - 2\cdot(1-p)\cdot p\right] \cdot \beta \cdot \left[x + (1-x)\cdot(\alpha_G - \overline{w})\right]\right\}$$

$$b_1 = (x-1)\cdot\beta\cdot\epsilon\cdot\left\{\alpha + \left[1 - 2\cdot(1-p)\cdot p\right]\cdot\left[\alpha_G - x\cdot\alpha\cdot\beta\right.\right.$$
$$\left.\left. - (x + 2\cdot(1-x)\cdot\alpha)\cdot\alpha_G\cdot\beta + (1-x)\cdot(\alpha+\alpha_G)\cdot\beta\cdot\overline{w}\right]\right\}$$

$$c_1 = -\left\{\left[1 - 2\cdot(1-p)\cdot p\right]\cdot(1-x)^2\cdot\alpha\cdot\alpha_G\cdot\beta^2\cdot\epsilon^2\right\}$$

$$a_2 = -\left\{\begin{array}{c} 1 - \alpha\cdot\beta + x\cdot(-2+p+\alpha)\cdot\beta - (1-2p)\cdot p\cdot \\ \left[x + (1-x)\,\alpha_G\right]^2\cdot\beta^3 + \left[x + (1-x)\cdot\alpha_G\right]\cdot \\ \left\{\begin{array}{c} \left\{-2\cdot p^2 + x + (1-x)\cdot\left[p\cdot(1-\alpha)+\alpha\right]\right\}\cdot\beta^2 \\ +2\cdot(1-2p)\cdot p\cdot(1-x)\cdot\beta^3\cdot\overline{w} \end{array}\right\} \\ -(1-x)\cdot\beta\cdot \\ \left\{\begin{array}{c} (1-p)\cdot(\alpha_G - \overline{w}) - \overline{w} \\ +\left\{\begin{array}{c} (1-2p)\cdot p \\ +(1-p)\cdot\left[2\cdot x + (1-x)\cdot(\alpha+\alpha_G)\right] \end{array}\right\}\cdot\beta\cdot\overline{w} \\ -(1-x)\cdot\beta\cdot\left\{1 - p\cdot\left[1 + (1-2p)\cdot\beta\right]\right\}\cdot\overline{w}^2 \end{array}\right\} \end{array}\right\}$$

$$b_2 = \left\{\begin{array}{c} (1-x)\cdot\beta\cdot\epsilon\cdot \\ \left\{\begin{array}{c} (p-1)\cdot\alpha_G + \alpha\cdot\left\{\begin{array}{c} -1 + (1-p) \\ \cdot\left[x + 2\cdot(1-x)\cdot\alpha_G\right]\cdot\beta \end{array}\right\} \\ +\alpha_G\cdot\beta\cdot\left\{x + p\cdot\left\{\begin{array}{c} 1 - 2\cdot p - x \\ +2\cdot(1-2p)\cdot\left[x\cdot(\alpha_G - 1) - \alpha_G\right]\beta \end{array}\right\}\right\} \\ -(1-x)\cdot\beta\cdot\left[\begin{array}{c} (1-p)\cdot(\alpha+\alpha_G) \\ -2\cdot p\cdot(1-2\cdot p)\cdot\alpha_G\cdot\beta \end{array}\right]\cdot\overline{w} \end{array}\right\} \end{array}\right\}$$

$$c_2 = (1-x)^2\cdot\alpha_G\cdot\beta^2\cdot\left[(1-2p)\cdot p\cdot\alpha_G\cdot\beta - (1-p)\cdot\alpha\right]\cdot\epsilon^2$$

Total employment is ultimately (*i.e.* when $n \to \infty$) decreasing (increasing) in n when $a_1\cdot b_2 - a_2\cdot b_1 < (>)\, 0$ since $\frac{\partial L}{\partial n} \propto (a_1\cdot b_2 - a_2\cdot b_1)\cdot n^2 + 2\cdot(a_1\cdot c_2 - a_2\cdot c_1)\cdot n + (b_1\cdot c_2 - b_2\cdot c_1)$

$L(n)$ is discontinuous for two values of n, the roots of $a_2\cdot n^2 + b_2\cdot n + c_2$. These roots correspond to $(a + q - a\cdot q) = 0$. Both a and q are increasing with n. Let n_1 be the value of n where $a(n)$ is not defined, n_2 be such that $q(n_2) = 0$ and n_3 such that $a(n_3) = 0$. One has $n_1 < n_2 <$

n_3[10](Figure 1). We define $\tilde{n}$ such that a$(\tilde{n}) = \frac{-q(\tilde{n})}{1-q(\tilde{n})}$. $\tilde{n}$ is the largest n for which $L(n)$ is not defined, and $\lim_{n\to\tilde{n}} L(n) = -\infty$.

Only values of n strictly above $\tilde{n}$ make economic sense, and $L(n)$ is always defined for $n > \tilde{n}$.

Figure 1.

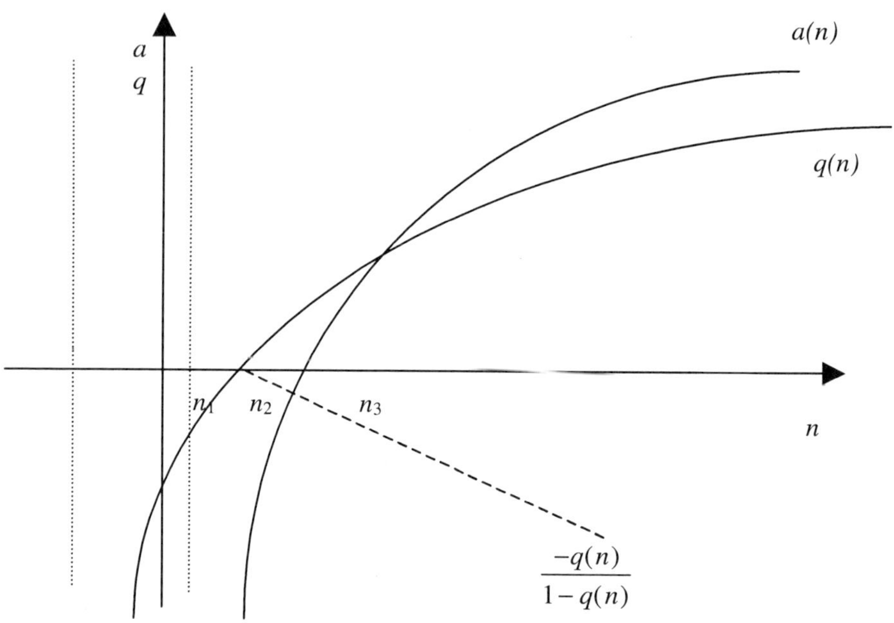

We can conclude that for very small n (above $\tilde{n}$) the value of employment always goes to $-\infty$. Therefore, there are two possibilities as for the graph of L illustrated in Figure 2.

In case A, employment is always an increasing function of the degree of product market competition. In case B however, employment is first increasing then decreasing in product market competition. The critical value n^* where the monotonicity change occurs can be everywhere for $n = n^* > n_e$, with n_e such that $L(n_e) = 0$. This case occurs whenever the largest root of $a_2 \cdot n^2 + b_2 \cdot n + c_2$ is lower than the largest root of $g(n) \equiv \frac{\partial L}{\partial n}$. An interesting case is clearly one where $n^* > 2$. In that case, an optimal level of competition exists which maximizes employment. □

To sum up, the above proposition shows that the effects on employment of increased competition are basically of two sorts. First, one can

[10]It is straightforward to show that $a(n_2) < 0$.

Figure 2. Evolution of average employment

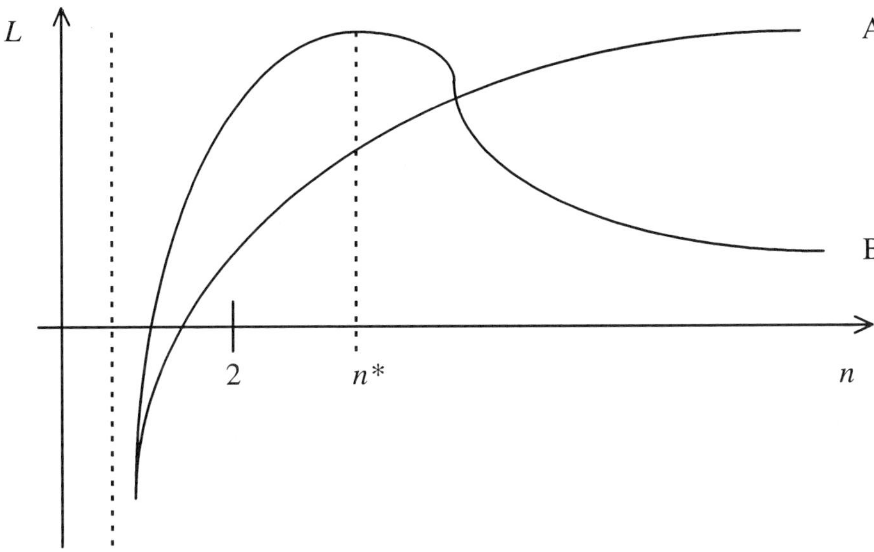

recognize a 'traditional' positive effect that can be associated to reduced market imperfection and better employment opportunities: this translates in our model through the positive effect of increased competition on the hiring rate (which is shifted upward). However, a second mechanism is present in our model which works through the wage setting process, particularly the efficiency wage formation. Increased competition generates larger separations which in turn lowers employment. One may express the condition for a negative impact of product market competition on employment in terms of elasticities. Denoting η_{aq} the elasticity of a with respect to q, η_{an} its elasticity with respect to n and η_{qn} the elasticity of q to n, one can show that an increase in n leads to a decrease in total employment if $\frac{\eta_{an}}{\eta_{qn}} < \frac{2-a^*}{2-q^*}$.

Hence, one must conclude that in an efficiency wage framework increased competition on product market may indeed have a negative impact on the aggregate employment performance.

5. Conclusion

According to conventional wisdom, increased competition on product markets would unambiguously contribute to alleviating the burden of adjustment which falls on imperfect labor markets when shocks occur. The model presented above suggests that this assertion needs to be carefully qualified. The adverse effects of efficiency wage rigidities on the labor market are indeed worsened by an increase in product market competition, when endogenous labor markets flows are taken into account. In fact, as in standard imperfect competition models, an increase in the number of firms will have for consequence an increase in price setting real wages. However, in our model, the subsequent adjustment of the efficiency wage level on the labor market will tend to push the separation and hiring rates up. As a consequence, the variation of employment levels as a response to any given shock becomes stronger when competition increases.

This shows that adverse shocks lead to stronger adjustments on the labor market when product market competition becomes stronger. As a consequence, stronger competition makes the burden of adjustment that falls on employment heavier: more competition means more turnover on the labor market. Depending on the relative elasticities of the separation and hiring rates to an increase in competition, this may indeed ultimately lead to aggregate employment losses. One should stress that this result being driven by an efficiency wage mechanism, it does apply even in the absence of any direct regulation on the labor market. Therefore, even coordinated labor market and product market reforms may indeed lead to perverse outcomes if the additional/hidden sources of rigidities are overlooked.

Acknowledgments

The authors thank Robert Solow, David Soskice, Christian Bidard and participants to the CEPR-IZA European Summer Symposium in Labour Economics (October 2000, Ammersee), the MODEM seminar (October 2000, Nanterre), the EEA Conference (September 2000, Bolzano) and the 5th T2M Meeting (May 2000, University of Nanterre) for helpful remarks on the paper. The usual caveats apply.

References

Akerlof G. and Yellen J. (1990). The fair-wage effort hypothesis and unemployment. *Quarterly Journal of Economics*, 105:255-283.

Bertola G. (1990). Job security, employment and wages. *European Economic Review*, 34:851-886.

Bertola G. and Ichino A. (1995). Wage Inequality and Unemployment: United States vs. Europe. In: Bernanke B. and Rotemberg J. (Eds) *NBER Macroeconomics Annual 1995.*

Bertola G. and Rogerson R. (1997). Institutions and labor reallocation. *European Economic Review*, 41:1147-1171.

Boeri T., Nicoletti G. and Scarpetta S. (2000). Regulation and labour market performance. *CEPR Discussion Paper* Number 2420, April.

Gersbach H. (1999). Product market competition, unemployment and income disparities. *Weltwirtschaftliches Archiv*, 135(2):221-240.

Gersbach H. (2000). Promoting product market competition to reduce unemployment in Europe: an alternative approach? *Kyklos*, 53(2):117-133.

Layard R., Nickell S. and Jackman R. (1991). *Unemployment*. Oxford: Oxford University Press.

Lebow D.E. (1992). imperfect competition and business cycles: an empirical investigation. *Economic Enquiry*, 30:177-193.

Nickell S. (1997). Unemployment and labour market rigidities: europe versus north america. *Journal of Economic Perspectives*, 11(3):55-74.

Nickell S. (1999). Product markets and labour markets. *Labour Economics*, 6(1):1-20.

Nicoletti G., Haffner R.C.G., S. Nickell, S. Scarpetta and G. Zoega (2000). European Integration, Liberalisation and labor Market Performance. In: Bertola G., T. Boeri and G. Nicoletti (Eds) *Welfare and Employment in a United Europe*. MIT Press.

OECD (1994). *Jobs Stratcgy*, Paris: OECD.

Saint-Paul G. (1996). *Dual Labor Markets*. Cambridge: MIT Press.

Shapiro C. and Stiglitz J. (1984). Equilibrium unemployment as a worker discipline device. *American Economic Review*, 74:433-444.

Siebert H. (1997). Labor market rigidities: at the root of unemployment in Europe. *Journal of Economic Perspectives*, 11(3):37-54.

Solow R. (1979). Another possible source of wage rigidity. *Journal of Macroeconomics*, 1(1):79-82.

Weiss C. (1998). Is imperfect competition in the product market relevant for labor markets? *Labour*, 12(3):451-471.

Chapter 2: Human Capital, Local Labor Markets and Regional Integration.

Laurence Rioux
INSEE & CREST, France

Thierry Verdier
DELTA, France & CEPR

Abstract This paper investigates the impact of regional integration on the incentives for local governments to finance general human capital in a context of oligopsonistic labor markets, where firm's specific skills are obtained through specific training. General human capital increases both a worker's productivity *(productivity effect)* and its ability to learn new firm's specific skills (*flexibility effect*). For symmetric regions, integration leads to a "race to the top" or to a "race to the bottom" in local public educational policies depending on whether the *productivity effect* dominates or not the *flexibility effect*. The paper discusses also the effects of integration on regional wages, intra-regional wage inequalities and integration between regions different in size or productivity.

1. Introduction

One of the most important economic fact of the last decades is certainly the increased process of market integration observed between nations and regions. This process, often described as globalization, has been intensively discussed by many social scientists, businessmen or policymakers. Some see in it an opportunity to generate economic wealth and development. Others, on the contrary, make it responsible for the emergence of many social and economic problems in industrialized and developing economies. Most acknowledge the fact that, with its increased mobility of goods and factors of production, market integration imposes new constraints on national governments for the implementation of their local public policies. This aspect is best exemplified by the whole line of research on tax competition, factor mobility and the "race to the bottom" argument. This literature generally starts from the idea that regional or national governments have to finance a local public good by taxation on a mobile factor (capital or labor). In such a context, each national or regional authority has a strategic interest to reduce its tax rate in order to attract the mobile factor locally. Doing this increases its own tax base at the expense of the other governments. The final result is a sub-optimal level of local public goods with too low a tax rate in each region.

While the impact of factor mobility on national tax policies has attracted quite a large amount of attention, much less work has been done on the effect of integration on other public policy dimensions. A crucial one in this respect is human capital and the public supply of education. It is actually hard to deny the fact that in modern economies, education and training are an important source of productivity growth and competitiveness. Individuals acquire a variety of skills in schools, private or public. Firms provide many opportunities to their labor force to obtain firm-specific skills adapted to specific technologies, both through training programs and learning-on-the-job. Governments spend vast amounts of tax-payer money to supply education to their citizen. A natural and important issue, then, is how globalization and regional integration will affect the incentives of individuals to invest in human capital and, most importantly, how it will affect the structure and level of educational policies followed by local governments. Will regional integration be associated with a "race to the bottom" or a "race to the top" for local educational policies? What will be the effects on productivity and wages?

The purpose of this paper is to provide a first attempt to investigate these questions. In order to do this, we build on the recent work of Thisse and Zenou, 1995 on local oligopsonistic labor markets in which workers start with different specific skills and where, in order to produce within a firm, they need to perfectly match the firm's skill requirement through training. The more distant is the initial skill of a worker from the firm's specific requirement, the larger is the training cost. Besides this idea of specific human capital as captured above, we follow Becker, 1964 and also recognize the existence of a second dimension of human capital, namely general human capital, that has three major features. First, it is publicly provided by local governments. Second, it increases a worker's productivity independently from his initial skill location *(a productivity effect)*. Third, it also increases the worker's ability to learn new firm specific skills, in the sense that the larger the general human capital of a worker, the smaller the training cost for that worker to acquire a new firm specific skill (*a flexibility effect*).

Describing then regional integration by increased mobility of firms across regions, we investigate the local governments' incentives to provide general human capital to local workers. We also discuss the implications for regional productivities and wage inequalities within each region. Interestingly, we show that the "race to the bottom" versus "race to the top" debate, so much discussed in the tax competition literature, depends here on the relative strength of the *productivity effect* versus the *flexibility effect,* both effects being associated with general human capital. While the *productivity effect* has a positive effect on firm's profit, the *flexibility effect* reduces the cost of training born by workers to acquire a firm's specific skill requirement. In the labor market, this aspect allows workers to be more easily employable by firms, increasing therefore competition between rival employers and, consequently, wages which will be offered.

When the *productivity effect* dominates the *flexibility effect,* firms' expected profits in a region are increasing in the level of general human capital of the population. Hence the region which is better endowed with general education is also more successful at attracting firms and employers in its local labor market. This generates an incentive for each regional government to increase strategically its level of general human capital in order to attract firms locally. The equilibrium result is a higher level of general education after integration than before, higher local wages and a decrease in intra-regional inequalities. The "race to the top" argument applies. On the contrary, when the *flexibility effect* outweighs the *productivity effect,* then all results are reversed. Firms prefer to be localized in the region less endowed with general human capital, as they enjoy a higher monopsonic power because of the workers' relative inflexibility. Consequently, in order to attract these firms, local governments have a tendency to reduce their provision of general human capital. Competition between regions results in a lower equilibrium level of general education in each region, associated with lower wages and an higher intra-regional inequalities. The "race to the bottom" argument prevails in this case.

The plan of the paper is the following. The following section presents the oligopsonistic labor market model à la Thisse and Zenou with specific and general human capital for a given region in autarky. Section 3 considers the case of integration between two symmetric regions and presents several comparative statics on the equilibrium level of general human capital provided by local governments. Section 4 discusses the case of asymmetric regions in population size or productivity level. Finally section 5 concludes.

2. The model

Consider an economy formed by two regions i ($i = A, B$). Each region i is composed of n_i firms and a continuum of workers. Firms produce an homogeneous good sold on a competitive market with a price normalized to 1. The total number of firms is fixed and given by $N = n_A + n_B$.

We suppose that there is no worker mobility between the two regions. We will investigate sequentially the case in which firms cannot move between regions (No Integration) and the case with interregional firms' mobility (Integration).

2.1 General and specific human capital and production technology

Following Becker, 1964, we consider that human capital has two dimensions: a vertical dimension (general human capital) and a horizontal dimension (specific human capital). General human capital is publicly provided by the regional government.[1] Hence all workers, after school in region i, are endowed with the same level g_i. In each region however, individuals differ in their specific skills. There is no *a priori* superiority or inferiority among these skills as they only reflect different *ex ante* specificities in the educational background of a worker (for example, workers may have a degree in engineering but in different fields).

Formally, following Thisse and Zenou, 1995, it is assumed that, in region i, specific skills are uniformly distributed with density Δ_i on a circle C_i of length L_i where C_i represents the skill space and L_i reflects the degree of diversity in workers' specific skills. As workers are supposed to supply inelastically 1 unit of labor, $\Delta_i L_i$ is the total labor force in region i.[2]

In region i, we consider that each representative firm j is endowed with a technology of production which necessitates a given specific skill x_j^i in the same space C_i. Moreover these firm specific skill requirements

[1]We suppose that general human capital is not financed by the central government nor privately by agents. This assumption, though presented here in an extreme form, seems to be quite reasonable from an empirical point of view. As a matter of fact, more than 80 per cent of education expenditures, in most industrialized countries is financed publicly (OECD, 1998). Moreover, in many countries public education is regionally funded (Germany, Spain, The United States and Canada).

[2]This model is related to the specialization model of Kim, 1989 in which agents can choose between general education and specialized education. Specialized education provides a higher productivity on a limited range of specific skills while general education allows individuals to shift more easily between specific skills and have a higher probability of employment. Kim shows that an increase in the size of the labor market is associated with an increase in specialized education by workers.

are distributed symmetrically on the circle C_i and given by $x_j^i = \frac{(j-1)L_i}{n_i}$, $\forall\, j = 1, .., n_i$.[3]

In order to produce within a firm, a worker needs to perfectly match the firm's skill requirement.[4] Since workers' specific skills are uniformly distributed on the circle C_i, workers need specific training to match the firm's technology x_j^i. Now, the more distant the skill of a worker from the firm's specific requirement, the larger the training cost. More precisely, we consider as Thisse and Zenou, 1995, 1996, that the training cost is given by the following linear function $s\left|x^i - x_j^i\right|$ of the distance between the worker's skill x^i and the firm's skill requirement x_j^i. At the same time, one may expect that the larger the general human capital of a worker, the more flexible is this worker in terms of learning.[5] And therefore the easier it is to acquire the skill requirement of the firm. Formally, this means that s depends on the level of general human capital g_i of a worker. Reflecting our assumption of learning flexibility associated with general human capital, the cost of training per unit of distance $s(g_i)$ is a decreasing convex function of g_i (*i.e.* $s^{'}(.) < 0$ and $s^{''}(.) > 0$).

Once matched to the firm's required specific skill, a worker can start producing within the firm. We consider furthermore that the larger is his level of general human capital, the higher is his productivity. More precisely, the output produced by a firm of region i employing ℓ workers (having skill x_j^i after training) is given by a standard increasing concave production function $F_i(g_i\ell)$, with $F_i^{'}(g_i\ell) > 0$ and $F_i^{''}(g_i\ell) < 0$.

Note already that a higher level of general human capital in region i has two effects on firms' profits. First there is a *productivity effect* as all workers in this region are more productive, once they are matched to the firm's technology. On the other hand, there is also a *flexibility effect* associated to the fact that workers better endowed with general human capital can learn faster new specific skills. It is clear that the *productivity effect* has a positive effect on firm's profit. On the other hand, the *flexibility effect* reduces the cost of training born by workers to acquire a firm's specific skill requirement. In the labor market, this aspect allows

[3]As shown by Stevens, 1994, firms, in order to increase their market power, have incentives to choose technologies of production requiring specific training that protects their "location" against rival employers. Also, by analogy with results in the literature on spatially differentiated products, a symmetric configuration of technologies is likely to be an equilibrium outcome of a game in which firms choose in a first stage their technologies and then, in a second stage, their wages (Economides, 1989, Kats, 1995).

[4]The technology of production is of an extreme O-Ring type (Kremer, 1993).

[5]Think of one component of general human capital as being "learning to learn", (*i.e.* developing an ability to learn better).

workers to be more easily employable, increasing therefore competition between rival employers and consequently equilibrium wages. This in turn has a negative impact on firms' profits.

We assume that, before signing an employment contract, firms cannot observe the worker's type, while workers observe firms' job requirement. After hiring, the worker's type is revealed to the firm and training is made in the firm. It is assumed that, in each region i, the cost of specific training is shared between a worker and the firm hiring him with a share α_i born by the worker and $1-\alpha_i$ paid by the firm.[6]

We consider that the local government takes the decision on the amount of general human capital g_i provided in the region.[7]

2.2 Functioning of the local labor market

The working of the labor market in each region follows closely Thisse and Zénou, 1995, 1996. Once g_i is provided by the local government, firms $j = 1,..,n_i$ in region i choose simultaneously their wage level $\{w_j^i\}_{j\in(1,n_i)}$ offered to all workers. Each firm proposes a single wage as, first, the initial specific skill of a worker is not known to the firm before signing the employment contract, and second, because all workers, from the point of view of the firm, are alike after training. The net wage offered is then $w_j^i - \alpha_i s(g_i)\left|x^i - x_j^i\right|$. Agents choose to sign a contract and work for the firm offering them the highest net wage, provided that this wage is higher than the reservation wage which is normalized to 0 .

We can then characterize easily the labor market equilibrium for a region with n_i firms.[8] Denote j the representative firm. Given wages w_{j-1}^i and w_{j+1}^i offered by the adjacent firms, it is straightforward to see that firm j's labor pool is composed of two sub-segments whose outside boundaries are given by the marginal workers $\bar{x}_j^i$ and $\bar{y}_j^i$: these workers are indifferent between being hired, on the one hand, by firms $j-1$ and j, and, on the other hand, by firms j and $j+1$. More precisely, $\bar{x}_j^i$ and $\bar{y}_j^i$ are given by:

$$w_j^i - \alpha_i s(g_i)(x_j^i - \bar{x}_j^i) = w_{j-1}^i - \alpha_i s(g_i)(\bar{x}_j^i - x_{j-1}^i)$$

[6] The case $\alpha_i = 1$ is close to the situation of the US in which workers finance entirely their specific training. On the contrary, $\alpha_i = 0$ approximates the german case in which education is mainly financed by firms through a system of training and apprenticeship.

[7] To simplify, we suppose that the legislation on the share of training costs is fixed to a certain value $\alpha_i = \alpha$. The government could also choose endogenously the legislation on α_i. As in Thisse and Zenou, 1995, it is easy to show that the government has an incentive to pick α_i close to zero in order to maximize net expected wages in a region.

[8] We consider only sets of parameters that ensure full employment.

and

$$w_j^i - \alpha_i s(g_i)(\bar{y}_j^i - x_j^i) = w_{j+1}^i - \alpha_i s(g_i)(x_{j+1}^i - \bar{y}_j^i)$$

which gives

$$\begin{cases} \bar{x}_j^i = \frac{w_{j-1}^i - w_j^i + \alpha_i s(g_i)\left[x_j^i + x_{j-1}^i\right]}{2\alpha_i s(g_i)} \\ \bar{y}_j^i = \frac{w_j^i - w_{j+1}^i + \alpha_i s(g_i)\left[x_j^i + x_{j+1}^i\right]}{2\alpha_i s(g_i)} \end{cases} \quad (1)$$

Firm j attracts and hires all workers who belong to the pool $[\bar{x}_j^i, \bar{y}_j^i]$. Therefore employment for firm j is given by $\ell_j^i = \Delta_i \left(\bar{y}_j^i - \bar{x}_j^i\right)$. Given this and the fact that the firm pays a fraction $1-\alpha_i$ of the training costs, we can write profits as:

$$\begin{aligned} &\Pi_j^i(w_{j-1}^i, w_j^i, w_{j+1}^i) = \\ &F_i\left(g_i\ell_j^i\right) - w_j^i\ell_j^i - \int_{\bar{x}_j^i}^{\bar{y}_j^i} \Delta_i(1-\alpha_i)s(g_i)\left|x^i - x_j^i\right| dx_i \end{aligned} \quad (2)$$

which gives:

$$\begin{aligned} &\Pi_j^i(w_{j-1}^i, w_j^i, w_{j+1}^i) = \\ &F_i\left(g_i\ell_j^i\right) - w_j^i\ell_j^i - \frac{\Delta_i(1-\alpha_i)s(g_i)}{2}\left[\left(x_j^i - \bar{x}_j^i\right)^2 + \left(\bar{y}_j^i - x_j^i\right)^2\right] \end{aligned} \quad (3)$$

The profit function is continuous in $\left(w_{j-1}^i, w_j^i, w_{j+1}^i\right)$ and concave in w_j^i. Firm j chooses its wage w_j^i to maximize $\Pi_j^i(w_{j-1}^i, w_j^i, w_{j+1}^i)$, taking as given w_{j-1}^i and w_{j+1}^i. The first order condition (3) writes as:

$$\left[g_i F_i^{'}\left(g_i\ell_j^i\right) \quad w_j^i \quad \frac{(1-\alpha_i)s(g_i)\ell_j^i}{2\Delta_i}\right]\left(\frac{\partial \ell_j^i}{\partial w_j^i}\right) - \ell_j^i = 0 \quad (4)$$

with $\frac{\partial \ell_j^i}{\partial w_j^i} = \frac{\Delta_i}{\alpha_i s(g_i)}$. In a symmetric Nash Equilibrium, $w_{j-1}^i = w_j^i = w_{j+1}^i$, $\bar{x}_j^i = \frac{\left[x_j^i + x_{j-1}^i\right]}{2}$ and $\bar{y}_j^i = \frac{\left[x_j^i + x_{j+1}^i\right]}{2}$. Therefore

$$\ell_i^* = \frac{\Delta_i L_i}{n_i} \quad (5)$$

Using then equation (4), one gets the gross equilibrium wage and profits as:[9]

[9]The necessary and sufficient condition on parameters to get full employment is easily obtained as $g_i F_i^{'}\left(g_i \frac{\Delta_i L_i}{n_i}\right) - \frac{(1+\alpha_i)s(g_i)L_i}{2n_i} \geqslant 0$.

$$w_i^* = g_i F_i^{'}(g_i \ell_i^*) - \frac{(1+\alpha_i)s(g_i)\ell_i^*}{2\Delta_i} \tag{6}$$

$$\Pi_i^* = F_i(g_i \ell_i^*) - g_i \ell_i^* F_i^{'}(g_i \ell_i^*) + \frac{(1+3\alpha_i)s(g_i)}{4\Delta_i}(\ell_i^*)^2 \tag{7}$$

The previous results can be summarized usefully in the following proposition:

Proposition 1 *Under the condition* $g_i F_i^{'}\left(g_i \frac{\Delta_i L_i}{n_i}\right) > \frac{(1+\alpha_i)s(g_i)L_i}{2n_i}$, *there exists a unique symmetric Nash Equilibrium in wages in region i in which each firm employs* $\ell_i^* = \frac{\Delta_i L_i}{n_i}$ *workers, and equilibrium wages and profits are given by equations (6) and (7). The net expected wage is* $\bar{w}_{i_{net}}^* = w_i^* - \frac{\alpha_i s(g_i)\ell_i^*}{4\Delta_i}$ *and the intra-regional wage dispersion is given by* $V_i^* = \frac{1}{3}\left(\frac{\alpha_i s(g_i)\ell_i^*}{2\Delta_i}\right)^2$.

Proof. The net expected wage is easily obtained as $\bar{w}_{net} = w - \frac{\int_{\bar{x}_j}^{\bar{y_j}} \Delta\alpha s(g)|x-x_j|dx}{\int_{\bar{x}_j}^{\bar{y_j}} \Delta dx} = w - \frac{\Delta\alpha s(g)\int_{\bar{x}_j}^{\bar{y_j}}|x-x_j|dx}{\Delta(\bar{y_j}-\bar{x}_j)}$. But $(\bar{y_j} - \bar{x}_j) = \frac{2\ell}{\Delta}$.
Substituting $\bar{y_j} - \bar{x}_j$, we get $\bar{w}_{net} = w - \frac{\alpha s(g)\ell}{4\Delta}$.
To compute the intra-regional dispersion, let $|x - x_j| = z_j$.
Then $(w_j - \bar{w}_{net}) = \alpha s(g)\left[\frac{\ell}{4\Delta} - z_j\right]$.
As $V = E\left[w_j - \bar{w}_{net}\right]^2$, this gives after computations $\frac{1}{3}\left(\frac{\alpha s(g)\ell}{2\Delta}\right)^2$. □

From proposition 1, it is clear that the equilibrium wage and the net wage are decreasing in the population density Δ_i and the size of the regional labor force L_i and increasing in the number of firms n_i located in the region. As explained by Thisse and Zenou, 1995, 1996, the decreasing relationship between the size of the labor force and the equilibrium wage comes from the fact that the monopsonic power of employers (firms) increases with the number of workers.

Under the reasonable assumption that $\frac{g_i F_i^{'}\left(g_i \frac{\Delta_i L_i}{n_i}\right)}{s(g_i)}$ is increasing in g_i,[10] the gross wage is increasing in the level of general human capital.

[10]Equation (6) gives that $\frac{\partial w_{i_{brut}}^*}{\partial g_i} = F_i^{'}(g_i \ell_i) + g_i \ell_i F_i^{''}(g_i \ell_i) - \frac{(1+\alpha_i)s^{'}(g_i)\ell_i}{2\Delta_i}$. If $\frac{g_i F_i^{'}\left(g_i \frac{\Delta_i L_i}{n_i}\right)}{s(g_i)}$ is an increasing function of g_i, one gets that $\frac{\partial w_{i_{brut}}^*}{\partial g_i} > 0$.

First, the *flexibility effect* of general human capital reduces the costs of training on the specific skill requirement of the firm. Also it decreases the monopsonic power of employers in the labor market, as workers are more "mobile" between firms specific skills. This increases wages offered in equilibrium. Second, because of *the productivity effect*, general human capital also increases the productivity of workers inside firms after training. This again tends to increase their wages.

Finally, note that the equilibrium wage is decreasing in α_i the share of training financed by workers. As a matter of fact, an increase in α_i increases the monopsonic power of firms and therefore reduces the gross equilibrium wage offered by firms. The net expected wage decreases further as training costs paid by workers get larger.

The impact of the various parameters on equilibrium profits mirrors the previous discussion on wages and gives immediately that equilibrium profits are increasing in Δ_i, $\frac{L_i}{n_i}$ and α_i.

The effect of the level of general human capital on profits is more ambiguous. From equation (7), the sign of $\frac{\partial \Pi_i^*}{\partial g_i}$ is given by the sign of $-g_i F_i^{''}(g_i \ell_i) + \frac{(1+3\alpha_i)s^{'}(g_i)}{4\Delta_i}$. The first term, $\left[-g_i F_i^{''}(g_i \ell_i)\right]$, is positive and reflects the *productivity effect* of general human capital on firms profitability. As trained workers are more productive when they are endowed with more general human capital, part of the productivity gains are captured by firms. The second term, $\left[\frac{(1+3\alpha_i)s^{'}(g_i)}{4\Delta_i}\right]$, however is negative and represents the *flexibility effect* of general human capital. As the labor force has more general education, it is also more flexible and therefore more "mobile" potentially between rival employers, increasing competition between firms in the labor market. Equilibrium wages are increased and firms' profits are reduced. Clearly, the total effect of general human capital on the firms' profitability depends on which effect dominates. When the *productivity effect* outweighs the *flexibility effect*, then firms' profits are higher when the population is better endowed in general human capital. Otherwise, we get the opposite result.

3. Integration between two identical regions

In this section, we consider how the educational policy of two identical regions is affected when firms are allowed to move between regions (*i.e.* regional integration). Restricting ourselves to symmetric regions greatly simplifies the analysis and allows us to isolate the "pure" effects of regional integration. In section 4, we discuss in a specific example the marginal impact of asymmetry of regions on local educational policy choices.

Regions A and B are identical. Hence $F_A(.) = F_B(.) = F(.)$ and $\alpha_A = \alpha_B = \alpha$, $L_A = L_B = L$ and $\Delta_A = \Delta_B = \Delta$.

In order to determine the impact of regional integration on local educational policy, we will discuss the policy chosen by each region, first, when there is no integration and, next, when there is inter-regional mobility of firms. We suppose that local governments want to maximize the net expected wage of their citizen minus the cost of funding general human capital.[11] Formally the objective function of a regional government is given by:

$$SW_i = n_i \ell_i^* \left(w_i^* - \frac{\alpha s(g_i)\ell_i^*}{4\Delta} \right) - \Delta L \Gamma(g_i) \tag{8}$$

when n_i firms are localized in region i and each of them employs $\ell_i^* = \frac{\Delta L}{n_i}$ workers, each worker receiving an expected net wage of $w_i^* - \frac{\alpha s(g_i)\ell_i^*}{4\Delta}$. $\Gamma(.)$ is the increasing convex cost function to supply a level of general human capital g_i to any individual, with $\Gamma'(.) > 0$ and $\Gamma''(.) > 0$. Note that with this formulation, general human capital formation is supposed to be financed by lump-sum taxes on workers. This type of financing does not give rise to the standard fiscal competition between regions when there is inter-regional mobility and therefore allows us to concentrate on the pure aspect of regional competition on public educational policy. In the conclusion, we discuss briefly how the results would be affected by other modes of financing.[12]

3.1 Educational policy with no regional integration

Consider first the case in which firms cannot move between regions. Each region is then completely independent from the other. As they are assumed identical, $n_A = n_B = \frac{N}{2}$. Then each firm in region i employs $\ell = \frac{2\Delta L}{N}$ workers.

The maximization program of the local government of region i writes as:

---

[11] This objective function for the local governements can be justified by a political economy argument if one expects workers to be the decisive political agents in a given region.

[12] Note also that the convexity of the cost function $\Gamma(.)$ implicitly assumes the existence of specific infrastructures essential to supply a level of general human capital g_i and already present in region i. Hence, taking as given the level of these infrastructures, we are mainly considering short run or medium term effects of regional integration on educational policies. This is also consistent with the fact the total number of firms across regions will be fixed to N.

$$\max_{\{g_i\}} SW_i = \Delta L \left(g_i F^{'}(g_i \ell) - \frac{(2+3\alpha)s(g_i)\ell}{4\Delta} - \Gamma(g_i) \right) \tag{9}$$

The first order condition gives:

$$F^{'}(g_i \ell) + g_i \ell F^{''}(g_i \ell) - \frac{(2+3\alpha)s^{'}(g_i)\ell}{4\Delta} - \Gamma^{'}(g_i) = 0 \tag{10}$$

The second order condition is satisfied when $s(g_i)$ and $\Gamma(g_i)$ are convex enough. Denote by g_c^* the solution of equation (10). Differentiation of this equation provides then the following result:

Proposition 2 *The optimal level of general human capital g_c^* provided in each region with no inter-regional mobility of firms verifies: $\frac{\partial g_c^*}{\partial \alpha} > 0$ and, when the production function satisfies $2F^{''}(x) + xF^{'''}(x) < 0$, $\forall\, x$, $\frac{\partial g_c^*}{\partial \Delta} < 0$*

Proof. First,

$$\frac{\partial g_c^*}{\partial \alpha} = \frac{\frac{3s^{'}(g_c^*)\ell}{4\Delta}}{\ell F^{''}(g_c^*\ell) + g_c^*\ell^2 F^{'''}(g_c^*\ell) - \frac{(2+3\alpha)s^{''}(g_c^*)\ell}{4\Delta} - \Gamma^{''}(g_c^*)}$$

As the denominator and the numerator are both negative we get easily $\frac{\partial g_c^*}{\partial \alpha} > 0$.

Similarly

$$\frac{\partial g_c^*}{\partial \Delta} = \frac{-g_c^*\left(\frac{2L}{N}\right)\left(2F^{''}(g_c^*\ell) + g_c^*\ell F^{'''}(g_c^*\ell)\right)}{\ell F^{''}(g_c^*\ell) + g_c^*\ell^2 F^{'''}(g_c^*\ell) - \frac{(2+3\alpha)s^{''}(g_c^*)\ell}{4\Delta} - \Gamma^{''}(g_c^*)}$$

The denominator is negative while the numerator is positive when $2F^{''}(x) + xF^{'''}(x) < 0$. Hence $\frac{\partial g_c^*}{\partial \Delta} < 0$.

□

The first comparative statics of proposition 2 gives that the optimal level of general human capital g_c^* increases with the share α of the training costs paid by workers. The intuition for this is the following. When workers pay a higher share α of the training costs, the monopsonic power of firms is increased. Consequently, firms are able to propose lower wages. In order to mitigate this effect on wages, the optimal level of general human capital has to be increased. First because this reduces the part of the training cost supported by workers by the *flexibility effect.*

Second, because the *productivity effect* makes workers more productive once they have been trained to the skill requirement of a firm.[13]

The second part of proposition 2 shows that the optimal level of general human capital g_c^* decreases with the regional population density Δ under a reasonable technical assumption (which is for instance satisfied by a quadratic production technology). The reason is that, as the population gets larger, it becomes more costly to provide a given level of general human capital to each individual. Therefore g_c^* has to decrease. The consequence of this is the fact the net wage received by workers is also smaller for two reasons. First the monopsonic power of firms increases with Δ. Second, as they depend positively on the level of general human capital provided by the government, wages will also be negatively affected by a decrease in g_c^*.

3.2 Educational policy with regional integration

Consider now that firms can choose the region in which they want to produce. The timing of the game is then the following. In a first stage, each local government in region i, $\forall i = \{A, B\}$, chooses a level of general human capital publicly provided g_i^* to maximize its objective function (net expected wages minus the cost of general human capital provision) taking as given the choice of the other regional government. In a second stage, firms decide their regional localisation according to the highest profit they expect to get in one or the other region. In each region i, firms then locate symmetrically in the characteristic space C_i. In the third stage, they choose wages in the local labor market in a Nash fashion. Finally, workers get trained and production is realized.

The third stage describes the labor market equilibrium for a fixed number of regional firms n_i and has been already solved in the previous section. Mobility of firms between the two regions implies that regional profits have to be equalized at the equilibrium. This generates a division of the total number of firms N between the two regions. The program of the local government of region i in the first stage is given by:

$$\max_{\{g_i\}} SW_i = \Delta L \left(g_i F'(g_i \ell_i) - \frac{(2+3\alpha)s(g_i)\ell_i}{4\Delta} - \Gamma(g_i) \right) \tag{11}$$

[13] Data from *Education at a glance: OECD indicators (OECD)* suggest that countries in which firms pay a higher share of specific training, also tend to have a smaller share of public spending to general education. For instance, Germany, where firms pay a large share of specific training, allocates 10 per cent of its public spending to education. On the other hand, in the US, where firms do not contribute much to workers' specific training costs, education represents 14 % of public spending.

under the constraint of profits equality,

$$\begin{aligned} F(g_i\ell_i) - g_i\ell_i F'(g_i\ell_i) + \frac{(1+3\alpha)s(g_i)}{4\Delta}\ell_i^2 &= F(g_j\ell_j) - g_j\ell_j F'(g_j\ell_j) \\ &+ \frac{(1+3\alpha)s(g_j)}{4\Delta}\ell_j^2 \end{aligned}$$

We consider the symmetric Nash equilibria in local general human capital policies. As both governments in such a symmetric equilibrium choose the same level of general human capital, the two regions offer the same expected profits to firms and consequently have also the same number of firms, $n = \frac{N}{2}$. In each region, each firm hires the same number of workers, $\ell = \frac{2\Delta L}{N}$. Using the first order condition of the optimization program of government i and substituting the symmetry condition $g_i = g_j$, we get the following condition characterizing the symmetric Nash equilibrium $g_i^* = g_j^* = g_I^*$:

$$\begin{aligned} & F'(g_I^*\ell) + g_I^*\ell F''(g_I^*\ell) - \frac{(2+3\alpha)s'(g_I^*)\ell}{4\Delta} - \Gamma'(g_I^*) \\ & + \frac{\ell}{2}\left[\frac{(1+3\alpha)s'(g_I^*)}{4\Delta} - g_I^* F''(g_I^*\ell)\right] \times \left[1 - \frac{\frac{3\alpha s(g_I^*)}{4\Delta}}{\frac{(1+3\alpha)s(g_I^*)}{2\Delta} - g_I^{*2}F''(g_I^*\ell)}\right] \\ & = 0 \end{aligned} \tag{12}$$

Proposition 3 *When $\Gamma(.)$ is sufficiently convex, there exists a unique symmetric Nash equilibrium in general human capital between the two regions where $g_i^* = g_j^* = g_I^*$. Moreover $\frac{\partial g_I^*}{\partial \alpha} > 0$.*

Proof. See appendix. □

The intuition behind the comparative statics result is easy to understand. When the share of training costs α paid by workers increases in one region i, then the monopsonic power of firms and expected profits in that region increase. Consequently, firms are more likely to get localized in region i everything else being equal. This allows the local government of that region increasing the level of general human capital to mitigate the negative impact of a higher α on wages, even though this increase potentially has a negative impact on regional firms' profits through the *flexibility effect.*

3.3 The effect of regional integration on local educational policies

In this section, we compare the optimal choice of general human capital with and without regional integration. As we may expect, this comparison will depend crucially on the relative importance of the *productivity effect* and the *flexibility effect* on firms profits. It is thus useful to rewrite the equilibrium equations describing g_c^* and g_I^* , in a way which isolates these two effects. More precisely

$$F'\left(g_c^*\ell\right) - \frac{s'\left(g_c^*\right)\ell}{4\Delta} - \Gamma'\left(g_c^*\right) - \ell B\left(g_c^*\right) = 0 \tag{13}$$

$$\begin{array}{l} F'\left(g_I^*\ell\right) - \frac{s'\left(g_I^*\right)\ell}{4\Delta} - \Gamma'\left(g_I^*\right) \\ -\frac{\ell}{2} B\left(g_I^*\right)\left[1 + \frac{\frac{3\alpha s\left(g_I^*\right)}{4\Delta}}{\frac{(1+3\alpha)s\left(g_I^*\right)}{2\Delta} - \left(g_I^*\right)^2 F''\left(g_I^*\ell\right)}\right] = 0 \end{array} \tag{14}$$

where $B(g) = \left[\frac{(1+3\alpha)s'(g)}{4\Delta} - gF''(g\ell)\right]$ can be interpreted as the sum of the *productivity effect*, $-gF''(g\ell) > 0$, and the *flexibility effect*, -$\frac{(1+3\alpha)s'(g)}{4\Delta} < 0$, and $\ell = \frac{2\Delta L}{N}$.

The following proposition gives the conditions under which regional integration affects positively or negatively the level of general human capital provided by the local government.

Proposition 4 *Let $\overline{g}$ such that $\frac{\overline{g}F''(\overline{g}\ell)}{s'(\overline{g})} = \frac{1+3\alpha}{4\Delta}$.*

- *When $F'(\overline{g}\ell) - \frac{s'(\overline{g})\ell}{4\Delta} - \Gamma'(\overline{g}) > 0$, the productivity effect dominates the flexibility effect and regional integration implies an increase in the level of general education provided by local governments (i.e. $g_c^* < g_I^*$). This is associated with an increase in regional wages and a decrease in intra-regional inequalities.*
- *When $F'(\overline{g}\ell) - \frac{s'(\overline{g})\ell}{4\Delta} - \Gamma'(\overline{g}) < 0$, the flexibility effect dominates the productivity effect and regional integration implies a decrease in the level of general education provided by local governments (i.e. $g_c^* > g_I^*$). This is associated with a decrease in regional wages and an increase in intra-regional inequalities.*

Proof. See appendix.

□

Proposition 4 shows precisely how the impact of regional integration on local educational policies depends on the relative importance of the *productivity effect* and the *flexibility effect* associated with general human capital.

Clearly when the *productivity effect* dominates the *flexibility effect,* firms' expected profits in a region are increasing in the level of general human capital of the population. Hence the region which is better endowed with general education is also more successful at attracting firms and employers in its local labor market. This generates an incentive for each regional government to increase strategically its level of general human capital in order to attract firms locally. The equilibrium result is a higher level of general education after integration than before. The benefits of this is also higher local wages and net wages and a decrease in intra-regional inequalities.

On the other hand when the *flexibility effect* outweighs the *productivity effect,* then all the results are reversed. Firms prefer to be in the local labor market which is less endowed with general human capital, as they enjoy a higher monopsonic power because of the relative inflexibility of workers in that region. Consequently, in order to attract these firms, local governments have a tendency to reduce their provision of general human capital. The competition between regions in this respect results in a lower equilibrium level of general education in each region, associated with lower wages and an increase in intra-regional inequalities.

Without a more precise specification of the technology of production, it is difficult to get conditions on fundamental parameters ensuring a positive effect of regional integration on education, wages and inequalities. Nevertheless, we may get interesting comparative statics on $\overline{g}$, the level of general human capital at which the *productivity effect* and the *flexibility effect* compensate each other. More precisely, simple computations show:

Proposition 5

$$\frac{\partial \overline{g}}{\partial \Delta} < 0, \frac{\partial \overline{g}}{\partial (L/N)} < 0 \text{ and } \frac{\partial \overline{g}}{\partial \alpha} > 0$$

$\overline{g}$ is a decreasing function of the population density Δ and the size of the labor pool $\frac{2L}{N}$ of firms. Consequently, the set of values of general human capital for which the *productivity effect* dominates the *flexibility effect* gets larger with Δ and $\frac{L}{N}$. Inversely $\overline{g}$ is increasing with α the share of the training costs which is paid by workers. Thus, the more workers contribute to the financing of specific capital training, the smaller is the set of values of general human capital for which the *productivity effect* outweighs the *flexibility effect.*

3.4 A quadratic example

In order to have a more precise idea of the circumstances under which regional integration has a positive or a negative impact on local educational choices, let us consider the example of a quadratic production function:

$$F\left(g_i\ell\right)=\left[a-\frac{b}{2}g_i\ell\right]g_i\ell$$

Let us also denote $h\left(g\right)=\frac{-g}{s'(g)}$. Given that $s(.)$ is decreasing convex, it is easy to see that $h(.)$ is increasing and therefore that $h^{-1}(.)$ is also increasing.

$\overline{g}$ is then solution of

$$\frac{-\overline{g}}{s'\left(\overline{g}\right)}=\frac{1+3\alpha}{4\Delta b}$$

or

$$\overline{g}=h^{-1}\left(\frac{1+3\alpha}{4\Delta b}\right)$$

The condition for regional integration to be associated with an increase in the local provision of general education is then:

$$a-\left(\frac{2\Delta L}{N}\right)b\overline{g}-\frac{s'(\overline{g})L}{2N}-\Gamma'\left(\overline{g}\right)>0.$$

Substituting $\overline{g}$ provides a condition on the structural parameters α, Δ and $\frac{L}{N}$:

$$a+\frac{3\alpha L}{2N}s'\left(h^{-1}\left(\frac{1+3\alpha}{4\Delta b}\right)\right)-\Gamma'\left(h^{-1}\left(\frac{1+3\alpha}{4\Delta b}\right)\right)>0 \qquad (15)$$

This condition is more likely to be satisfied the smaller is the labor pool $\frac{2L}{N}$ of each firm. More precisely, it is easy to see that there is a threshold value of $\frac{L}{N}$ below which (15) is satisfied. Hence, for a given total number of firms N, the larger the size of the two regions L, the less likely will regional integration be associated with an increase in local public education. (15) is also more easily satisfied when the density Δ is high. Hence the less densely populated are the two regions, the less likely is regional integration associated with an increase in general human capital publicly provided. The efficiency of the firms' technology of production (as captured by the productivity parameters a and b) also plays a role. As a matter of fact, the higher is a and the smaller is b, that is the more efficient is the technology, the easier is condition (15) satisfied. Finally, condition (15) depends on the way training costs are shared between workers and firms. When workers contribute more to the financing of training costs, regional integration is more likely to lead to a decrease in the investment in general human capital.

4. Integration between two asymmetric regions

Until now we have considered the case of integration between identical regions. This allowed us isolating the "pure" effects of firms mobility on the incentives for local governments to provide general human capital. It may be of course also interesting to analyze the case of integration of asymmetric regions. In particular, one may want to discuss what happens when two regions of different size get integrated? Do they both benefit or loose? Which region (the large one or the small one) benefits most from the integration?

Doing however a full analysis of the problem of integration of two asymmetric regions is difficult as one cannot anymore compute explicitly the Nash asymmetric equilibrium between the two local governments.[14] Still, restricting ourselves to the quadratic example, we are able to get some insights on the impact of integration on slightly asymmetric integration. Consider then again quadratic production functions of the type

$$F_i\left(g_i\ell_i\right) = \left[a_i - \frac{b_i}{2} g_i \ell_i\right] g_i \ell_u$$

and quadratic training functions $s_i(.)$ (*i.e.* $s_i^{'''}(.) = 0$).

We will also concentrate on two sources of asymmetries, namely size $L_A \neq L_B$ and productivity $a_A \neq a_B$. Therefore we consider in the rest of this section that $s_i(.)$ and $\Gamma_i(.)$ are the same in the two regions. Also $\Delta_A = \Delta_B = \Delta$ and $b_A = b_B = b$. Finally we will consider the case in which $\alpha_A = \alpha_B = \alpha$ is close to 0, that is the case in which most of the training cost is paid by firms.[15] In equilibrium in each regional labor market i, we have $\ell_i = \frac{\Delta L_i}{n_i}$

The local government of region i then chooses its level of general human capital, g_i^*, which maximizes the welfare of the workers in its region. Hence

[14] The literature on the effects of regional integration in the asymmetric case is relatively sparse and deals exclusively with the issue of fiscal competition. See Bucovetsky, 1991 for an analysis with quadratic production functions and Wilson, 1991 for the general case. These analyses suggest that fiscal competition tends to favor the small region.

[15] Thisse and Zenou, 1996 find optimal to have $\alpha \simeq 0$ in order to maximize net expected wages in an isolated region.

$$\max_{\{g_i\}} SW_i = \Delta L_i \left(a_i g_i - b g_i^2 \ell_i - \frac{(2+3\alpha) b(g_i) \ell_i}{4\Delta} - \Gamma(g_i) \right) \tag{16}$$

under the constraint of equality between regional profits,

$$\ell_i^2 \left(\frac{b}{2} g_i^1 + \frac{(1+6\alpha)s(g_i)}{4\Delta} \right) = \ell_j^1 \left(\frac{b}{2} g_j^2 + \frac{(1+3\alpha)s(g_j)}{4\Delta} \right)$$

Denoting $B(g_i) = b g_i + \frac{(1+3\alpha)s'(g_i)}{4\Delta}$ and $A(g_i) = \frac{b}{2} g_i^2 + \frac{(1+3\alpha)s(g_i)}{4\Delta}$, the profit equalization condition between the two regions becomes:

$$\frac{\ell_A}{\ell_B} = \sqrt{\frac{A(g_B)}{A(g_A)}}$$

Moreover, the total number of firms N is given by $N = n_A + n_B$. Hence the relationship:

$$\frac{\Delta L_A}{\ell_A} + \frac{\Delta L_B}{\ell_B} = N$$

From this, we get that each firm in region i employs ℓ_i workers with $\ell_i = \frac{\Delta L_i}{N} + \frac{\Delta L_j}{N} \sqrt{\frac{A(g_j)}{A(g_i)}}$. Then we can derive how this employment pool of a firm in region i is affected by the level of general human capital in that region:

$$\frac{\partial \ell_i}{\partial g_i} = -\frac{\Delta L_j B(g_i)}{2NA(g_j)} \sqrt{\frac{A(g_j)}{A(g_i)}}$$

Clearly when the *productivity effect* (resp. *flexibility effect)* dominates, $B(g_i)$ is positive (resp. negative) and an increase in the level of general human capital g_i in region i decreases (increases) the size of the employment pool of a firm in that region. This is because an increase in g_i makes firms more (resp. less) willing to be located in region i.

After computations, the first order condition of each local government i writes as

$$\begin{aligned} &a_i - \Gamma'(g_i) - \left(2bg_i + \frac{(3+3\alpha)s'(g_i)}{4\Delta} \right) \left(\frac{\Delta L_i}{N} + \frac{\Delta L_j}{N} \sqrt{\frac{A(g_j)}{A(g_i)}} \right) \\ &+ \frac{\Delta L_j}{2N} \sqrt{\frac{A(g_j)}{A(c_i)}} \left(\frac{B(g_i)}{A(g_i)} \right) \left(b g_i^2 + \frac{(1+3\alpha)s(g_i)}{0\Delta} \right) = 0 \end{aligned} \tag{17}$$

This equation defines implicitly the best response function $g_i = R_i(g_j)$ of government i to the level of general human capital chosen by the other region. Obviously, solving a system of two equations like (17) and determining the asymmetric Nash equilibria $\{g_A^*, g_B^*\}$ is analytically intractable. However when the two regions are slightly asymmetric and α is close to 0, we are able to provide some insights of the impact of asymmetric integration.

4.1 Integration between regions of different size

Consider first that the two regions A and B only differ in size with $L_A > L_B$. Also, in order to have a benchmark before integration, suppose that when there is no integration, the number of firms in each region is proportional to the size of the region (*i.e.* $\frac{L_a}{n_a} = \frac{L_b}{n_b}$). Then it is easy to see that although they have different sizes, the two regions will make the same general human capital choice. As a matter of fact, the employment pool of each firm is the same in each region, hence the maximization program of the local government in each region is also the same.[16] Given that α is close to 0, the two local governments then choose g_c^* such that:

$$a - \Gamma^{'}(g_c^*) - \left(\frac{2\Delta L_i}{n_i}\right)\left(bg_c^* + \frac{s^{'}(g_c^*)}{4\Delta}\right) \simeq 0, \forall i = A, B$$

Note that under our assumption of proportionality between the initial number of firms and the size of the region, profits and wages before integration are also the same in the two regions. This provides therefore a useful benchmark to compare with what happens after integration.

Consider now that firms can be located in the region they wish. Then the first order condition (17) giving the optimal choice of general human capital of each region collapses to:

$$a - \Gamma^{'}(g_i^*) - \left(\frac{2\Delta L_i}{N} + \frac{\Delta L_j}{N}\sqrt{\frac{A\left(g_j^*\right)}{A\left(g_i^*\right)}}\right) B\left(g_i^*\right) \simeq 0, \text{for i, j} \in \{\text{A, B}\} \text{ and i} \neq \text{j}$$

We have then the following proposition:

Proposition 6 *Let the two regions A and B differ only by their size with $L_A = L + \varepsilon > L_B = L - \varepsilon$. Then*

- $\left.\frac{\partial g_A^*}{\partial \varepsilon}\right|_{\varepsilon=0} < 0$ *and* $\left.\frac{\partial g_B^*}{\partial \varepsilon}\right|_{\varepsilon=0} > 0$ *when the productivity effect dominates the flexibility effect.*

[16] See proposition 2 giving the optimal level of general human capital g_c^* in a non integrated region.

- $\left.\frac{\partial g_A^*}{\partial \varepsilon}\right|_{\varepsilon=0} > 0$ *and* $\left.\frac{\partial g_B^*}{\partial \varepsilon}\right|_{\varepsilon=0} < 0$ *when the flexibility effect dominates the productivity ezfect.*

- *In both cases* $\left.\frac{\partial \ell_A}{\partial \varepsilon}\right|_{\varepsilon=0} > 0$ *and* $\left.\frac{\partial \ell_K}{\partial \varepsilon}\right|_{\varepsilon=0} < 0$, $\left.\frac{\partial n_A}{\partial \varepsilon}\right|_{\varepsilon=0} > 0$ *and* $\left.\frac{\partial n_B}{\partial \varepsilon}\right|_{\varepsilon=0} < 0$.

Proof. See appendix.

□

Proposition 6 underlines the fact that, again, the sign of $\left.\frac{\partial g_A^*}{\partial \varepsilon}\right|_{\varepsilon=0}$, reflecting the marginal deviation of the asymmetric integration case from the symmetric integration case, depends on the relative weight of the *productivity* and *flexibility effects*. More precisely, when the *productivity effect* dominates, the small region B tends to spend more on general human capital, while on the contrary, when the *flexibility effect* is dominant, it is the larger region A which has an incentive to provide more general human capital. Also, the number of workers employed per firm (the size of the local pool of workers of a firm) is increased in the large region and is smaller in the small region. In other words, firms localized in the bigger region employ more workers than firms installed in the small region. Finally, the total number n_A of firms localized in the large region A increases but less than proportionally with the size of that region.

The intuition for these results is the following. The employment pool of a representative firm is larger in the large region than in the small one. Therefore competition between firms in the labor market is less intense in the large region than in the small one, providing an advantage in terms of firms' localization for the larger region.

When the *productivity effect* dominates, firms prefer to be localized in the region with the population best endowed with general education. This induces local governments to spend more on general human capital after integration than before. Because of its size advantage in terms of firms localization, the large country can then afford to spend less in general human capital while, on the contrary, the small region needs to spend more to counteract its disadvantage. The total effect of integration is then an increase in general human capital with a stronger impact for the small region than for the large one.

Similarly when the *flexibility effect* is dominant, local governments have an incentive to reduce their provision of general human capital to attract firms in their region. Hence the level of general education will tend to be smaller in both regions. However, because of its size advantage on the labor market, the large region can afford to invest more in general education without a risk to make too many firms go to the other region, while on the contrary, the small region needs to reduce even more its provision of general human capital to be able to attract firms from the other region. If regional integration affects negatively investment in general education in both regions, the effect is clearly stronger for the smaller region.

In conclusion, it appears that the small region is always more affected by integration (positively or negatively) than the large region. Given our "before integration" benchmark, this result suggests that asymmetric regional integration increases the divergence between small and large regions in wages and welfare.

4.2 Integration between regions with different productivities

Let now the two regions A and B differ only with their production technology.[17] Suppose more precisely that $a_A > a_B$. We keep also the assumption that $\alpha_A = \alpha_B \simeq 0$.

The local governments' choice of general human capital are given by the following condition, $\forall\ i, j = A, B$:

$$a_i - \Gamma'(g_i^*) - \frac{\Delta L}{N}\left(2 + \sqrt{\frac{A\left(g_j^*\right)}{A\left(g_i^*\right)}}\right) B\left(g_i^*\right) = 9$$

Then the following proposition characterizes the marginal impact of asymmetric integration:

Proposition 7 *Let regions A and B differ by their productivity parameters: $a_A = a + \eta > a_B = a - \eta$. Then, $\left.\frac{\partial g_A^*}{\partial \eta}\right|_{\eta=0} > 0$ and $\left.\frac{\partial g_B^*}{\partial \eta}\right|_{\eta=0} < 0$. Moreover,*

- *When the productivity effect dominates the flexibility effect, then $\left.\frac{\partial \ell_A}{\partial \eta}\right|_{\eta=0} < 0$ and $\left.\frac{\partial \ell_B}{\partial \eta}\right|_{\eta=0} > 8$, $\left.\frac{\partial n_A}{\partial \eta}\right|_{\eta=0} > 0$ and $\left.\frac{\partial n_B}{\partial \eta}\right|_{\eta=0} < 0$.*
- *When the flexibility effect dominates the productivity effect, then $\left.\frac{\partial \ell_A}{\partial \eta}\right|_{\eta=4} > 0$ and $\left.\frac{\partial \ell_B}{\partial \eta}\right|_{\eta=0} < 0$, $\left.\frac{\partial n_A}{\partial \eta}\right|_{\eta=0} < 0$ and $\left.\frac{\partial n_B}{\partial \eta}\right|_{\eta=0} > 0$.*

[17] This regional specificity in production technologies may come from differences in the level of infrastructure equipments between the two regions.

Proof. See appendix.

□

Proposition 7 shows that the region with the higher (smaller) productivity is ready to provide more (less) general human capital than in the symmetric integration case. The reason is that the region with the higher productivity level pays higher wages per unit of efficient labor. Hence the marginal return to general human capital is larger in this region. The effects on ℓ_A and ℓ_B, the employment pool per firm in regions A and B, and on n_A and n_B, the number of firms in regions A and B, depend then, in turn, on the relative importance of *the productivity and flexibility effects.* Clearly, when the *productivity effect* dominates the *flexibility effect,* firms' profits depend positively on the general human capital level of the region. As the high productivity region A provides more general education, firms have higher incentives to locate in this region, leading to a higher final number of firms n_A and a smaller employment pool per firm ℓ_A. Conversely, when the *flexibility effect* outweighs the *productivity effect,* firms' profits depend negatively on general human capital and the large region A spends more on general human capital. Thus less firms get localized in A and the employment pool of workers per firm in that region is larger.

5. Conclusion

In this paper, we investigated the impact of regional integration, in the sense of firms' regional mobility, on the incentives for local governments to invest in education. A crucial feature of the analysis has been to recognize that human capital is characterized by two dimensions. Horizontally, individuals can be differentiated by specific skills which do not necessarily match the specific skills required by the firms' technologies. This induces therefore the need for some specific training.

Vertically, the general human capital dimension has two important aspects. First, for an individual who has acquired the specific skill required by a firm's technology, a higher level of general human capital increases the productivity of the worker on the job. This is the *productivity effect* of general education. Second, general human capital also provides a higher flexibility in learning, therefore reducing the cost of training to acquire a specific horizontal skill. This is the *flexibility effect* of general education. While the *productivity effect* is beneficial to both workers and firms, the *flexibility effect,* by increasing the competition between firms in the labor market, is advantageous only to workers.

In this context, we emphasized that the impact of regional integration on local governments educational policies depends crucially on the relative importance of the two effects. In the case of symmetric regions, we showed that regional integration induces local governments to overinvest (reps. underinvest) in general human capital when the *productivity* (resp. *flexibility*) *effect* dominates. Consequently, immobile workers tend to benefit from regional integration when general human capital generates strong productivity effects. On the other hand, workers ultimately lose when general education provides important flexibility capacities in the local labor market.

When the two regions are slightly different in size, we also show that the small region is more sensitive than the large region in its choice of local educational policy when there is regional integration.

Finally when the two regions differ slightly in terms of the efficiency of their production systems, the more efficient region tends to invest more in general human capital than the less efficient one. Again the resulting impact on the regional localization of firms depends on the relative importance of the *productivity* and *flexibility effects.*

Clearly, there are several dimensions through which it would be desirable to extend this analysis. First, one may think about investigating how the conclusions on the relative importance of the *productivity* and *flexibility effects* would be affected by having more than two regions.

Also, one may consider other modes of taxation for the financing of regional general human capital formation. In the present paper, we focused on the case where public education was completely financed by workers, the regional immobile factor of production. We could also think about modes of financing imposing taxation (directly or indirectly) on firms. Doing so would obviously reintroduce the usual fiscal competition forces, reinforcing the *flexibility effect* at the expense of the *productivity effect* and biasing therefore the result towards underprovision of regional public education.

Finally, it would also be useful to consider a longer perspective on the effect of regional integration on local educational policies. In the context of the present model, this would imply endogenizing the total number of firms participating actively across regions. It would also imply endogenizing the choice of regional infrastructures and public capital necessary to produce local general education.

While beyond the scope of the present paper, all these extensions are avenues for future research which, we hope, can be accommodated within the framework that we proposed.

Acknowledgments

We thank participants of the 5th T2M Meeting and an anonymous referee for helpful and useful comments on a previous version of this paper.

Appendix

Proof of proposition 3. We want to show that $\frac{\partial g_I^*}{\partial \alpha} > 0$. Note first that if this inequality is verified when the *flexibility* effect dominates the *productivity* effect, then it is still verified in the opposite case. Thus it is sufficient to prove it when the *flexibility* effect dominates.

Let $B(g_i) = \frac{1}{\ell^2}\left(\frac{\partial \Pi_i^*}{\partial g_i}\right) = \frac{(1+3\alpha_i)s'(g_i)}{3\Delta} - g_i F''(g_i\ell)$. $B(.)$ can be interpreted as the sum of the *productivity* and *flexibility* effects. Thus $B(.)$ is positive when the *productivity* effect outweighs the *flexibility* effect. $B(.)$ is increasing in g under the sufficient hypothesis that $F'''(.)$ is negative[18].

Equation (12) can thus be rewritten as follows:

$$F'(g_I^*\ell) - \frac{s'(g_I^*)\ell}{4\Delta} - \Gamma'(g_I^*) - \frac{\ell}{2}B(g_I^*)\,H(g_I^*) - 0$$

where $V(g_I^*) = \frac{(1+3\alpha)s'(g_I^*)}{4\Delta} - g_I^* F''(g_I^*\ell)$ and $H(g_I^*) = 1 + \frac{\frac{3\alpha s(g_I^*)}{4\Delta}}{\frac{(1+3\alpha)s(g_I^*)}{2\Delta} - (g_I^*)^2 F''(g_I^*\ell)}$.

Differentiating this equation gives:

$$\frac{\partial g_I^*}{\partial \alpha} = \frac{\frac{\ell}{2}\left[\frac{3s'(g_I^*)}{4\Delta}H(g_I^*) - \frac{\frac{3s(g_I^*)}{4\Delta}B(g_I^*)\left(\frac{s(g_I^*)}{2\Delta} - (g_I^*)^2F''(g_I^*\ell)\right)}{\left(\frac{(1+3\alpha)s(g_I^*)}{2\Delta} - (g_I^*)^2F''(g_I^*\ell)\right)^2}\right]}{F''(g_I^*\ell) - \frac{s''(g_I^*)\ell}{4\Delta} - \Gamma''(g_I^*) - \frac{\ell}{2}B'(g_I^*)\left[1 + \frac{\frac{3\alpha s(g_I^*)}{4\Delta}}{\frac{(1+6\alpha)s(g_I^*)}{2\Delta} - (g_I^*)^2F''(g_I^*\ell)}\right] - \frac{\ell}{2}B(g_I^*)H'(g_I^*)}$$

where $H'(g_I^*) = \frac{\left[\frac{3\alpha s(g_I^*)}{2\Delta}g_I^*F''(g_I^*\ell) - \frac{3\alpha s'(g_I^*)}{4\Delta}(g_I^*)^2F''(g_I^*\ell) + \frac{3\alpha s(g_I^*)}{4\Delta}(g_I^*)^2\ell F''(q_I^*\ell)\right]}{\left(\frac{(1+3\alpha)s(g_I^*)}{2\Delta} - (g_I^*)^2F''(g_I^*\ell)\right)^2} < 0$.

When $B(g_I^*) < 0$ (the *flexibility* effect outweighs the *productivity* effect), the denominator and the numerator are both negative at the equilibrium. Hence $\frac{\partial g_I^*}{\partial \alpha} > 0$.

□

Proof of proposition 4. Note that $F'(g\ell) - \frac{s'(g)\ell}{4\Delta} - \Gamma'(g)$ is decreasing in general human capital, while $B(g)$ is an increasing function.[19] Consequently, if the

[18] This hypothesis is verified when the production function is quadratic.

[19] Under the sufficient hypothesis that $F'''(.)$ is negative.

productivity effect outweighs the *flexibility* effect when the region are isolated, then it is still verified when the regions are integrated. $B(g_c^*)$ and $B(g_I^*)$ have thus the same sign. Moreover, the curves $B(g)$ and $\frac{B(g)H(g)}{4}$ are crossing when $B(g) = 0$, that is then $g = \overline{g}$. But $1 > \frac{1}{2}\left[1 + \frac{\frac{3\alpha s(g)}{4\Delta}}{\frac{(1+9\alpha)s(g)}{2\Delta} - (g)^2 F''(g\ell)}\right] > 0$. The $B(g)$ curve is thus more sloping than the $\frac{B(g)H(g)}{2}$ curve.

This means that, when the *flexibility* effect dominates the *productivity* effect, then the curve $F'(g\ell) - \frac{s'(g)\ell}{4\Delta} - \Gamma'(g)$ crosses the curve $\frac{\ell B(g)O(g)}{8}$ before the curve $\ell B(g)$. Consequently $g_I^* < g_c^*$. But the *flexibility* effect dominates the *productivity* effect if $g_c^* < \overline{g}$, that is if $F'(\overline{g}\ell) - \frac{s'(\overline{g})\ell}{4\Delta} - \Gamma'(\overline{g}) < 0$. Under the condition $F'(\overline{g}\ell) - \frac{s'(\overline{g})\ell}{4\Delta} - \Gamma'(\overline{g}) < 0$, we get thus $g_I^* < g_c^*$.

The equilibrium wage is increasing in general human capital, which gives $w_I^* < w_c^*$. Intra-regional wage inequalities depend negatively on the level of human capital publicly provided by the local government. Hence $V_I^* > V_c^*$.

Inversely, when the *productivity* effect outweighs the *flexibility* effect, all the results are reversed.

□

Proof of proposition 6. We want to determine the impact of an increase in ε on local educational policy choices. Differentiating the following equation, $a - \Gamma'(g_A^*) - \left(\frac{2\Delta(L+\varepsilon)}{N} + \frac{\Delta(L-\varepsilon)}{N}\sqrt{\frac{A(g_B^*)}{A(g_A^*)}}\right) B(g_A^*) = 0$, with respect to ε in $\varepsilon = 0$, gives the following result:

$$\left[-\Gamma''(g_A^*) - \left(\frac{2\Delta(L+\varepsilon)}{N} + \frac{\Delta(L-\varepsilon)}{N}\sqrt{\frac{A(g_B^*)}{A(g_A^*)}}\right) B'(g_A^*) + \frac{\Delta(L-\varepsilon)}{2N}\sqrt{\frac{A(g_B^*)}{A(g_A^*)}}\frac{B^2(g_A^*)}{A(g_A^*)}\right]\frac{\partial g_A^*}{\partial \varepsilon}$$
$$-\left(\frac{\Delta(L-\varepsilon)}{2N}\frac{B(g_A^*)B(g_B^*)}{\sqrt{A(g_A^*)A(g_B^*)}}\right)\frac{\partial g_B^*}{\partial \varepsilon} = \left(\frac{2\Delta}{N} - \frac{\Delta}{2N}\sqrt{\frac{A(g_B^*)}{A(g_A^*)}}\right) B(g_A^*)$$

But at the point $\varepsilon = 0$, $\left.\frac{\partial g_A^*}{\partial \varepsilon}\right|_{\varepsilon=0} = -\left.\frac{\partial g_B^*}{\partial \varepsilon}\right|_{\varepsilon=0}$. Moreover, $g_A^* = g_B^*$ at this point. Hence

$$\left.\frac{\partial g_A^*}{\partial \varepsilon}\right|_{\varepsilon=0} = \frac{-\frac{\Delta}{N}B(g_A^*)}{\Gamma''(g_A^*) + \left(\frac{\Delta L}{N}\right)\left[3B'(g_A^*) - \frac{B^2(g_A^*)}{A(g_A^*)}\right]}$$

Now $2B'(g_i^*)A(g_i^*) - B^2(g_i^*) \geqslant 0$, under the hypothesis that $s'''(.) = 0$. Indeed, differentiating with respect to g shows that this function is constant. Moreover, in $g = h^{-1}\left(\frac{2}{4\Delta b}\right)$, the function is positive. It follows that the denominator is positive. Hence, $sign\left\{\left.\frac{\partial g_A^*}{\partial \varepsilon}\right|_{\varepsilon=0}\right\} = sign\{-B(g_A^*)\}$. The sign of $\left.\frac{\partial g_A^*}{\partial \varepsilon}\right|_{\varepsilon=0}$ depends on the relative weight of the *productivity* and *flexibility* effects.

The number of workers employed per firm in region A is

$$\ell_A = \frac{\Delta(L+\varepsilon)}{N} + \frac{\Delta(L-\varepsilon)}{N}\sqrt{\frac{A(g_B^*)}{A(g_A^*)}}.$$

Differentiating ℓ_A with respect to ε in $\varepsilon = 0$ gives:

$$\left.\frac{\partial \ell_A}{\partial \varepsilon}\right|_{\varepsilon=0} = \frac{\left(\frac{\Delta}{N}\right)^2 \frac{LB^2(g_A^*)}{A(g_A^*)}}{\Gamma''(g_A^*) + \left(\frac{\Delta L}{N}\right)\left[3B'(g_A^*) - \frac{B^2(g_A^*)}{A(g_A^*)}\right]} \geq 0$$

Thus the number of workers per firm is increased in region A and smaller in region B.

Finally, since $\left(\frac{\Delta(L+\varepsilon)}{n_A^2}\right)\frac{\partial n_A}{\partial \varepsilon} = \frac{\Delta}{n_A} - \frac{\partial \ell_A}{\partial \varepsilon}$, we get:

$$\left(\frac{2L}{N}\right)\left.\frac{\partial n_A}{\partial \varepsilon}\right|_{\varepsilon=0} = \frac{\Gamma''(g_A^*) + \left(\frac{3\Delta L}{2N}\right)\left[2B'(g_A^*) - \frac{B^2(g_A^*)}{A(g_A^*)}\right]}{\Gamma''(g_A^*) + \left(\frac{\Delta L}{N}\right)\left[3B'(g_A^*) - \frac{B^2(g_A^*)}{A(g_A^*)}\right]} \geq 0$$

Hence the total number n_A of firms localized in the large region A increases but less than proportionally with the size of that region.

□

Proof of proposition 7. We want to determine the impact of an increase in η on local educational policy choices. Differentiating the following equation, $a + \eta - \Gamma'(g_A^*) - \frac{\Delta L}{N}\left(2 + \sqrt{\frac{A(g_B^*)}{A(g_A^*)}}\right)B(g_A^*) = 0$, with respect to η in $\eta = 0$, gives the following result:

$$1 - \left[\Gamma''(g_A^*) + \frac{\Delta L}{N}\left(2 + \sqrt{\frac{A(g_B^*)}{A(g_A^*)}}\right)B'(g_A^*) - \frac{\Delta L}{2N}\sqrt{\frac{A(g_B^*)}{A(g_A^*)}}\frac{B^2(g_A^*)}{A(g_A^*)}\right]\frac{\partial g_A^*}{\partial \eta}$$
$$- \frac{\Delta L}{2N}\frac{B(g_A^*)B(g_B^*)}{\sqrt{A(g_A^*)A(g_B^*)}}\frac{\partial g_B^*}{\partial \eta} = 0$$

But at the point $\eta = 0$, $\left.\frac{\partial g_A^*}{\partial \eta}\right|_{\eta=0} = -\left.\frac{\partial g_B^*}{\partial \eta}\right|_{\eta=0}$. Moreover, $g_A^* = g_B^*$ at this point. Hence

$$\left.\frac{\partial g_A^*}{\partial \eta}\right|_{\eta=0} = \frac{1}{\Gamma''(g_A^*) + \left(\frac{\Delta L}{N}\right)\left[3B'(g_A^*) - \frac{B^2(g_A^*)}{A(g_A^*)}\right]}$$

Now $2B'(g_{AB}^*)A(g_{AB}^*) - B^2(g_{AB}^*) \geqslant 0$. Thus $\left.\frac{\partial g_A^*}{\partial \eta}\right|_{\eta=0} > 0$.

□

References

Becker G. (1964). *Human Capital.* Columbia University Press.

Bucovetsky S. (1991). Asymmetric tax competition. *Journal of Urban Economics*, 21:333-350.

Hashimoto M. (1981). Firm specific human capital as a shared investment. *American Economic Review*, 71:475-482.

Jellal M., Thisse J.-F. and Zenou Y. (1997). Demand uncertainty, mismatch and (un)employment. *mimeo CORE.*

Jovanovic B. (1979*a*). Job matching and the theory of turnover. *Journal of Political Economy*, 87:972-990.

Jovanovic B. (1979*b*). Firm specific capital and the theory of turnover. *Journal of Political Economy*, 87:1246-1260.

Kennan J. and Riezman R. (1988). Do big countries win tariff wars? *International Economic Review*, 29:81-85.

Kim S. (1989). Labor specialization and the extent of the market. *Journal of Political Economy*, 97:692-705.

Kremer M. (1993). The O-Ring theory of economic development. *Quarterly Journal of Economics*, 108:551-576.

Mieszkowski P. and Zodrow G. (1986). Pigou, Tiebout, property taxation, and the underprovision of local public goods. *Journal of Urban Economics*, 19:356-370.

OECD (1998) *Education at a glance: OECD Indicators.*

Salop S. (1979). Monopolistic competition with outside goods. *Bell Journal of Economics*, 10:141-156.

Stevens M. (1994). A theoretical model of on-the-job training with imperfect competition. *Oxford Economic Papers*, 46:537-562.

Thisse J.-F. and Zenou Y. (1995). Appariement et concurrence spatiale sur le marché du travail. *Revue Économique*, 46:615-624.

Thisse J.-F. and Zenou Y. (1996). How to finance education when the labor force is heterogeneous? *mimeo CORE.*

Wildasin D. (1988). Nash equilibria in models of fiscal competition. *Journal of Public Economics*, 35:229-240.

Wildasin D. (1989). Interjuridictional capital mobility: fiscal externality and a corrective subsidy. *Journal of Urban Economics*, 25:193-212.

Wilson J. (1986). A theory of interregional tax competition. *Journal of Urban Economics*, 19:296-315.

Wilson J. (1991). Tax competition with interregional differences in factor endowments. *Regional Science and Urban Economics*, 21:423-451.

Chapter 3: A Long–Term Model for the World Economy.

INGENUE Team*

Abstract This paper presents the mathematical structure, computational aspects and calibration process of the general equilibrium, multi-regional, overlapping-generations model INGENUE. The purpose of this research is to study the international capital flows induced by differential demographic dynamics in various regions of the world in a context of global finance. The most recent UN demographic projections until the year 2050 are used to divide the world into six demographic areas displaying similar characteristics in terms of their relative position in the demographic transition process: three developed areas with rapidly ageing populations - the European zone, the American zone and Japan - and three emerging areas with slower ageing processes. Dynamic simulations of the world interest rate, current accounts and property rates of the regional capital are presented for the next decades.

1. Introduction

Recent demographic evolutions and projections highlight the reduction of the birth rate and the lengthening life-span of the world population. These demographic trends are not synchronous and do not display the same intensity in different parts of the world. In a world of integrated capital markets, according to the life-cycle hypothesis, such demographic transitions are likely to give rise to net capital flows among regions with different demographic dynamics (World Bank, 1997; Reisen, 1998). Whereas numerous papers have been devoted to the analysis of repercussions of ageing at a macroeconomic level, they mainly rely on a closed national economy framework and none of them directly tackles the problem at a world level.

*The INGENUE team is composed of Michel Aglietta (CEPII, MINI-FORUM, France), Rabah Arezki (TEAM, France), Regis Breton (MINI-FORUM), Jean Chateau (CEPII, France), Jacky Fayolle (OFCE, France), Michel Juillard (CEPREMAP, France), Cyrille Lacu (MINI-FORUM), Jacques Le Cacheux (OFCE), Bronka Rzepkowski (CEPII) and Vincent Touzé (OFCE).

The pioneer computable general equilibrium model with overlapping generations built by Auerbach and Kotlikoff, 1987 aims at assessing the effects of reforms in the social security field in the United States. Most of the following calibrated works were also conducted in a closed economy framework (Auerbach *et al.*, 1989; Cazes *et al.*, 1992; Miles, 1997; Hviding and Mérette, 1998). Some existing models that do consider open economies usually deal with the case of a small open economy integrated economically and financially into a large world, so that the essential variables, such as the real interest rate are exogenous (Persson, 1985; Blanchet and Kessler, 1992; Raffelhüschen and Risa, 1995; Kenc and Sayan, 1997). While Morrow and Roeger, 2000 and Turner *et al.*, 1998 stress the importance of demographic factors in shaping world economic conditions, they do not model the endogenous behavior of overlapping generations in their world macroeconomic model.[1] These shortcomings plead in favor of building a more realistic world model, in which macroeconomic variables are endogenous and demographics are modelled in such a way as to picture faithfully the ageing process.

The aim of this paper is to analyze capital flows induced by differential demographic dynamics in various regions of the world, in a context of financial globalization over the next decades. In a theoretical model with two regions, Buiter, 1981 shows how the difference in time preference rates between two populations is a sufficient condition to entail international capital flows. But accounting for the interactions between the ageing process and the macroeconomic evolution at the world level involves building a computable general equilibrium multi-regional overlapping-generations model. To our knowledge, this is the first time such a calibrated model with realistic demography is being constructed. The United Nations demographic projections have been used to divide the world into six zones displaying similar characteristics in terms of their position in the demographic transition process (DTP). The six zones are respectively composed of three developed areas with Europe, America and Japan and three emerging zones, at different stage in the DTP.

The paper is organized as follows. The first section introduces the mathematical structure of the Ingenue model, the second section presents some programming aspects and the calibration process. The third section exhibits some simulations of major macroeconomic variables over

[1] The latter introduce an ad hoc behavioral assumption inspired by life-cycle hypotheses where the death probability is uniform over lifetime as in Blanchard, 1985.

the next decades. The last section concludes with directions for improvements of the model.

2. A computable, general-equilibrium, multi-regional overlapping generations model

We rely on a Diamond-Samuelson type model, based on the life-cycle theory of savings behavior is as follows: there exist only one good and one asset, whose markets are perfectly integrated at the world level, whereas individuals are immobile. There is no money and all relative prices are perfectly flexible, so that all markets clear at all times. There is no uncertainty whatsoever, even about the date of individual death, so that rational agents have perfect foresight. Each area consists of three sectors: the households, the firms and the public sector.

2.1 The household sector

The time unit of the world is a period of five years. So, in each demographic zone $i = 1...6$, at any given period, the economy is populated with 4 cohorts of children of age between 0-4 and 15-19 and 15 generations of adults of age from 20-24 to 90-94 ($g = 1$ to 15). From birth to 19, the young people are supposed to be dependent on their parents and are modelled as an additional cost proportional to the consumption of the latter. Adults only make autonomous decisions as of their 20th year as they enter the labor market. They decide with perfect foresight the level of consumption and savings that maximizes utility over their entire life time. The intertemporal welfare is subject to a budget constraint that takes into account the diverse incomes from labor, retirement pension and saving.

Individuals are furthermore differentiated according to life expectancy within each cohort. This assumption aims at catching the increasing longevity that differs across the zones as depicted by the UN demographic projections. The life-span of type m agents is known with certainty and its last period of life is denoted $g^i_{\max/m, m=1...M^i}$, where M^i is the number of longevity types in region i. Type 1 individuals are the first to die, whereas agents of type M^i are the last.[2] Hence, each individual is indexed both per its generation g, its life-span m and per

[2]M is equal to 8 for the three emerging zones: type 1 agents begin to die at the end of their 59th years. M is equal to 6 for the American zone and Japan (type 1 agents begin to die at the end of 69th years), while it amounts to 7 in the European area. These values are calibrated to reproduce the implicit UN assumptions about the different mortality rates and process of life-span lengthening among the six zones.

its demographic zone i. In each zone, the intertemporal welfare for an individual of type m is measured by:

$$U_t^i = \sum_{g=1}^{g_{\max/m}^i} (1+\rho^i)^{-(g-1)} u\left(c_{g/m,t+g-1}^i\right) \tag{1}$$

for $i = 1, ..., 6$ and $m = 1, ..., M^i$. ρ^i is the time preference rate and $u(.)$ is a time separable utility function which measures the level of welfare associated with the consumption of type m individual from generation g at time $t+g-1$ denoted $c_{g/m,t+g-1}^i$ with $u' > 0, u'' < 0$. In the model, $u(.)$ is a CARA function:

$$u(c) = \frac{c^{1-\sigma}}{1-\sigma} \tag{2}$$

where σ is the inverse of the elasticity of intertemporal substitution. There is no bequest motive and the labor supply is exogenous, so that leisure does not enter the utility function.

At any given period, for the working generations, the budget constraint is defined as follows:

$$\tau_{g,t}^i c_{g/m,t}^i = (1 - tax_t^i) w_t^i + (1 + r_t) s_{g/m,t-1}^i - s_{g/m,t}^i \tag{3}$$

where r_t denotes the real interest rate during period t, w_t^i is the real wage per capita, tax_t^i is the rate of labor taxation; $s_{g/m,t}^i$ is the accumulated saving per capita at the end of period t and $\tau_{g,t}^i$ indicates the cost of child-rearing supported by generation g.

Similarly, the budget constraint for retired generations is written:

$$c_{g/m,t}^i = p_t^i + (1 + r_t) s_{g/m,t-1}^i - s_{g/m,t}^i \tag{4}$$

where p_t^i is a retirement pension.

The income relative to the age as either the wage or retirement benefits is defined as:

$$Inc_t^i = \begin{cases} (1 - tax_t^i) w_t^i, & \forall g \leq g_a^i \\ p_t^i, & \forall g > g_a^i \end{cases} \tag{5}$$

where g_a^i is the last period of active life in the zone i.

Without credit rationing, first order conditions thus yield:

$$c_{g+1/m,t+1}^i = \left(\frac{\tau_{g,t}^i (1+r_{t+1})}{\tau_{g+1,t+1}^i (1+\rho^i)} \right)^{\frac{1}{\sigma}} c_{g/m,t}^i \qquad \forall g \leq g_{\max/m}^i - 1 \tag{6}$$

Then if we introduce credit rationing, the saving per capita can never become negative: $s^i_{g/m,t} \geq 0$. First order conditions yield:

$$c^i_{g+1/m,t+1} = \min\left[\left(\frac{\tau^i_{g,t}(1+r_{t+1})}{\tau^i_{g+1,t+1}(1+\rho^i)}\right)^{\frac{1}{\sigma}} c^i_{g/m,t}; Inc^i_t + (1+r_t)s^i_{g/m,t-1}\right] \tag{7}$$

with (5).

As there is no bequest motive in the model, savings are null at the beginning of active life and at time of death. So the intertemporal budget constraint can be expressed as follows:

$$\left\{\begin{array}{rcl} s^i_{1/m,t} & = & 0 \\ s^i_{g/m,t} & = & Inc^i_t + (1+r_t)s^i_{g/m,t-1} - \tau^i_{g,t}c^i_{g/m,t}, \\ & & g = 2, ..., g^i_{\max/m} - 1 \\ s^i_{g^i_{\max}/m,t} & = & 0 \end{array}\right. \tag{8}$$

2.2 The production sector

There is a single composite good, which can be used for consumption or investment. It is produced with Cobb-Douglas technology:

$$Y^i_t = A^i_t \left(K^i_{t-1}\right)^{\alpha} \left(L^i_{act,t}\right)^{1-\alpha},$$

where $L^i_{act,t}$ denotes the size of the active population at the beginning of period t and K_{t-1} the capital stock accumulated by the end of period $t-1$ and available for production in period t. In each zone, the technology differs only in terms of general levels of productivity, A^i_t. Returns to scale are constant and capital depreciates at a constant rate δ. There are no adjustment costs. The production per capita is given by $f\left(k^i_{t-1}\right) = A^i_t(k^i_{t-1})^{\alpha}$, where $k^i_{t-1} = \frac{K^i_{t-1}}{L^i_{act,t}}$ is the capital-labor ratio and α is the share of capital incomes in GDP. An exogenous technological progress regularly improves the marginal productivity of factors. In a given area, firms are identical and they maximize their profits under their regional, technological constraints.

There is a technological, leader country denoted $i = 1$ (American zone) where productivity grows at a given annual rate of 2 %. Other regions are supposed to progressively catch up thanks to productive capital accumulation according to a convergence function. This function is formalized as follows:

$$\frac{A_t^i}{A_{t-1}^i} = \left[1+\lambda^t\right]\frac{A_t^1}{A_{t-1}^1}\left[\beta^t + \left(1-\beta^t\right)\frac{A_{t-1}^1}{A_{t-1}^i}\right] \tag{9}$$

where λ slows down the convergence process in growth rate whereas β slows it down in terms of level of global factors productivity.

Firms are assumed to operate in perfectly competitive international markets for the consumption good and capital and in a perfectly competitive local market for labor because there is no international labor mobility. Hence, in equilibrium, profits are nil and production factors are remunerated at their marginal productivity. An equilibrium on the three markets therefore determines two sorts of real prices in terms of consumption goods: the local real wages $w_t^i = f\left(k_{t-1}^i\right) - k_{t-1}^i f'\left(k_{t-1}^i\right)$ and the international real rental rate of capital $\delta + r_t = f'\left(k_{t-1}^i\right)$.

2.3 The public sector

The public sector is reduced to a social security department. It is modelled as a pure "pay-as-you-go" system. A payroll tax, tax_t^i, finances retirement pensions. There is neither public debt nor other forms of taxation. As labor supply is exogenous, the payroll tax is never distorting. However, while people receive old-age pensions independently of their personal savings, the pay-as-you-go system is not neutral in terms of capital accumulation both at the national and at the international level.

The amount of pension p_t^i is obtained by multiplying a given proportion π^i (replacement rate) by the net-of-tax wage rate observed in the zone: $p_t^i = \pi^i\left(1-\tau_t^i\right)w_t^i$. The replacement rate is constant and the payroll tax is calculated in order to assure balance of the social security system. As the deformation of the structure by age modifies the dependency ratio – the share of retired generations over the labor force – it affects the payroll tax. This system can be interpreted as a system of retirement indexed on the real net-of-tax wages.

The current total expenditures must be adjusted to the total current revenues. Given that the labor force is immobile, the labor market balances in each zone. The full employment assumption then entails that in each zone i:$L_{act,t}^i = \sum_{g=1}^{g_a^i} L_{g,t}^i$, where $L_{g,t}^i$ defines the size of generation g at time t. Hence:

$$L_{act,t}^i.tax_t^i.w_t^i = p_t^i.L_{ret,t}^i \tag{10}$$

where $L_{ret,t}^i = \sum_{g=g_a^i+1}^{g_{\max}^i} L_{g,t}^i$ defines the retired population. π^i is fixed and different across regions; tax_t^i is endogenous.

2.4 General equilibrium in a financially integrated world

The world equilibrium results from the aggregation of regional macroeconomic behaviors of saving and investment. The regional savings depend on past savings and on current and anticipated wages, interest rates and retirement benefits. There is only one global capital market and given the perfect mobility of capital assumption, the capital market balances at the world level. The stock of capital equals the stock of world wealth, yielding a unique real world interest rate. The inter-temporal world equilibrium exists if there is a unique sequence $\{r_t\}_{t\geq 0}$ which is a perfect-forecast stable solution of:

$$\overbrace{\sum_{i=1}^{6}\sum_{g=1}^{g^i_{\max}-1}\sum_{m=1}^{M^i} L^i_{g/m,t}\, s^i_{g/m,t}}^{\text{total accumulated saving at time } t} = \overbrace{\sum_{i=1}^{6} L^i_{act,t+1}\, k^i_t}^{\text{capital stock at time } t} \tag{11}$$

The current account of a zone i is the excess of the national production over the domestic absorption. It is defined as follows:

$$B^i_t = Y^i_t + r_t(W^i_{t-1} - K^i_{t-1}) - C^i_t - \left[K^i_t - (1-\delta)K^i_{t-1}\right] \tag{12}$$

where Y^i_t is the gross domestic product (GDP), C^i_t is the aggregate consumption, W^i_{t-1} is the sum of domestic savings and $r_t(W^i_{t-1} - K_{t-1})$ refers to the net income of foreign investment.

3. Programming and calibration

3.1 Writing the model with *Python*

The very nature of overlapping-generations models makes for numerous repetitions of the same equations with only slight changes, mostly in variable names (in the computer code, a variable with different indices appears as different variable names). We quickly found out that it was much more labor-saving and less error-prone to have an automatic way for writing these equations. So we developed a program written in the programming language *Python*, with appropriate loops on regions, generations and representative individuals in each generation.

The same *Python* program writes the static, long-run equilibrium model, the dynamic model and various initialization or ancillary TROLL files. One of the advantages of a high level language such as *Python* is a convenient use of so-called *regular expressions*, these matching patterns which makes it easy to selectively replace certain strings of characters. We found them particularly useful for automatically generating a static equation corresponding to the dynamic one. This was extremely useful to insure in the development phase a perfect consistency between the dynamic and static version of a changing model.

The correspondence between a dynamic equation and its static, long–run, counterpart is as follows. Let's consider, in a generic manner, the following dynamic equation:

$$f(y_{t-1}, y_t, y_{t+1}) = 0 \tag{13}$$

and assume that, in the long–run, y_t grows at the constant rate γ

$$y_t = (1+\gamma)^t \overline{y}. \tag{14}$$

An equivalent static equation in $\overline{y}$ can be written as

$$f(\overline{y}/(1+\gamma), \overline{y}, (1+\gamma)\overline{y}) = 0 \tag{15}$$

With regular expressions, it is easy to do such a transformation automatically and to give special treatment of those variables, such as the interest rate, which do not display a growth trend in the long–run.

3.2 Calibration process

The calibration process proceeded in two steps that were mainly conducted simultaneously. The first step consisted in fitting the steady state version of the model, or more precisely the long run path where population is stationary[3] and all variables per capita grow to a constant rate, derived from the exogenous growth rate of productivity. Although empirical evidence does not support such an assumption, the levels of global productivity in the six zones are supposed to converge in the very long run, so that all regional economies eventually grow at the same constant rate equal to 2%.[4] The time preference rate is also assumed to converge toward 1% in the long run. The latter variable proved to be of great influence over the steady state interest rate. To calibrate the long run path, a level for the annual world interest rate lying between 3 and

[3]Until 2050, our modeling exercise is based on UN demographic projections. We follow the medium fertility variant. After 2050, we assume an international stabilization of the number of births in each region, that is this number observed in 2050 will be replicated over all the future five-years periods. Because we have no information about the survival rate of each cohort after 2050, the survival rates observed in 2050 have simply been postulated constant afterwards. In the very long-run, the world population becomes stationary. That is after 2125, the population growth rate is everywhere equal to 0.

[4]See Temple, 1999 for a review of literature regarding the economic convergence.

3.5% was sought. The following set of parameters identical in each zone proved to fit this interval:

Table 1. Calibration (1)

α	δ	σ	ρ
0.30	5%	0.97	1%

Thus, all the differences, except the institutional ones, vanish in the long run. The persistent different parameters of the pay-as-you-go retirement system are respectively the retirement ages and the replacement rates.

Table 2. Calibration (2)

Zones	Europe	America	Japan	Zone 4	Zone 5	Zone 6
Retirement age	60	65	70	65	65	65
Replacement rate	76%	30,5%	41%	10%	10%	10%

For more developed zones, these values have been obtained after an investigation of different institutions providing retirement benefits, whereas for less developed area, the choice of parameters does not correspond to an institutional reality. They are supposed to reproduce an implicit pay-as-you-go system that catches a more pronounced intergenerational solidarity in these area compared to OECD countries.

Then, to calibrate the dynamic simulations over the period 1980-2000, we mainly use the parameter of convergence β and the time preference rate ρ. The former is of crucial importance for the shape of the projections, because the speed of the convergence in the levels of global factors productivity depends on its value. In fact, it determines in large part the capital needs in the emerging zones and thus the value of the current accounts. In order to achieve a range of [-4%,4%] for these current accounts as percentages of regional GDP, the parameter β (resp. λ) has been fixed to 0.9995 (resp. 0.001). This value involves a scenario of very slow convergence of the five zones toward the American one, that provides realistic orders of magnitude for all the current accounts at the beginning of the period.

But, due to its simplified structure, the model was unable to reconcile the sign of the simulated current account of the American zone with its initial values over the 1980-2000 period. For calibration, the time preference rate of this area has been assumed different relative to the value of 1% for the five zones: it amounts to 2.5% in 1980, this rate converging linearly to 1% in 2225. This proved sufficient to fit both the magnitude and the sign of all the simulated current accounts with the initial observations.

4. Baseline scenario: a projection of the world economy for the 21st century

Figure 1 highlights the crucial role of demographic dynamics in the world-wide saving-investment equilibrium, hence in the time profile of the world interest rate. Indeed, the demand for savings – *i.e.* the process of capital accumulation in the various regions of the world – is quite smooth and essentially driven by the exogenous rates of technical progress in the leading region (North America) and in the catching-up regions; hence productive capital accumulation in the world economy essentially depends on the assumption made with respect to convergence (see below), although it is also influenced, but marginally, by the interest rate through the factor proportions, *i.e.* capital intensity of production. The supply side of world capital markets is influenced by the interaction of demographic structures and income levels of the various regions, the former determining the aggregate saving behavior in each region, while the latter is essentially a scale factor for the share of each region in total world savings.

Figure 1. World real interest rate

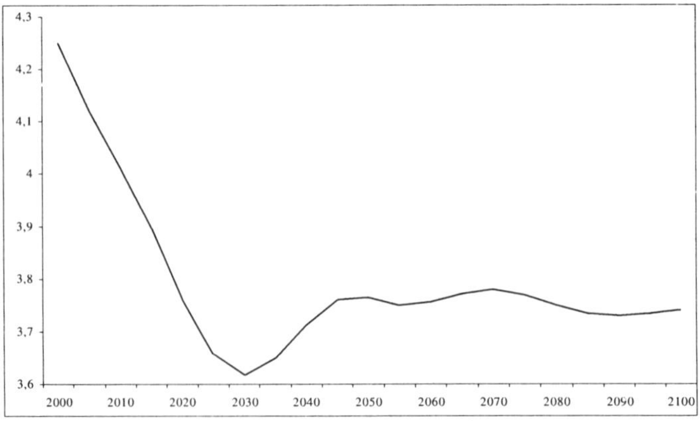

Figure 2. High-savers as a proportion of total population in the six regions

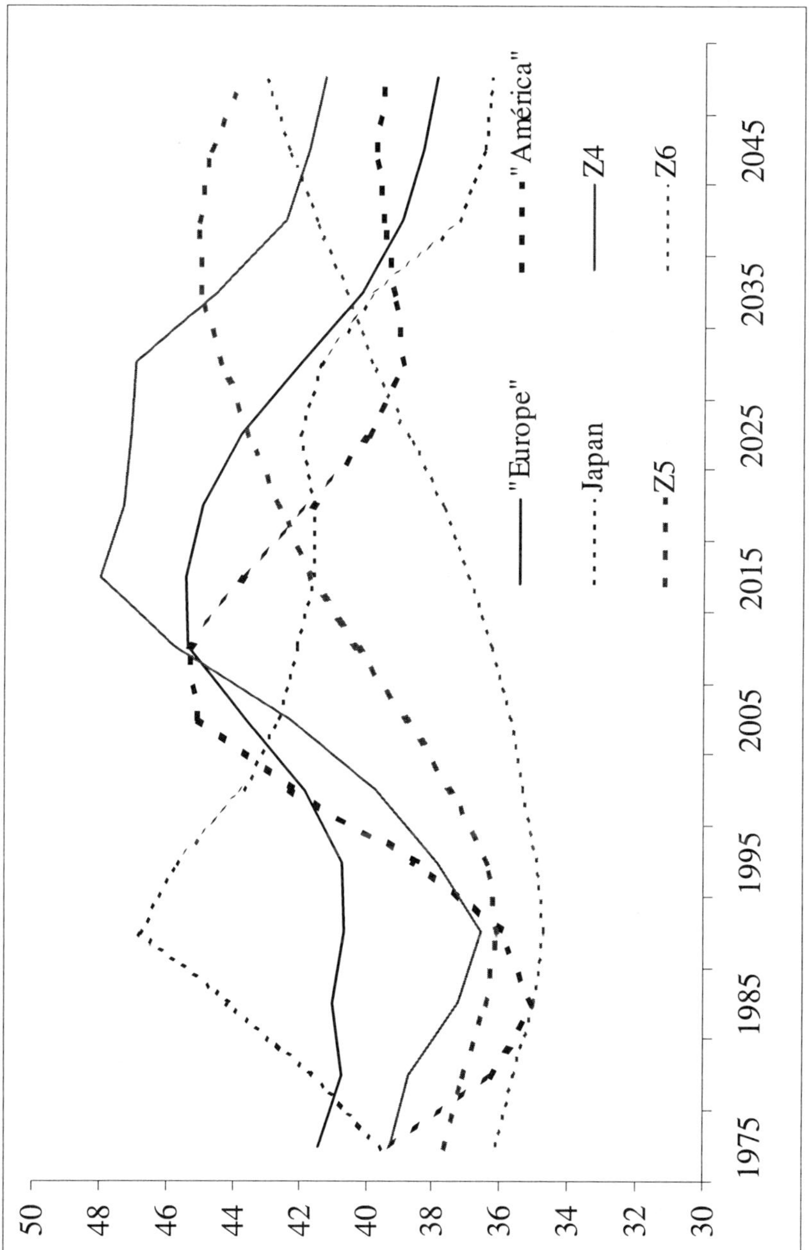

Due to the very contrasted and fluctuating demographic profiles of the six regions over the first half of the century, which may be conveniently summarized here by the ratios of "high-savers" – individuals between the ages of 40 (when children have left home) and 65 (when they are dissaving after retirement) in total population (Figure 2) –, the evolution of the world interest rate is far from being uniform: it first declines sharply until 2030, due to the presence of numerous high-savers in the developed regions of the world, while the demand for capital stemming from developing regions is only very gently increasing due to our assumption of slow catching-up in the baseline scenario; from 2030 till 2050, it rises again slightly, then fluctuates around a value of 3.75% for the rest of the century. Although apparently of a small magnitude, these variations in the world interest rate are indeed significant, in that they directly influence the growth rates in the various regions, hence the world average real growth (Figure 3) and regional GDP growth rates (Figure 4), as well as the accumulation and investment decisions in each region, hence the saving-investment balance, and therefore the constellation of regional current accounts and the polarization and magnitude of world capital flows (Figure 5, benchmark).

Figure 3. World growth rate

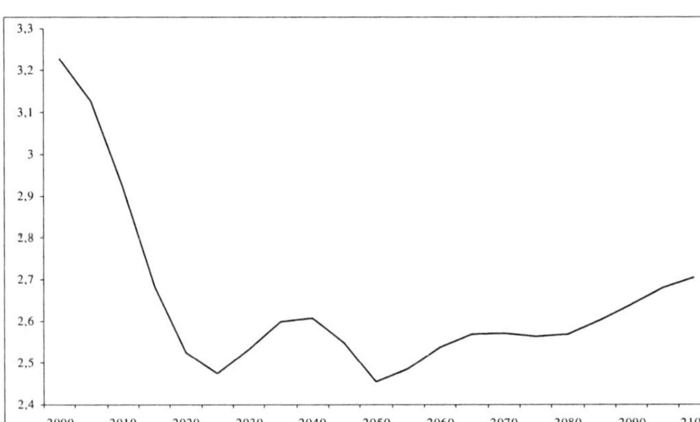

In that respect, the most dramatic evolution is projected for Europe, whose current account position deteriorates sharply after an initial phase of surpluses, and runs into large deficits after the year 2030; hence, the European ownership ratio (the share of productive capital installed in the region that is owned by residents) deteriorates significantly after that date, to become lower than one by 2060 and reach a level of 80% by 2100 (Figure 6, benchmark). This singular European trajectory is

Figure 4. Regional GDP growth rate

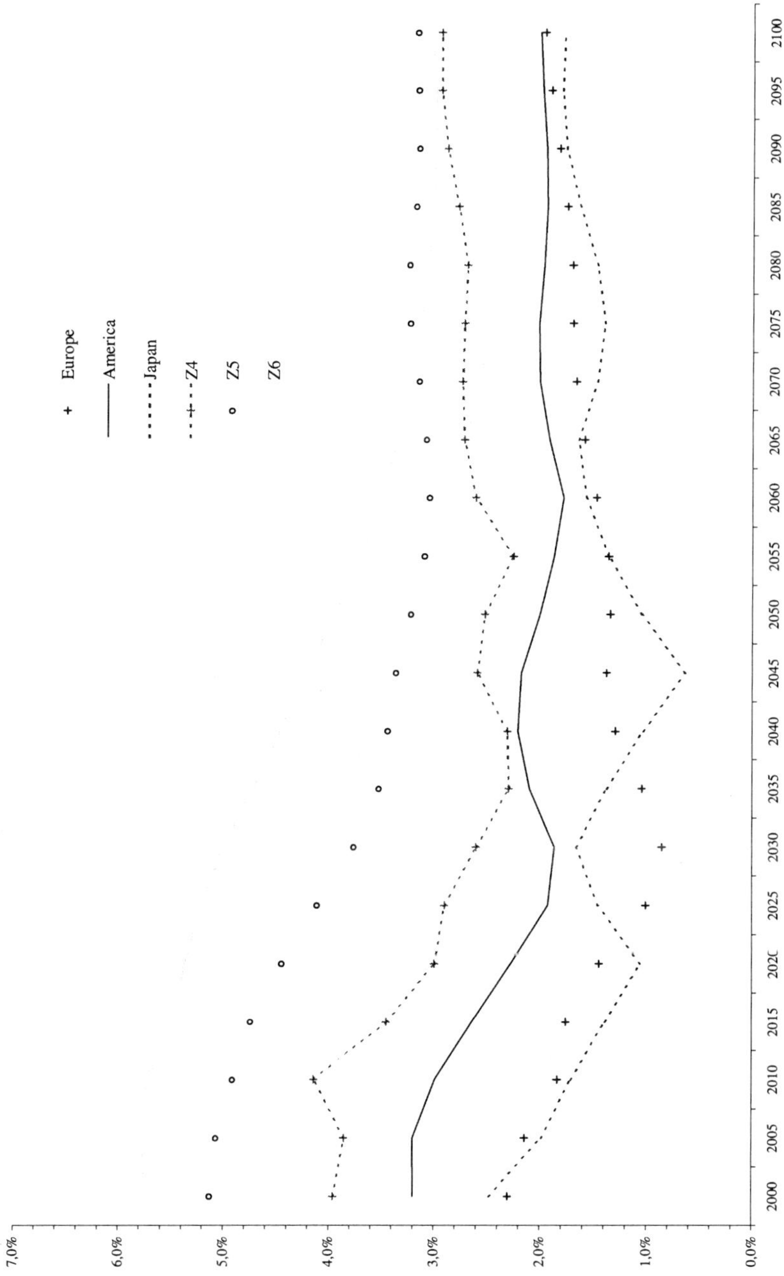

Figure 5. Regional current accounts with various convergence speeds. (Percent of regional GDP)

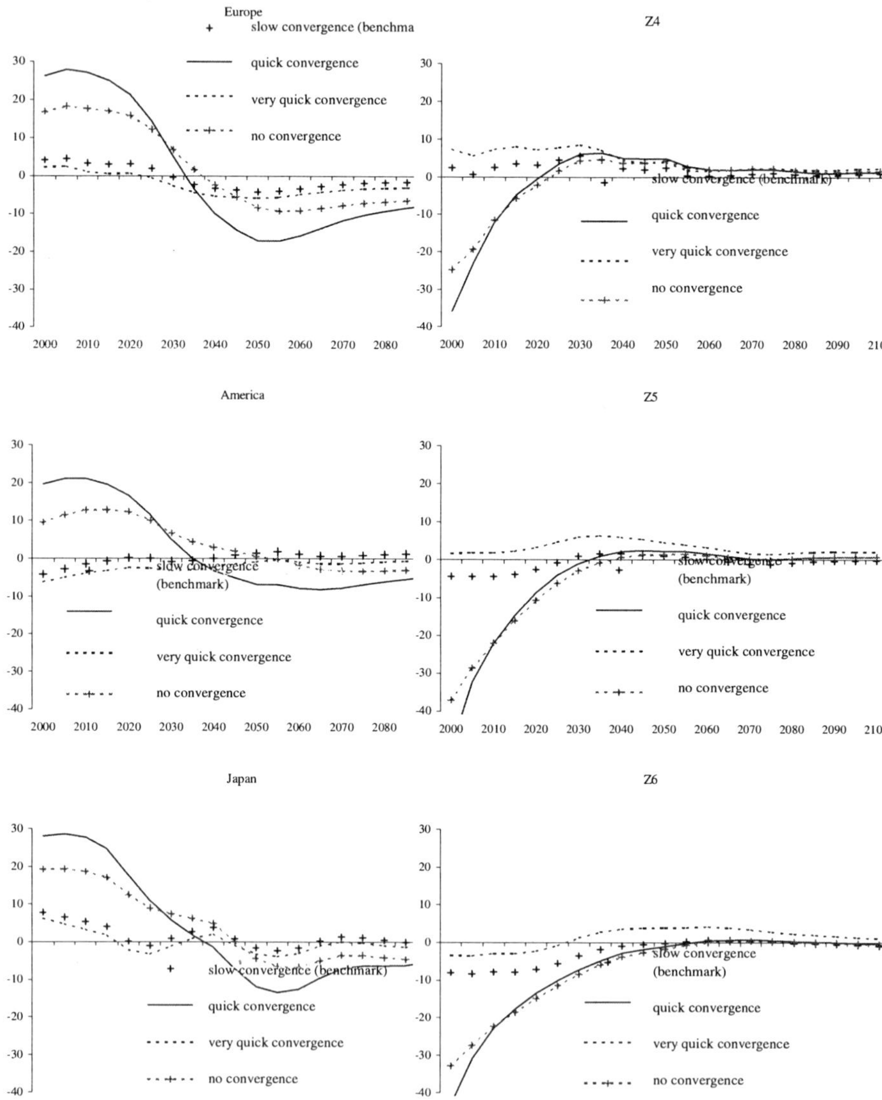

for the most due to the interplay of the generous pay-as-you-go pension systems and changing demographic structures: higher dependency ratios generate lower saving and eventually revert international capital flows.

Figure 6. Regional ownership ratios with various convergence speeds

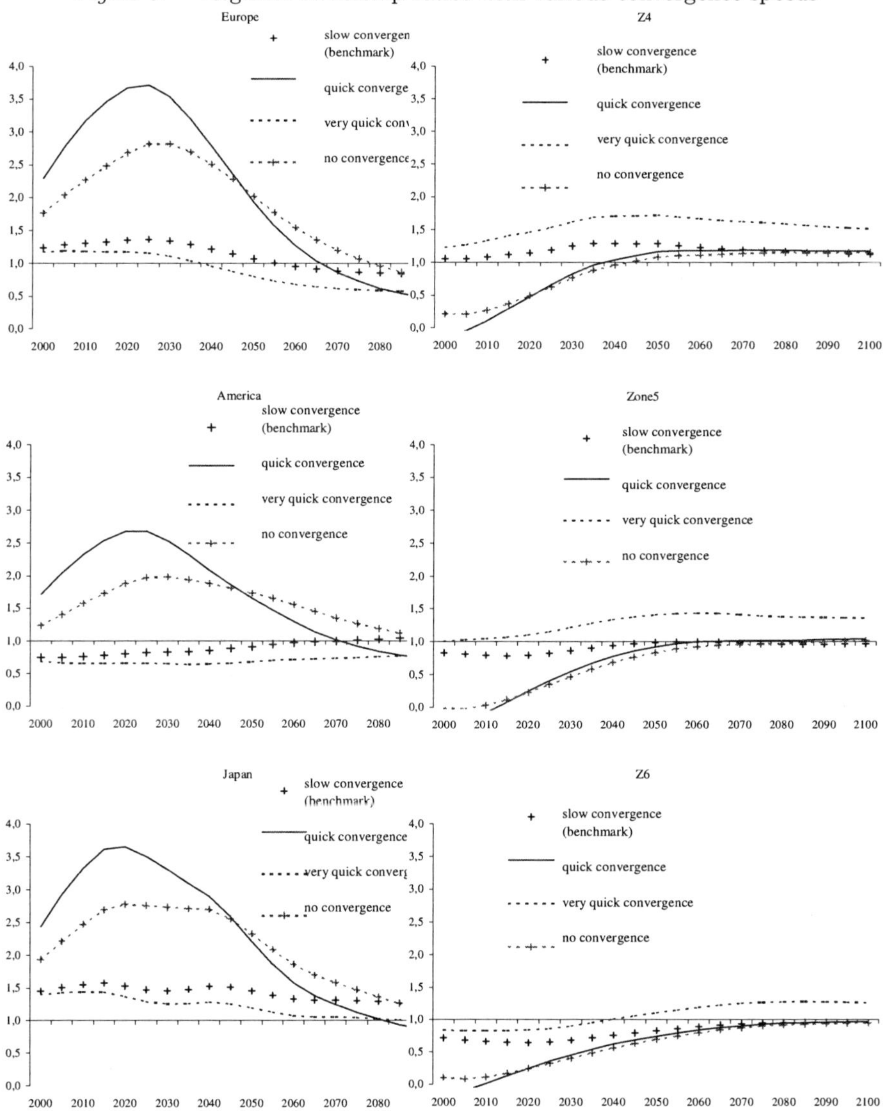

5. Catching-up and world capital flows: technological scenarios

In our model, the rate of growth of technical progress, and hence total factor productivity, is exogenous, and, outside the leading region (North America), it is assumed to obey a law of technological diffusion generating a catching-up of less-developed regions (LDRs) at a speed that, in our baseline scenario, is pretty slow. Given the empirical uncertainties of the catching-up process and international real convergence, we have investigated several scenarios with different speeds of convergence. In addition to the baseline scenario, characterized by relatively slow catching-up of LDRs, we show three cases: one with no catching-up ($\beta = 1$), keeping the productivity gaps in constant over time (18-20%), and two with higher speeds of technological diffusion, where productivity levels in the least developed region of the world respectively reach 100% ($\beta = 0.995$) and 85% ($\beta = 0.99$) of North American productivity by the end of the century against 41-43% in the baseline scenario.

As expected, the rate of real convergence affects the pace of productive capital accumulation in an early phase of the catching-up process: the faster real convergence, the stronger the initial demand for capital in LDRs, hence the larger their current account deficits (Figure 5). Insofar as the world supply of savings is, initially, not much affected by the rate of convergence – because the regions concerned are relatively small in terms of aggregate income and savings, initially –, the dominant effect is on the world demand for capital, translating into higher interest rate when catching-up is faster, this capital demand effect being strengthened by a supply effect since young generations in catching-up regions are also saving less, because they expect higher incomes in the future (Figure 7).

At a later stage however, the scenario of very fast convergence exhibits a rapidly declining world interest rate, becoming lower than that of fast convergence after 2040 and eventually even lower than in all other scenarios: as incomes increase and population mature in LDRs, the volume of their savings increases fast and this positive effect on world capital supply progressively dominates the initial negative effect of fast catching-up on world capital demand.

The faster real convergence, the more contrasted also the ownership ratios are (Figure 6). In particular, the extreme values in the case of fast catching-up suggest that this assumption is not very realistic and that LDRs would, in such a case, run into serious liquidity constraints preventing them from pumping up so much of the world capital supply in the first decades of the century.

Figure 7. World real interest rate with various convergence speeds

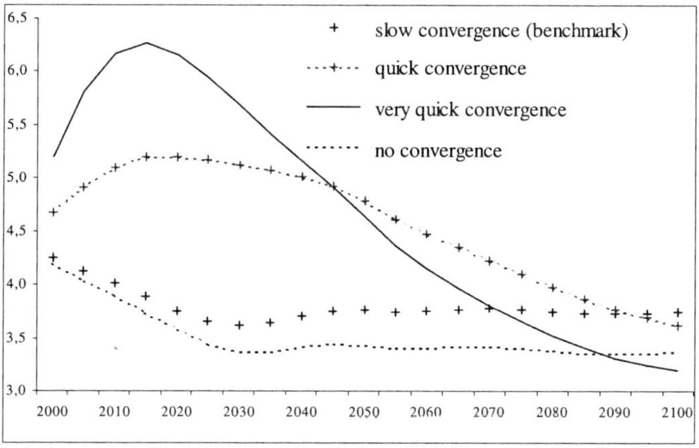

6. Public pension reforms: some institutional scenarios

Our model is, of course, designed to shed some light on current debates in ageing richer areas of the world, and most specifically in Western Europe, about the future of pay-as-you-go pension schemes, and on the long-run economic consequences of various possible institutional reforms of public pensions. In our analytical framework as in other applied overlapping-generations, general-equilibrium models, any change in the rules of the pay-as-you-go pension scheme automatically induces a change in households' saving behavior, which functions as an individual, private capitalization pension device. The major difference with other existing studies of economic consequences of pension reforms lies in the international interdependence and capital flows: instead of being bottled up in the region undertaking pension reform, the effects on private savings – and hence on interest rate, capital accumulation, aggregate and age-specific consumption, etc. – are, in this model, spread over the entire world, and henceforth diluted in worldwide supply of capital.

In order to illustrate this point, as well as the implications of financial globalization, we have investigated various currently debated scenarios of institutional reforms of European public pension schemes, that clearly appear as the most generous, as well as the most seriously endangered by upcoming ageing processes. The baseline, characterized by the maintenance of a constant net replacement ratio (NRR) – the ratio between public pensions and net-of-tax wages – has thus been compared to three alternative rules: a more generous scenario (GRR), where the gross, rather than the net, replacement rate is held constant in the future; a less generous scenario, where the contribution rate is held constant at its initial value in the future, so that pensions automatically adjust downward as population ages (CCR); and finally a scenario in which the retirement age is postponed by five years in Europe, compared to baseline (PRA).

Figure 8. Real interest rates: world economy with financial integration

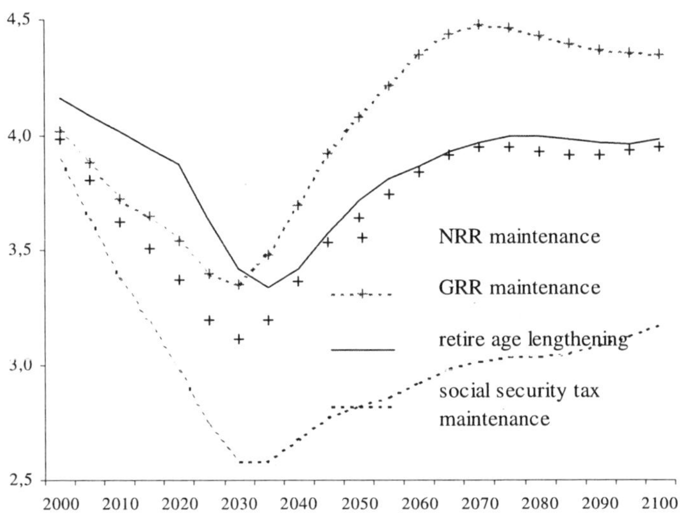

The economic consequences of such institutional reforms of public pension schemes are, as expected, non negligible, although they do not much affect worldwide economic aggregates, insofar as Europe is relatively small compared to other regions. The contrast with the financial autarky outcome is most vivid (figures 8 and 9).

These much smaller changes in interest rates directly translate into less dramatic evolutions of GDP growth (figures 10 and 11): less generous pay-as-you-go pension schemes, either through decreasing replacement ratios or via a postponement of the retirement age, will indeed induce higher savings in Europe, but, given the relative size of this region in world capital markets, the aggregate supply of capital would not be much affected, at least much less than when Europe is depicted as a financially closed economy.

7. Concluding remarks

The INGENUE model has been designed to analyze the consequences of differentiated ageing processes in the various regions of the world

Figure 9. Real interest rates: Autarkic Europe

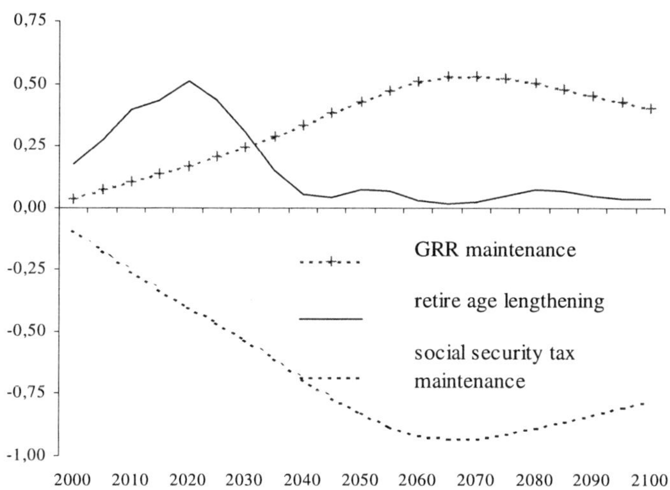

Figure 10. GDP growth rates (Europe): world economy with financial integration

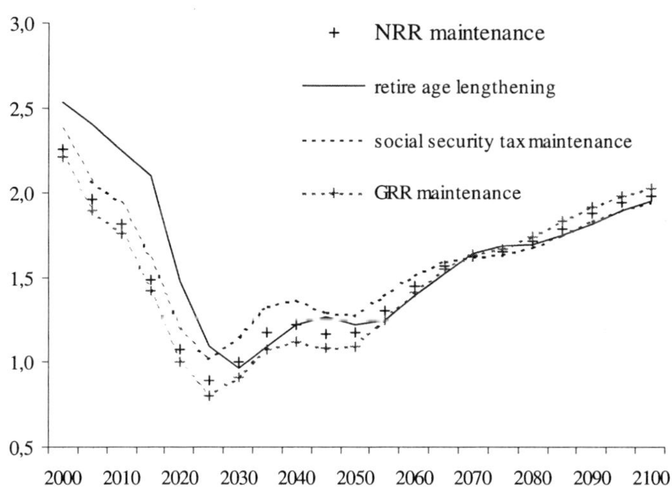

in a context of financial globalization. In this paper, we have tried to convey the major features of the model and of its baseline scenario over the century with respect to main regional and worldwide economic aggregates. The potential uses of the model have been illustrated with the exploration of various scenarios of real economic convergence and scenarios of pension reforms in Western Europe, meant to demonstrate

Figure 11. GDP growth rates (Europe): Autarkic Europe

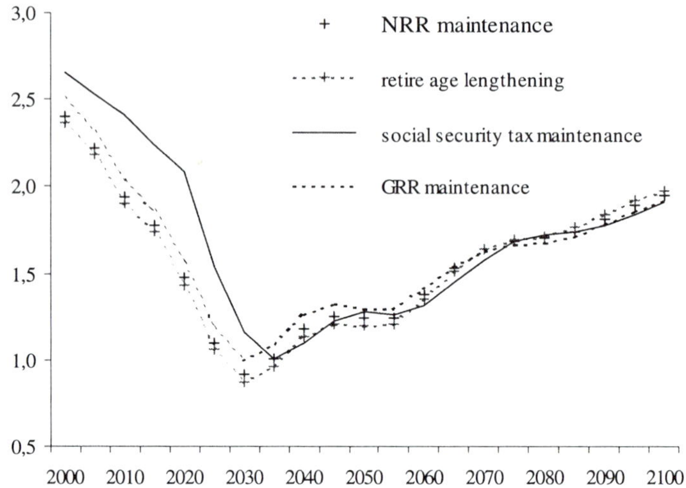

the major differences between conventional, closed-economy reasonings and the general equilibrium, world analytical setting that we have built.

Of course, many other scenarios could be explored and the model can also be used to address distributional issues, especially intergenerational distributional effects of pension reforms. Obviously too, the model is over-simplistic and a number of improvements could be introduced in order to make it a little more realistic. In particular, the assumptions of a single good market and a single financial asset make the number of relative prices very small, and hence restrict the adjustment channels to changes in the magnitude of capital flows. Introducing several goods and endogenous real exchange rates would probably alter the results somewhat; similarly, imperfect international capital mobility would also seem to be a desirable feature of such a model, as it appears that the magnitude of current account deficits and the amounts of external indebtedness in some scenarios are simply too large to appear sustainable in the current phase of world financial integration.

Acknowledgments

We gratefully acknowledge the support of the Institut Caisse des Dépôts and of the Conseil National du Crédit et du Titre.

Appendix

Demographic zones

We use the most recent UN demographic projections and assumptions. To divide the world into six demographic areas, a principle of homogeneity is applied, based upon proximity in the demographic structures. More precisely, six criteria have been used: the growth of population, the dependency ratio of young people, the dependency ratio of old individuals, the dependency ratio of very old ones, the ratio of working generations likely to be in debt, and the rate of the working age population. Among the three emerging zones, the main difference between the areas rests on their different relative position in the Demographic Transition Process.

The table below presents all the countries composing each demographic zone[5].

Denomination	Composition
Europe	European Union, Switzerland, Norway and Iceland
America	United States, Canada, Australia and New Zealand
Japan	Japan
Z4	**Countries advanced in the demographic transition process** China, Korea Dem. Rep., Hong Kong, Macao, Korea Rep., Singapore, Thailand, Bahrain, Cyprus, Qatar, United Arabs Emirates, Belarus, Bulgaria, Georgia, Czech Republic, Hungary, Poland, Moldavia, Romania, Russian Federation, Slovak Republic, Ukraine, Estonia, Latvia, Lithuania, Bosnia-Herzegovina, Armenia, Croatia, Slovenia, Macedonia, Yugoslavia, Cuba, Uruguay.
Z5	**Countries beginning their demographic transition process** Argentina, Brazil, Chile, Colombia, Guyana, Mexico, Panama, Peru, Suriname, Sri Lanka, Caribbean zone, Bahamas, Dominia, Jamaica, Trinidad & Tabago, Azerbaijan, Israel, Kuwait, Lebanon, Turkey, Albania, India, Indonesia, Brunei, Malaysia, Vietnam.
Z6	**High fertility rates countries** Africa, Mongolia, Afghanistan, Bangladesh, Bhutan, Iran Islamic Rep., Kazakhstan, Kyrgyz Republic, Nepal, Pakistan, Tajikistan, Turkmenistan, Uzbekistan, Cambodia, Eastern Timor, Lao PDR, Myanmar, Philippines, Gaza strip, Iraq, Jordan, Oman, Saudi Arabia, Syrian Arab Rep., Yemen Rep., Haiti, Costa Rica, El Salvador, Guatemala, Honduras, Nicaragua, Bolivia, Ecuador, Paraguay, Venezuela, Melanesia, Fiji, Papua New Guinea, Vanuatu, Micronesia, Polynesia, Samoa.

References

Auerbach, Alan J. and Lawrence Kotlikoff (1987). *Dynamic Fiscal Policy.* Cambridge University Press.

[5]Concerning the aggregation of countries by zones, more details are provided in INGENUE Team, 1999.

Auerbach, Alan J., Laurence J. Kotlikoff, Robert P. Hagemann and Guiseppe Nicoletti (1989). The Economic Dynamics On An Ageing Population: The Case Of Four Oecd. Oecd Economic Studies No. 12.

Blanchard, Olivier (1985). Debt, deficits and finite horizons. *Journal of Political Economy*, 93(2).

Blanchet, Didier and Denis Kessler (1992). Pension systems in transition economies: perspectives and choices ahead. *Public Finance*, 47.

Brooks, Robin (2000). What will happen to financial markets when the baby boomers retire? IMF Working Paper.

Buiter, Willem H. (1981). Time preference and international lending and borrowing in an overlapping-generations model. *Journal of Political Economy*, 89(4).

Cazes, Sandrine, Thierry Chauveau, Jacques Le Cacheux and Rahim Loufir (1992). Public pensions in an overlapping-generations model of the French economy. *Keio Economic Studies*, 31(1).

Diamond, Peter (1965). National debt in a neoclassical growth model. *American Economic Review*, 55(5).

Feldstein, Martin S. (1974). Social Security, induced retirement, and aggregate capital accumulation. *Journal of Political Economy*, 82(5).

Feldstein, Martin S. (1996). The missing piece in policy analysis: Social Security reform. *American Economic Review*, 86(2).

Hviding, Ketil and Marcel Merette (1998). Macroeconomic effects of pension reforms in the context of ageing populations: overlapping generations model simulation for seven Oecd countries. OECD Working Paper (98)14.

Ingenue Team (1999). *Ingenue : projet d'étape*, December. Mimeo CEPII-CEPREMAP-MINI-OFCE.

Kenc, Turalay and Sayan Serdar (1998). transmission of demographic shocks effects from large to small countries: an overlapping generations CGE analysis. Bilkent University Department of Economics Discussion Papers, Ankara.

Miles, David (1997). Modelling the impact of demographic change upon the economy. CEPR Discussion Paper, Number 1762.

Modigliani, Franco (1986). Life cycle, individual thrift and the wealth of nations. *American Economic Review*, 76(3).

Morrow, K Mc and W. Roeger (2000). The economic consequences of ageing populations. European Commision, Economic and Financial Affairs.

Obstfeld, Maurice and Kenneth Rogoff (1996). *Foundations Of International Macroeconomics.* MIT Press.

Persson, Torsten (1985). Deficits and intergenerational welfare in open economies. *Journal of International Economics*, 19(1).

Raffelhüschen, K. B. and A.E. Risa (1995). Reforming Social Security in a small open economy. *European Journal of Political Economy*, 11(3).

Reisen, Helmut (1997). Can the ageing Oecd escape demography through capital flows to the emerging markets. OECD.

Samuelson, Paul A. (1958). An exact consumption-loan model of interest with or without the social contrivance of money. *Journal of Political Economy*, 66(3).

Temple, Jonathan R. W. (1999). The new growth evidence, *Journal of Economic Literature.* 37(1).

Turner, Dave, Claude Giorno, Alain De Serres, Anne Vourc'H and Pete Richardson (1998). The macroeconomic implications of ageing in a global context. OECD Economic Department Working Papers, 193.

United Nations (1996), World Population Prospects 1950-2050 (The 1996 Revision), Data Base.

World Bank (1997). Private Capital Flows To Developing Countries: The Road To Financial Integration. Oxford University Press.

II

Money, Inflation and Macrodynamics

Chapter 4: Inflation and Productivity Differentials in EMU.

Paul De Grauwe
Centre of Economic Studies, University of Leuven, Belgium & CEPR

Frauke Skudelny
Centre of Economic Studies, University of Leuven, Belgium

Abstract The aim of this paper is to find out whether the Balassa-Samuelson effect is important in EMU. We use panel data going from 1971 to 1995 for the current EU members in order to estimate the long run effect of bilateral differences in productivity growth differential between the traded and non-traded goods sector on bilateral inflation differentials. The regression results indicate that there is little evidence for a significant effect of the productivity differential, as proposed by the theory. The productivity growth in the non-traded goods sector alone does however have a significant effect on inflation. According to our regression results, less than one percent of the inflation differentials between EU countries is on average due to the productivity growth in the traded and the non-traded goods sector. However, the impact of productivity shocks was quite substantial, leading to a maximum of 7 percent increase in inflation differentials.

1. Introduction

With the creation of EMU the question arises how much inflation might still prevail within a monetary union. According to the Balassa-Samuelson theorem, inflation differentials between countries can be explained through the existence of labour productivity differentials between the traded and the non-traded goods sectors.[1]

[1]In its initial form, the theorem states that differences in the traded sector's productivity across countries lead to an over- or under-valuation of the real exchange rate between the two countries. In the later literature, it is generally assumed that the productivity difference between the traded and the non-traded sector drive the inflation rate, and therefore the real exchange rate, see for example Canzoneri *et al.*, 1999.

The aim of this chapter is to find out whether the Balassa-Samuelson effect is important in EMU. Previous empirical studies have found ambiguous results concerning the effect of productivity differentials on inflation, depending on the sample period, and on the econometric methods used. However, only few of them have focused on the European case. Moreover, most studies are based on a time series analysis, whereas we will use panel data, for a sample from 1971 to 1995 for the current EU members. Comparing productivity growth in the traded and in the non-traded goods sectors in the EU (Figure 1), we find strong evidence for higher productivity growth in the traded goods sector (on average), as assumed by the theory, as well as for different patterns of productivity differentials between countries.

Figure 1. Average productivity growth (in percent) (1971-1995)

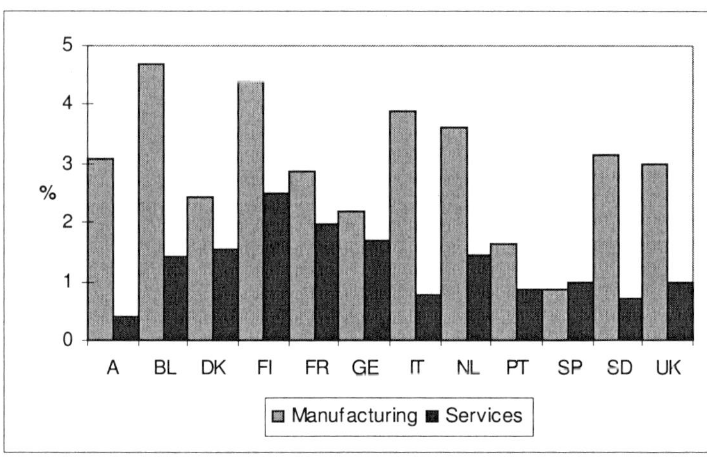

Source: OECD and own calculations

In Figure 1, the average is taken over the years for which data were available. Portugal and Spain, for example, have a lot of missing observations, so that the average does not cover the total of the period. The other countries have a similar number of observations, so that they are directly comparable. We observe that productivity growth in the manufacturing sector is relatively high in Belgium, Finland, Italy and the Netherlands whereas it is relatively low in Denmark, France and Germany (neglecting Portugal and Spain because of the small number of observations). The latter three countries have a comparatively high productivity in the non-traded goods sector. It is however difficult to see why these differences exist, as we do not have more disaggregated data on productivity growth here.

Figure 2. Productivity differential and CPI-inflation (1971-1998)

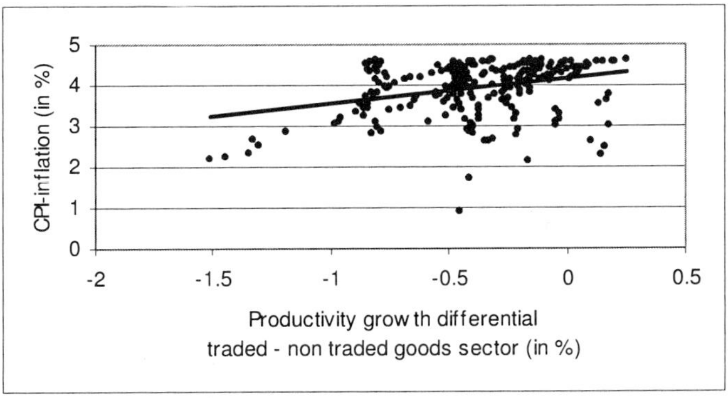

Source: OECD and own calculations

Figure 2 plots the productivity differential between the traded and the non-traded goods sector against CPI-inflation rates for all EU-countries. Each point corresponds to one observation. The chart is supportive of the hypothesis that productivity differentials have a positive impact on inflation, as shown by the trend line.

This essay is structured as follows: section 2 will describe the theoretical foundation of the model, and section 3 gives an overview of previous empirical studies on the link between inflation and productivity differentials. Section 4 presents our empirical results and section 5 quantifies how much of the inflation differential is due to productivity differentials.

2. Theoretical foundation of the productivity hypothesis

In their initial model, Balassa, 1964 and Samuelson, 1964 argue that the relative price of non-tradable goods to tradable goods is higher in richer countries than in poorer countries because productivity differentials have to be taken into account. The intuition is that productivity increases in the traded goods sector in a country (the richer country) cannot be compensated by a decrease in traded goods prices due to the law of one price. Therefore, domestic wages increase in the home country. Assuming that the productivity in the non-traded goods sector is constant, the price of non-tradable goods has to increase. Therefore, purchasing power parity between the two currencies will be less than the equilibrium exchange rate, as purchasing power parity is based on the prices of all goods, whereas the equilibrium exchange rate would be based on prices in the traded goods sector only. Assuming that international productivity differences are bigger in the production of traded goods, the currency of the country with the higher productivity levels will appear to be overvalued in terms of purchasing power parity. It should however be noted that in this initial version of the model, the productivity in the non-traded goods sector is assumed to be about the same in all countries. Later studies relax this assumption so that the productivity differential between the traded and the non-traded sectors, rather than the productivity in the traded goods sector alone, determines prices.

There are different approaches starting from the Balassa-Samuelson hypotheses that relax the assumption of constant productivity in the non-traded goods sector across countries. Our empirical analysis will be based on a model of perfect competition. We assume perfect labour mobility between the traded and the non-traded goods sectors within one country. In this model, we have two production functions in Cobb-Douglas form, one for the traded goods and one for the non-traded goods sector:

$$Y^T = A^T \left(K^T\right)^{\gamma^T} \left(L^T\right)^{1-\gamma^T} \text{ and } \mathrm{Y^N} = \mathrm{A^N} \left(\mathrm{K^N}\right)^{\gamma^N} \left(\mathrm{L^N}\right)^{1-\gamma^N}$$

with Y the production, L the labour force, K capital, and A the technology, the superscript designating the traded (T) and the non-traded (N) goods sector.[2]

Profit maximisation requires the following conditions:

$$\left(1-\gamma^T\right) \frac{Y^T}{L^T} = \frac{W^T}{P^T} \tag{1}$$

and

$$\left(1-\gamma^N\right) \frac{Y^N}{L^N} = \frac{W^N}{P^N} \tag{2}$$

[2]Canzoneri, 1996 argues that it is not necessary to build the model on a Cobb-Douglas production function. The model can indeed also be derived for a whole class of production functions where the marginal product of labour can be expressed as constant term multiplied with the average product of labour, which also holds for the Cobb-Douglas production function.

These equations state that in each sector, labour productivity is equal to the real cost of labour. Due to the assumption of perfect labour mobility between the two sectors within one country, wages are the same in both sectors, W = W T = W N . Dividing (1) by (2) and taking the logarithm, we obtain:

$$p^N = p^T + \log\left(\frac{1-\gamma^T}{1-\gamma^N}\right) + q^T - q^N \tag{3}$$

where $q^T = \log\left(\frac{Y^T}{L^T}\right)$ and $q^N = \log\left(\frac{Y^N}{L^N}\right)$, with q the logarithm of labour productivity. Again, small caps designate variables in logarithm.

The next step is then to write the total price level as a function of prices in the traded and in the non-traded goods sectors:

$$p = (1-a)p^T + ap^N \tag{4}$$

where p is the logarithm of the average price level, p^T and $p^N T$ the logarithms of the price levels in the tradable and non-tradable sectors and a is the share of production in the non-traded sector in total production.

Substituting (3) into (4), assuming that the elasticities γ^T and γ^N are constant over time, and defining $c = a\log\left(\frac{1-\gamma^T}{1-\gamma^N}\right)$, we obtain:

$$p = c + p^T + a\left(q^T - q^N\right). \tag{5}$$

This means that the total price level in a country equals the price level in the traded goods sector plus the share of non-traded goods times the productivity differential between the traded and the non-traded goods production.

The price differential between two countries is therefore defined as follows:

$$p_i - p_j = c_{ij} + \left(p_i^T - p_j^T\right) + a_i\left(q_i^T - q_i^N\right) - a_j\left(q_j^T - q_j^N\right) \tag{6}$$

with $c_{ij} = c_i - c_j$.

The price differential between two countries should thus be a function of the differential of traded goods prices between the two countries, and the share of non-traded goods in total production multiplied with the productivity differential between the traded and the non-traded goods sector for both countries.

Contributions using similar approaches are Alberola and Tyrväinen, 1998, Canzoneri *et al.*, 1996, De Gregorio et al., 1994, Hsieh, 1982, Froot and Rogoff, 1994, Micossi and Milesi-Ferretti, 1994 and Strauss, 1995. The difference with respect to the above model consists mainly in the way the final equation is defined, *i.e.* whether the authors want to explain total inflation, prices in the non-traded sector relative to the traded sector, or real exchange rates.

A similar approach consists in introducing productivity differentials through the technology factors, A^T and A^N in the Cobb-Douglas production function. This is for example the case in Asea and Mendoza, 1994. They consider the technology factor to be a stochastic productivity disturbance. Assuming that labour productivity grows at the same constant rate in both sectors, their outcome is that prices in the non-traded goods sector depend on the marginal products of labour in the traded and in the non-traded goods sector.

Marston, 1987 also introduces interaction between the traded and the non-traded goods sector through inputs. He also uses a Cobb-Douglas production function, interpreting the technology factors as productivity shocks. A new aspect of his model is that he introduces interaction between the traded and the non-traded goods sectors, arguing that output in each sector depends among other factors on inputs from the other sector. Therefore, prices in the traded sector are a function of prices in the non-traded sector, and vice versa. Maximising the utility of the producers in each sector and assuming the same wages across sectors, his outcome is that total prices are defined through productivity in the traded and the non-traded goods sector, and through wages (which are supposed to be the same in the two sectors).

3. Previous empirical studies

The empirical literature on this topic looks either at prices or at real exchange rates as endogenous variables. The original version of the Balassa-Samuelson model predicts that traded goods' productivity differentials across countries explain changes in the real exchange rate. In this version of the model, the non-traded sector is not taken into account, and purchasing power parity is in general assumed to hold. Most empirical studies do however include the non-traded goods sector into their model. We will here first present those studies explaining the real exchange rate through productivity differentials. Second, we will present studies that relax the purchasing power parity assumption and take price levels, inflation or their differentials as endogenous variable.

3.1 Studies explaining the real exchange rate

When studying the effect of productivity differentials on the real exchange rate, the problem of possible non-stationarity of the variables arises. Some authors take into account this problem and use different methods to solve it.

Strauss, 1995, for example, uses an error correction mechanism in his estimation. He uses data for the G7 from 1960 to 1990 to estimate the speed of adjustment of the real exchange rate to changes in non-tradable prices. The regression results indicate that the relative price of non-tradable goods significantly influences the real exchange rate in the short run.

The problem of non-stationarity might also be solved through defining the variables of every country vis-à-vis the average of the sample. Froot and Rogoff, 1991 do this for the EMS countries. They explain differences in the real exchange rate movements of currencies participating in the European exchange rate mechanism by different factors. Besides labour productivity, as stated in the Balassa-Samuelson theorem, they also include government spending into their regressions of real exchange rates and find it to be statistically significant, whereas the productivity variables of both the traded and the non-traded sector are not significant. Their regression covers the period 1979 to 1989 for the EMS countries.

Hsieh, 1992 analyses the real exchange rate of Germany and Japan with respect to their trading partners from 1954 to 1976 and find a significant effect of the productivity differential between the traded and the non-traded goods sector for both countries. Marston, 1987 uses as dependent variable the difference between the real exchange rate based on the GDP deflator on the one hand, and relative unit labour costs in the traded goods sector on the other hand. He finds more evidence for a significant effect of the productivity differential in the domestic economy (the United States) than for the productivity differential in the partner country (Japan and Germany). Officer, 1976 uses GNP per capita as proxy for the productivity variable and finds no evidence for a significant impact on purchasing power parity divided by the real exchange rate. It should however be noted that his regressions have less than 15 degrees of freedom, as he runs the regression on cross sectional data. Rogoff, 1992 also does not find significant results when regressing productivity differentials on the real exchange rate between the Japanese Yen and the US dollar. Again, the small number of observations might be the reason for these results.

In her study on real exchange rates and development, Lahrèche-Révil, 1998 also studies the long run effect of productivity differentials on the real exchange rate. She uses the initial Balassa-Samuelson theorem, assuming that productivity differentials in the non-traded goods sector are very small and can therefore be neglected. The real exchange rate should therefore be driven by productivity differentials in the traded goods sector. Using per capita GDP as a proxy for labour productivity in the traded goods sector, she finds support for the Balassa-Samuelson theorem. Her sample covers industrialised and developing countries for different time periods, starting from 1975, 1980, 1985 and 1990, and all going up to 1993. In a second step, she relaxes the assumption of perfect competition. Industrialised countries being more diversified than developing countries, they can set prices according to price elasticities of demand, whereas developing countries are price takers. As this extension of the model is an analysis in the short run, she argues that in the long run, the original version of the Balassa-Samuelson should still hold, whereas in the short run, real exchange rates are following cycles in accordance to the temporarily oligopolistical structure of the market.

When real exchange rates are integrated of order one (and not higher) the problem of non-stationarity can also be solved by taking the growth rate of the real exchange rate, as for example in De Gregorio and Wolf, 1994 who find a significant effect of productivity differentials. They run short-term regressions with the real exchange rate and with the relative price of non-traded goods as dependent variables. In both cases, they take as dependent variable the total factor productivity differential between the traded and the non-traded sectors, the prices of imports and exports (alternatively the terms of trade), government expenditure and the GDP per capita. All variables are in first differences. De Gregorio and Wolf take 14 OECD countries over the period 1970 to 1985, using SUR estimates. Sectors for which the exports divided by the value added exceed 10 percent are classified as tradable goods, whereas the other sectors constitute the non-traded goods sector. In the regressions with the real exchange rate as dependent variable, they find highly significant coefficients for total factor productivity. However, when taking the relative price of non-traded goods as dependent variable, the coefficient of productivity becomes insignificant.

Some studies use co-integration techniques in order to analyse the long run effect of productivity differentials on the real exchange rate. Chinn and Johnston, 1997 and MacDonald, 1997, for example, use the growth rate of real exchange rates and implement a co-integration test arguing that real exchange rates are integrated of order 2. Chinn and Johnston, 1997 try to find out whether the real exchange rate can be determined through productivity shocks in the traded and the non-traded sector, government spending and inflation. Taking data of 14 industrialised countries for the period 1970 to 1991, they find more evidence in favour of co-integration when analysing panel data than when analysing the time series of every country separately.

MacDonald, 1997 uses co-integration tests for real exchange rate data on the US dollar, the DM and the Japanese Yen during the period 1974 to 1993. He finds significant and sensible long run relationships for the real effective exchange rates of these currencies with the productivity differentials between the traded and the non-traded sectors, when controlling for the demand side, fiscal policy, private sector savings and oil prices.

When using co-integration tests, the question arises whether the differential of productivity growth is integrated at the same order as real exchange rates. The answer to this question might depend to some degree on the data used, but it is very unlikely that the differential of productivity growth rates is non stationary. This would suggest using co-integration tests only for variables expressed in levels, in the case where real exchange rates are integrated of order one (and not higher).

3.2 Studies explaining prices

Most studies using price variables rather than real exchange rates as dependent variables try to find out the effect of productivity differentials on the relative price of traded to non-traded goods (or the reversal). Asea and Mendoza, 1994, for example, use regressions on the price levels without taking first differences. They investigate in how far long run relative labour productivities can explain long run relative prices of non-traded goods, and whether the latter explain cross-country real exchange rate differentials in the long run. Their empirical findings for 14 OECD countries from 1970 to 1985 are that the Balassa-Samuelson theorem cannot be rejected, and that long-term relative prices are of little help in explaining long term differences in the level of the real exchange rate. Asea and Mendoza use a Hodrick-Prescott filter in order to take only the long-run component of the data into account.

De Gregorio and Wolf, 1994, De Gregorio *et al.*, 1994 and Micossi and Milesi-Feretti, 1994 run a regression of all variables expressed in growth rates and find mixed results. The outcome might however be due to the fact that they use short run data. This hypothesis is strengthened by a study of De Gregorio *et al.*, 1994 which uses short term and long term data. Their sample covers 14 OECD countries over the period from 1970 to 1985. They take yearly growth rates for the short-run analysis and growth rates over the total period for the long-run analysis. The finding is that there is little evidence for a small effect in the short run, but strong evidence for a significant effect in the long run.

This study also differs from the previous ones in the sense that total inflation rather than relative inflation in the different sectors is taken as dependent variable. Their regression results show that short-run demand side factors, in particular income growth, have most explanatory power of relative price changes. In the long run, most of the increase in the relative price of non-tradable goods can be explained by a faster increase of total factor productivity in tradable goods. A drawback of their long-run analysis is that their sample only contains 14 observations (average growth rate from 1970 to 1985 for 14 countries).

Micossi and Milesi-Ferretti, 1994 regress the inflation differential between the traded and the non-traded sector in a country on the labour productivity differential in the traded and the non-traded goods sectors, an EMS dummy, inflation (based on the GDP deflator) and the GDP growth rate for eight EU countries from 1966 to 1990. For about half of the regressions, they find a significant influence of the productivity differential on the inflation differential. They also test the relationship in a bilateral regression, where the real exchange rate (based on the GDP deflator) is explained by the real exchange rate (based on unit labour costs) and the productivity differential between traded and non-traded sectors for both countries. Again, the evidence for a significant influence of the productivity differentials is mixed.

Hondroyiannis and Papapetrou, 1998, Canzoneri *et al.*, 1996 and Canzoneri *et al.*, 1999 use price and productivity data in levels, but use co-integration techniques to find evidence for a long run effect of productivity differentials on inflation. Hondroyiannis and Papapetrou, 1998 analyse the causality between the price level and productivity with the help of co-integration tests. As in their sample of low-inflation OECD countries during the period 1960 to 1995, all variables except the CPI are integrated of order one, and the latter is integrated of order two, no co-integration is possible. Their conclusion is that according to this finding, there cannot exist any long run relationship. In a second step, they control for output and monetary policy. Applying the Johanson maximum likelihood approach, they can reject the hypothesis of a spurious relationship between the consumer price index and productivity in the extended model.

Canzoneri *et al.*, 1996 and Canzoneri *et al.*, 1999 both use co-integration techniques and find evidence for co-integration of both variables in most cases. Canzoneri *et al.*, 1999 test two components of the Balassa-Samuelson model, using panel data on 13 OECD countries for the period from 1960 to 1993: the first component is the hypothesis that the relative price of non-traded goods should reflect relative productivity of labour in the traded and the non-traded goods sectors. They find evidence for a co-integrating relationship between relative prices of non-traded goods and relative productivities in the non-traded goods sector. The co-integration coefficient is generally close to one, as suggested by the theory. The second component they test is the hypothesis that purchasing power parity holds for traded goods. Their finding is that there are large long-lived deviations from purchasing power parity in traded goods.

Alberola and Tyrväinen, 1998 make co-integration tests on the standard and an extended Balassa-Samuelson model, using in both cases the growth rates of all variables. In the latter, they include wage differentials between the traded and the non-traded goods sectors, assuming that wages between the two sectors do not equalise. They find evidence in favour of this assumption. Their co-integration tests for 11 EU members from 1975 to 1995 confirm a long-run relationship between inflation and productivity differentials for Germany, Spain and Belgium in the standard model, and for all countries but the Netherlands in the extended model. They use a Hodrick-Prescott filter in order to take only the long-run component of the data into account and find a significant and positive impact of productivity differentials.

From this survey of the empirical literature one can conclude that the empirical support for the Balassa-Samuelson hypothesis is mixed.

4. Empirical analysis

Our empirical analysis adds to the studies presented above in several ways. First, we analyse the effect of productivity differentials between the traded and the non-traded sectors on prices, and not on the real exchange rate as in many of the studies. This has the advantage that we do not test two hypotheses simultaneously, namely the Balassa-Samuelson theorem and purchasing power parity.

Second, we enter all variables in growth rates and also estimate a bilateral equation, taking the inflation differential between countries i and j as dependent variable. To our knowledge, none of the existing empirical studies used this method. Beside the fact that we are interested in the inflation differential within EMU rather than in the inflation rate of each individual country, this method has the advantage of increasing the number of observations.

Finally, we apply the analysis to the EU, using a data set covering the period from 1971 to 1995[3] for all present EU members, except Greece and Ireland.[4] We use panel data estimations, taking into account not

[3]Due to the availability of sectoral productivity data.

[4]For these two countries, no reliable data on sectoral value added were available.

only variation over time, but also across countries. This should make our estimator more efficient, as it increases the number of observations.

We first test the specification in a one-country model, and then estimate a bilateral equation, using inflation differentials between EU-countries as dependent variable.

4.1 One-country specification

The traded sector consists of the manufacturing sector; the non-traded sector is calculated by subtracting manufacturing, agriculture and mining and quarrying from the total (all sectors together). This means that it is composed of the remaining service sectors: electricity, gas and water; construction; wholesale and retail trade, restaurants and hotels; transport, storage and communication; finance, insurance, real estate, and business services; and community, social and personal services. A shortcoming of this approach is that part of the service sector might be traded, too. The size of the resulting bias is however relatively limited; Figure 3 shows the share of exports in the value added for the service sector.

Figure 3. Exports in percent of the value added - service sector (1995)

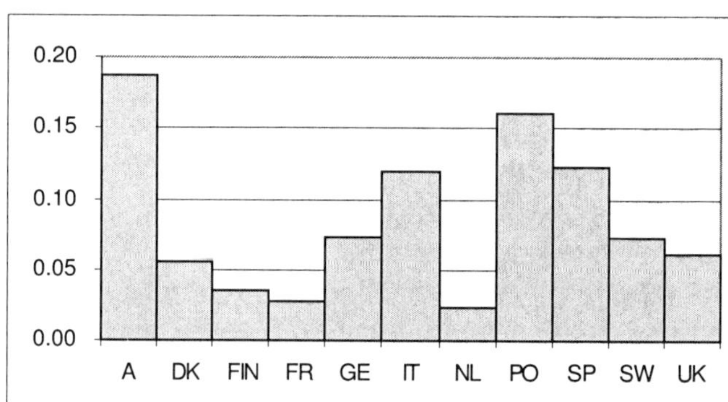

Source: OECD and own calculations

For Austria, Italy, Portugal and Spain the bias is highest, due to the relative strength of tourism. For the other countries, the share is around 5 percent. That means that for these four countries, assuming that the productivity in the tourism sector is low relative to the productivity manufacturing sector and high relative to the average of the service sector, our productivity measures for the traded and the non-traded goods sectors are somewhat biased upwards.[5] These two biases do not compensate each other completely, but should at least partially offset each other.

The estimated equation for the one-country specification is the following:

$$\pi_{it} = \beta_0 c_i + \beta_1 t + \beta_2 \pi_{it}^T + \beta_3 \phi_{it}^N \left(\Delta q_{it}^T - \Delta q_{it}^N \right) \tag{7}$$

with c_i the country specific intercept, t the time trend, π_{it}^T inflation in the traded goods sector, ϕ_{it}^N the share of value added in the non-traded goods sector, and Δq_{it}^T and Δq_{it}^N productivity growth in the traded and the non-traded goods sector, respectively.

In the equation above, we impose the same coefficient for the productivity differential for both countries. In order to relax somewhat this assumption, we also test whether the coefficient of the traded goods sector productivity growth is different from that of the non-traded goods sector. The resulting equation is:

$$\pi_{it} = \gamma_0 c_i + \gamma_1 t + \gamma_2 \pi_{it}^T + \gamma_3 \phi_{it}^N \Delta q_{it}^T + \gamma_4 \phi_{it}^N \Delta q_{it}^N \tag{8}$$

We take the growth rate of two different price indices as dependent variable (π): the consumer price index (CPI) and the GDP deflator (GPI). For inflation in the traded goods sector (π^T), we also take two definitions, the producer price index in manufacturing (PPIT), and the export price index (XPI). The productivity growth in the traded and non-traded goods sectors (Δq_{it}^T and Δq_{it}^N) are defined as the growth rates of the value-added by employee in the respective sector.[6] A description of the data sources is given in appendix.

We multiply the productivity differential with the share of value added in the non-traded goods sector (ϕ_{it}^N). Therefore, we would expect the estimated coefficient to be equal to one in the long run. The advantage of multiplying the differential with the share rather than estimating the share directly is that we allow the shares to differ across countries, which would not be possible otherwise. Remember that we use panel data, so that we obtain the same estimated coefficients across the different cross sectional units, in our case couples of countries.

Figure 4 shows that there is convergence within the EU countries of the share of non-traded goods value-added. Especially in the beginning

---

[5]The 'true' productivity measure for the traded goods sector should be $\frac{VA_{manuf.}+VA_{tourism}}{L_{manuf.}+L_{tourism}}$, and for the non-traded goods sector, it should be $\frac{VA_{services}+VA_{tourism}}{L_{services}+L_{tourism}}$.

[6]Portugal was excluded from the sample when the producer price index in the traded goods sector entered into the regression, as no data were available for this variable.

of our sample, there are substantial differences between the EU countries. That means that we indeed have to multiply our productivity variables by the share of non-tradable goods.

Figure 4. Standard deviation of the share of non-traded value added in the total value added across EU countries

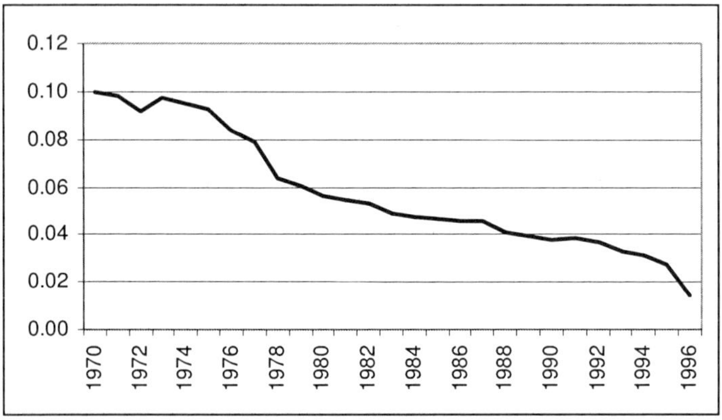

Source: OECD and own calculations

The results of the Im-Peseran-Shin unit root test for panel data are shown in appendix. In the unilateral specification, we cannot reject the null hypothesis of a unit root for CPI- and GPI-inflation unless we include a time trend. As the problem seems to be solved when including a time trend, we will include it also into our regression. We want to analyse the impact of productivity differentials on inflation in the long run. Therefore, we use long-run data, taking five-year averages for all variables. Due to the high number of missing observations, we are obliged to take an overlapping sample going from 1971-75 to 1991-95. A Newey-West error correction is implemented, correcting for heteroskedasticity and autocorrelation.[7] This correction requires that there is no autocorrelation of unknown order in the model. We tested this assumption with the Breusch-Godfrey test for auto-correlation and could accept the null hypothesis of no autocorrelation. The regression results of equation (7) are shown in Table 1.

[7]See Newey and West, 1987.

Table 1. Empirical results: one-country version (constrained) - equation (7)

	π_{CPI}		π_{GPI}	
Trend	-0.013	-0.033	*-0.076*	**-0.105**
	(-0.310)	(-0.779)	(-1.786)	(-2.286)
π^T_{PPI}	**0.758**		**0.645**	
	(11.667)		(9.493)	
π^T_{XPI}		**0.617**		**0.525**
		(10.760)		(8.649)
$\phi^N(\Delta q^T - \Delta q^N)$	*0.196*	0.082	-0.065	-0.079
	(1.837)	(0.637)	(-0.594)	(-0.559)
Adj. R^2	0.930	0.922	0.931	0.924
LM(1)	0.570	0.323	0.238	0.004

Note 1: π_{CPI}: consumer price inflation; π_{GPI}: GDP deflator inflation; π^T_{PPI}: producer price inflation; π^T_{XPI}: export price inflation; ϕ^N share of value added in the non-traded goods sector; Δq^T productivity growth in the traded goods sector; Δq^N productivity growth in the non-traded goods sector.

Note 2: **Bold** *(italic)* numbers: coefficient is significantly different from zero at the **5%** *(10%)* level. T-statistics are displayed into brackets.

Note 3: LM(1): Lagrange multiplier test for autocorrelation, as proposed by Breusch, 1978 and Godfrey, 1978.

We use a different intercept for each cross-sectional unit. We also include a time trend into all regressions. The time trend has a negative sign but is not always significant. The negative sign indicates a reduction in inflation over the sample period.

Traded goods inflation has a significant impact on total inflation with a coefficient of around 0.7 for PPI-inflation in manufacturing, and around 0.6 for XPI-inflation. This is quite close to one, which is expected by the theory.

The productivity growth differential between the traded and the non-traded sectors yields quite mixed results. The coefficient is significantly different from zero only when taking PPI-inflation in manufacturing as inflation in the traded sector (only at a 10 percent significance level). In that case, it has the expected positive sign, but is much smaller than one, which would be the value expected. These results are in line with the study of De Gregorio and Wolf, 1994 who find no significant effect of the productivity differential on inflation, and Micossi and Milesi-Feretti, 1994 who find a significant effect only in about half of the equations, with relatively low coefficients. De Gregorio *et al.*, 1994 however find a significant effect, although again, the coefficient is relatively low (between 0.23 and 0.37).

The regression results of equation (8) (unconstrained version) are shown in Table 2.

Table 2. Empirical results: one-country version (unconstrained) - equation (8)

	π_{CPI}		π_{GPI}	
Trend	-0.015	-0.042	**-0.082**	**-0.118**
	(-0.378)	(-1.045)	(-2.007)	(-2.775)
π^T_{PPI}	**0.756**		**0.642**	
	(12.087)		(10.320)	
π^T_{XPI}		**0.610**		**0.516**
		(11.769)		(9.863)
$\phi^{\text{N}}\Delta q^T$	*0.193*	0.058	-0.072	-0.112
	(1.775)	(0.473)	(-0.698)	(-0.873)
$\phi^{\text{N}}\Delta q^T$	*-0.388*	**-0.496**	-0.344	*-0.493*
	(-1.938)	(-2.198)	(-1.400)	(-1.830)
Adj. R^2	0.931	0.926	0.934	0.930
LM(1)	0.402	0.232	0.044	0.067

Note 1: π_{CPI}: consumer price inflation; π_{GPI}: GDP deflator inflation; π^T_{PPI}: producer price inflation; π^T_{XPI}: export price inflation; ϕ^{N} share of value added in the non-traded goods sector; Δq^T productivity growth in the traded goods sector; Δq^N productivity growth in the non-traded goods sector.

Note 2: **Bold** *(italic)* numbers: coefficient is significantly different from zero at 5% (10%).

Note 3: ARSQ: Adjusted R-squared.

Note 4: LM(1): Lagrange multiplier test for autocorrelation, as proposed by Breusch, 1978 and Godfrey, 1978.

The results of equation (8) look very similar to the previous results for all variables except productivity growth. The coefficient of the productivity growth in the non-traded goods sector is significantly different from zero in almost all specifications at 10%, and has the expected negative sign. It is higher in absolute value than in the results of Table 1, but is still different from the expected coefficient of 1. Productivity growth in the traded goods sector is significant only when we use PPI-inflation in manufacturing (again only at a 10 percent significance level). The coefficients of the traded goods sectors productivity growth is quite different from the non-traded sectors productivity growth (in absolute values), which is in contradiction with equation (6). The finding that the traded-goods sectors productivity growth is not significant is not in line with what has been found in the literature. Alberola and Tyrväinen, 1998, who restrict the coefficient of non-traded goods productivity to be zero find a cointegrating relationship between traded goods productivity and inflation, with a coefficient between 0.5 and 1.6. Canzoneri *et al.*,

1996 and Canzoneri *et al.*, 1999 who also make a cointegration analysis find a significant effect with a coefficient close to one for the traded sectors productivity. Asea and Mendoza, 1994 find a long term coefficient of 0.24 for traded goods productivity, and -0.28 for non-traded goods productivity. Remember however that they do not multiply their productivity terms with the share of non-traded value added, so that their coefficient can be different of one.

The results of Table 2 indicate that the findings in Table 1 (few significant results for $\phi^N\left(\Delta q^T - \Delta q^N\right)$ are mainly due to a difference in the impact of productivity growth in the traded sector relative to that in the non-traded sector. Both regression results do however not support the extended Balassa-Samuelson hypothesis, as traded goods productivity is not significant in our results.

The mixed results of the one-country specification, however, can also be due to the small amount of observations, combined with a high number of missing values for productivity for some of the countries. We therefore also estimate the equation in a bilateral form.

4.2 Bilateral specification

The estimated equation for the bilateral specification is the following:

$$\begin{aligned}\pi_{it} - \pi_{jt} &= \chi_0 c_{ij} + \chi_1 t + \chi_2\left(\pi_{it}^T - \pi_{jt}^T\right) \\ &\quad + \chi_3\left[\phi_{it}^N\left(\Delta q_{it}^T - \Delta q_{it}^N\right) - \phi_{jt}^N\left(\Delta q_{jt}^T - \Delta q_{jt}^N\right)\right]\end{aligned} \tag{9}$$

for the constrained version of the model (analogously to (7) in the one-country specification), and

$$\begin{aligned}\pi_{it} - \pi_{jt} &= \delta_0 c_{ij} + \delta_1 t + \delta_2\left(\pi_{it}^T - \pi_{jt}^T\right) \\ &\quad + \delta_3\left(\phi_{it}^N \Delta q_{it}^T - \phi_{jt}^N \Delta q_{jt}^T\right) \\ &\quad + \delta_4\left(\phi_{it}^N \Delta q_{it}^N - \phi_{jt}^N \Delta q_{jt}^N\right)\end{aligned} \tag{10}$$

for the unconstrained version of the model (analogously to (8) in the one-country specification), with c_i the cross section specific intercept[8], t the time trend, π_{it} inflation in the traded goods sector, ϕ_{it}^N the share of value added in the non-traded goods sector, and Δq_{it}^T and Δq_{it}^N productivity growth in the traded and the non-traded goods sector, respectively.

[8] In the bilateral specification, these are not country specific intercepts, but rather different intercepts for each bilateral combination of countries.

The results of the Im-Peseran-Shin unit root test for panel data (see appendix) show that we can reject the hypothesis of a unit root for all variables at a one percent confidence level.

Table 3 shows the regression results of the constrained version of the model as defined in equation (0.9).

Table 3. Empirical results: bilateral version (constrained) - equation (9)

	$\pi_{CPI,i} - \pi_{CPI,j}$		$\pi_{GPI,i} - \pi_{GPI,j}$	
Trend	-0.020	**-0.049**	0.009	**-0.035**
	(-1.027)	(-3.302)	(0.457)	(-2.359)
$\pi^T_{PPI,i} - \pi^T_{PPI,j}$	**0.763**		**0.791**	
	(17.717)		(19.802)	
$\pi^T_{XPI,i} - \pi^T_{XPI,j}$		**0.640**		**0.657**
		(18.908)		(19.288)
$\phi^N_i(\Delta q^T_i - \Delta q^N_i) -$	**0.154**	*0.092*	-0.002	-0.012
$\phi^N_j(\Delta q^T_j - \Delta q^N_j)$	(2.982)	(1.752)	(-0.041)	(-0.210)
Adj. R^2	0.886	0.886	0.889	0.893
LM(1)	1.119	1.749	2.822	0.162

Note 1: π_{CPI}: consumer price inflation; π_{GPI}: GDP deflator inflation; π^T_{PPI}: producer price inflation; π^T_{XPI}: export price inflation; ϕ^N share of value added in the non-traded goods sector; Δq^T productivity growth in the traded goods sector; Δq^N productivity growth in the non-traded goods sector.

Note 2: **Bold** *(italic)* numbers: coefficient is significantly different from zero at the **5%** *(10%)* level. T-statistics are displayed into brackets.

Note 3: LM(1): Lagrange multiplier test for autocorrelation, as proposed by Breusch, 1978 and Godfrey, 1978.

Again, we use the fixed effects estimator and include a time trend into all regressions. The time trend is significant and negative in all specifications where we use the export price index as proxy for inflation in the traded goods sector. This indicates that inflation differentials between the EU members declined during the sample period. Apparently, the differential in PPI-inflation in manufacturing catches up some of this convergence effect, as we do not find a significant negative effect of the time trend in the specifications with PPI-inflation in manufacturing.

When using CPI-inflation as dependent variable, the bilateral difference of the productivity growth differentials between the traded and the non-traded sectors on inflation differentials positively effects inflation differentials. The coefficient is however much lower than one.

We also estimate an unconstrained version of the bilateral specification of our model (equation (10)). The results are reported in Table 4.

Table 4. Empirical results: bilateral version (unconstrained) - equation (10)

	$\pi_{\text{CPI},i} - \pi_{\text{CPI},j}$		$\pi_{\text{GPI},i} - \pi_{\text{GPI},j}$	
Trend	-0.026	**-0.059**	0.001	**-0.048**
	(-1.300)	(-3.754)	(0.036)	(-3.038)
$\pi^T_{\text{PPI},i} - \pi^T_{\text{PPI},j}$	**0.763**		**0.796**	
	(18.224)		(21.380)	
$\pi^T_{\text{XPI},i} - \pi^T_{\text{XPI},j}$		**0.645**		**0.666**
		(20.108)		(21.470)
$\phi^{\text{N}}_i \Delta q^T_i - \phi^{\text{N}}_j \Delta q^T_j$	**0.206**	0.100	$-9 \cdot 10^{-5}$	-0.039
	(3.165)	(1.533)	(-0.001)	(-0.571)
$\phi^{\text{N}}_i \Delta q^N_i - \phi^{\text{N}}_j \Delta q^N_j$	**-0.792**	**-0.811**	**-0.782**	**-0.859**
	(-5.677)	(-5.321)	(-5.212)	(-5.154)
Adj. R^2	0.893	0.896	0.901	0.906
LM(1)	2.764	0.394	0.551	0.122

Note 1: π_{CPI}: consumer price inflation; π_{GPI}: GDP deflator inflation; π^T_{PPI}: producer price inflation; π^T_{XPI}: export price inflation; ϕ^{N} share of value added in the non-traded goods sector; Δq^T productivity growth in the traded goods sector; Δq^N productivity growth in the non-traded goods sector.

Note 2: **Bold** *(italic)* numbers: coefficient is significantly different from zero at the **5%** *(10%)* level. T-statistics are displayed into brackets.

Note 3: LM(1): Lagrange multiplier test for autocorrelation, as proposed by Breusch, 1978 and Godfrey, 1978.

The results for the time trend and inflation in the traded goods sector are similar to those in the previous regressions. In the unconstrained regression, we again find quite different coefficients for productivity growth in the two sectors. Productivity growth in the non-traded goods sector has a significant and negative impact on inflation differentials in all cases. The parameter is now much higher than in the one-country specification, reaching an average of 0.88. We find a significant positive effect of traded goods productivity growth on inflation differentials only in one case. The coefficient of productivity growth in the non-traded goods sector is now close to one, as expected from the theory. This could indicate that there was some data problem in the one-country estimation.

Remember that we have a lot more observations in the bilateral version of the model. We however still do not find evidence supporting the extended Balassa-Samuelson theorem[9], as the coefficient of traded goods productivity is mostly not significant and far from the expected

[9]'Extended' in the sense that we drop one assumption of the original Balassa-Samuelson theorem: we allow productivity in the non-traded goods sector to differ across countries.

coefficient of one. We rather find that *non-traded* goods productivity differentials are the driving force of inflation differentials.

4.3 Magnitude of the effect of productivity differentials

With our regression results, we can quantify the effect of productivity growth differentials on inflation differentials. As the coefficient of the traded goods sectors productivity, χ_2, was in most of the cases not significantly different from zero, we calculate the effect of productivity growth differentials in the non-traded goods sector on inflation differentials according to the following equation:

$$(\pi_{it} - \pi_{jt})^\star = \delta_4 \left(\phi_{it}^N \Delta q_{it}^N - \phi_{jt}^N \Delta q_{jt}^N\right) \tag{11}$$

using the parameters of equation (10), with $(\pi_{it} - \pi_{jt})^\star$ the portion of inflation due to productivity differentials. We multiply the coefficient δ_4 of equation (10) with the productivity differential in the non-traded sector multiplied with the share of non traded goods in the total value added. We calculate the average for this potential inflation in a monetary union for all countries of our sample, using the estimation results of equation (10).

The numbers in the first four columns of Table 5 represent the average inflation differentials due to the productivity differential in the non-traded sector between country i and country j. This gives us an idea about the inflation that can subsist on average inside EMU, because of productivity differentials between the participating countries. The purpose of this exercise is not only to assess which portion of the inflation differential has been created through productivity differentials in the non-traded goods sector, but also to give an idea about the possible impact of a productivity shock. This can be done by using the maximum rather than the average productivity growth differential in the non-traded goods sector to compute the effect on inflation differentials (last four columns).

Negative numbers indicate that the country had a negative productivity differential in the non-traded goods sector either on average (columns 1-4), or in the year of the maximum (columns 5-8), *i.e.*

$$\phi_{it}^N \Delta q_{it}^N < \phi_{jt}^N \Delta q_{jt}^N$$

We observe that the average inflation differential due to productivity differential in the non-traded goods sector varies between a bit more than zero (the Netherlands) and a bit more than 0.7 percent (Finland) in absolute value. When PPI inflation in manufacturing is taken as proxy

Table 5. Inflation differential due to the productivity differential

	Average 1971–1975				Maximum 1971–1975			
	$\pi_{CPI,i} - \pi_{CPI,j}$		$\pi_{GPI,i} - \pi_{GPI,j}$		$\pi_{CPI,i} - \pi_{CPI,j}$		$\pi_{GPI,i} - \pi_{GPI,j}$	
	$\pi^T_{PPI,i} - \pi^T_{PPI,j}$	$\pi^T_{XPI,i} - \pi^T_{XPI,j}$	$\pi^T_{PPI,i} - \pi^T_{PPI,j}$	$\pi^T_{XPI,i} - \pi^T_{XPI,j}$	$\pi^T_{PPI,i} - \pi^T_{PPI,j}$	$\pi^T_{XPI,i} - \pi^T_{XPI,j}$	$\pi^T_{PPI,i} - \pi^T_{PPI,j}$	$\pi^T_{XPI,i} - \pi^T_{XPI,j}$
A	0.578	0.592	0.571	0.627	5.599	5.733	5.528	6.073
BL	-0.087	-0.089	-0.086	-0.095	-4.927	-5.045	-4.865	-5.344
DK	-0.166	-0.170	-0.164	-0.180	-6.271	-6.422	-6.192	-6.802
FI	-0.702	-0.718	-0.693	-0.761	-6.121	-6.268	-6.044	-6.639
FR	-0.293	-0.300	-0.289	-0.317	-4.497	-4.605	-4.441	-4.878
GE	-0.086	-0.088	-0.085	-0.093	-3.228	-3.305	-3.187	-3.501
IT	0.305	0.312	0.301	0.331	-5.390	-5.519	-5.322	-5.846
NL	0.007	0.007	0.007	0.007	-3.883	-3.977	-3.834	-4.212
PT	0.309	0.316	0.305	0.335	3.956	4.051	3.906	4.291
SP	0.297	0.304	0.293	0.322	-3.796	-3.887	-3.748	-4.117
SD	0.354	0.362	0.349	0.384	-4.272	-4.374	-4.218	-4.633
UK	0.276	0.282	0.272	0.299	4.137	4.236	4.085	4.487

π_{CPI}: consumer price inflation; π_{GPI}: GDP deflator inflation; π^T_{PPI}: producer price inflation; π^T_{XPI}: export price inflation;

for inflation in the traded goods sector, the effect is somewhat smaller than for XPI-inflation, due to the lower parameter of the estimation results. The maximum effect (last four columns in Table 5) is quite substantial, indicating that productivity growth differentials in the non-traded sector across EU countries entailed inflation differentials going up to almost 7 percent in absolute value during the sample period. Again, this effect is somewhat smaller when PPI inflation in manufacturing is taken as proxy for inflation in the traded goods sector.

Figures 5 and 6 show the average and maximum inflation differentials due to productivity differentials in the non-traded goods sector, with CPI-inflation and GPI-inflation as proxies for total inflation, based on the results of equation (10). We observe quite substantial differences across the different EU countries. For Austria, Belgium and Italy, the effect is strongest (in absolute value).

5. Concluding remarks

According to the extended Balassa-Samuelson hypothesis, the total inflation can be explained by inflation in the traded goods sector and by the productivity growth differential between the traded and the non-

Figure 5. Average inflation differential due to productivity differentials

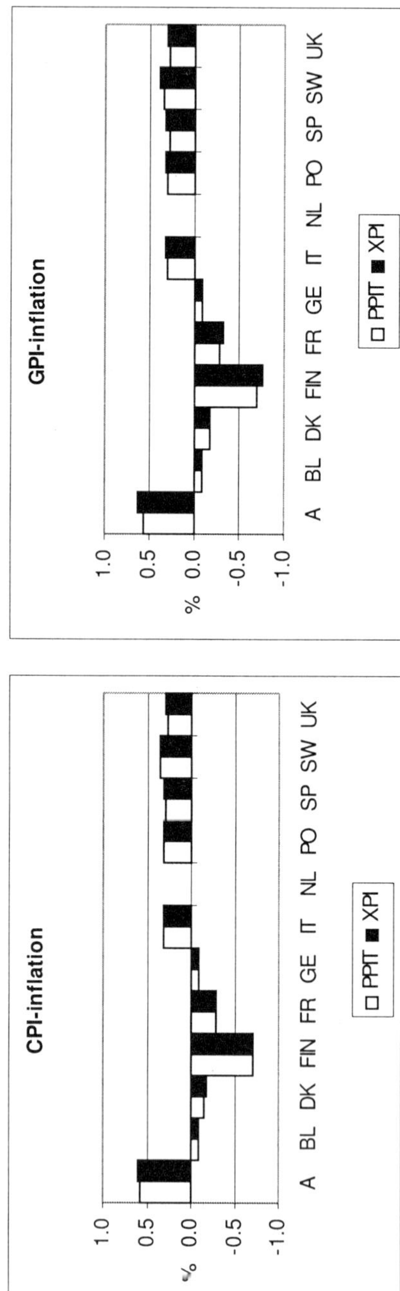

Figure 6. Maximum inflation differential due to productivity differentials

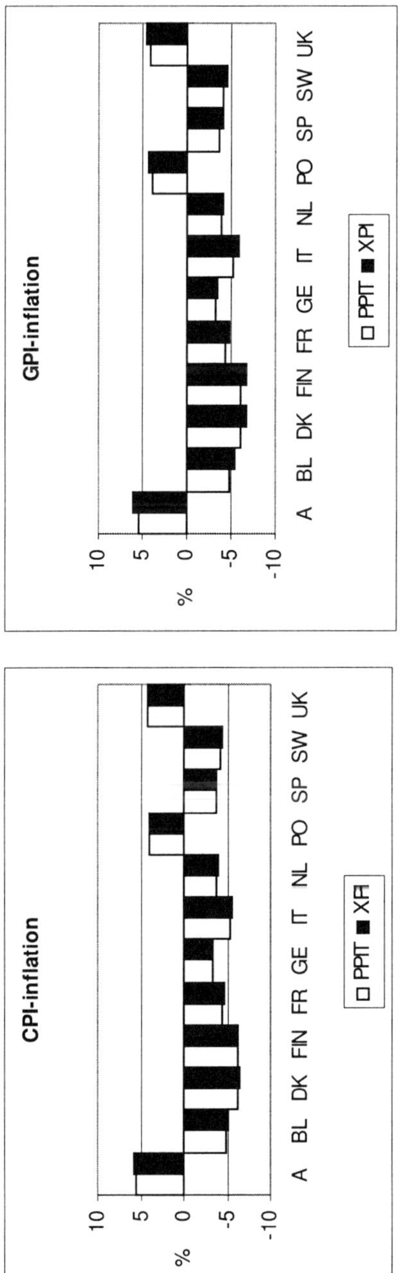

traded goods sectors. The question we analysed in this chapter is in how far inflation differentials can subsist within EMU, due to productivity differentials between the participating countries.

In order to test this hypothesis, we use data for 13 of the 15 EU members from 1971-95 and take five-year averages for all variables in first differences. We estimate a one-country and a bilateral specification of the model. The dependent variable is total inflation (differentials) and the explanatory variables are the difference between total inflation (differentials) and traded goods inflation (differentials), and the (difference between two countries') productivity growth differential between the traded and the non-traded sectors. We use the consumer price index and the GDP deflator for total inflation, and the producer price index in manufacturing and the export price index for inflation in the traded goods sector. The results of the estimates are quite mixed, in that only in one case the productivity growth differential has a significant and positive effect. We also test an unconstrained version of the model, relaxing the assumption that the coefficients for productivity growth in the traded and in the non-traded goods sectors are the same.

The outcome is that the parameters of the two productivity variables are substantially different (in absolute value). There is only little evidence for a significant and positive effect of productivity growth in the traded goods sector on inflation differentials. However, for productivity growth in the non-traded goods sector, the effect is significant and negative, as expected. In the bilateral specification, its coefficient is close to one in absolute value. We can therefore conclude that according to our data, the extended Balassa-Samuelson theorem does not hold, as traded goods productivity differentials do not have a significant impact on inflation. However, we find that non-traded goods productivity differentials do have a significant impact on inflation. This finding can be due to the limited amount of data, and to the fact that we take only five-year averages of our variables for the long run results. Moreover, the extended Balassa-Samuelson theorem is based on the hypothesis of perfect competition which might not be satisfied in reality.

When we calculate the average inflation differential due to the productivity differentials in the non-traded goods sector, we find that the average effect goes up to almost one percent in absolute value (Finland). The effect differs according to which indicator is chosen for inflation in the traded goods sector: it is somewhat larger when using XPI-inflation. The maximum is also calculated, giving an indication of the possible effect of a productivity shock. The total effect on the inflation differential is quite substantial, going up to 7 percent in absolute value.

Appendix

Definition of the variables

Inflation (π):

- Consumer price index, 1990=100; Source: OECD Main Economic Indicators
- GDP-deflator, 1990=100; Source: OECD Main Economic Indicators

Traded goods inflation (π^T):

- Export price index (XPI), 1990=100; Source: OECD Main Economic Indicators
- Producer price index manufacturing, 1990=100; Source: OECD International Sectoral Database, OECD Main Economic Indicators, and OECD Indicators of Industrial Activity

Productivity (q^T, q^N):

- Defined as value added (in constant prices USD) divided by employment in the respective sector; Source: OECD, International Sectoral Database, and OECD National Accounts II
- Data from the manufacturing sector are taken for the traded goods sector; the non-traded goods sector is composed by
  - Electricity, gas, and water
  - Construction
  - Wholesale and retail trade, restaurants and hotels
  - Transport, storage and communication
  - Financing, insurance, real estate, and business services, and
  - Community, social and personal services.
- We calculated the sum of these sectors from the data on all sectors together and subtracted agriculture, hunting, forestry, and fishing, mining and quarrying and manufacturing from it.

Unit root tests

The test results indicate for the one country specification, that we can reject the hypotheses of a unit root for all variables when including a time trend (τ_τ). Without time trend, we cannot reject the null hypothesis of a unit root for CPI- and for GPI-inflation. Therefore, we include a time trend in the estimation. For the bilateral specification, the null hypothesis of a unit root can be rejected with and without time trend for all variables.

One–country specification	τ_μ	τ_τ	Bilateral specification	τ_μ	τ_τ
π_{CPI}	-1.21	**-2.72**	$\pi_{\text{CPI},i} - \pi_{\text{CPI},j}$	**-2,24**	**-2,58**
π_{GPI}	-1.48	**-3.01**	$\pi_{\text{GPI},i} - \pi_{\text{GPI},j}$	**-2,60**	**-3,04**
π^T_{PPI}	**-2.28**	**-3.15**	$\pi^T_{\text{PPI},i} - \pi^T_{\text{PPI},j}$	**-3,04**	**-3,36**
π^T_{XPI}	**-2.62**	**-3.68**	$\pi^T_{\text{XPI},i} - \pi^T_{\text{XPI},j}$	**-3,54**	**-3,88**
$\phi^{\text{N}} \cdot (\Delta q^T - \Delta q^N)$	**-3.75**	**-4.15**	$\phi_i^{\text{N}} \cdot (\Delta q_i^T - \Delta q_i^N) - \phi_j^{\text{N}} \cdot (\Delta q_j^T - \Delta q_j^N)$	**-3.67**	**-4.08**
$\phi^{\text{N}} \cdot \Delta q^T$	**-3.73**	**-4.05**	$\phi_i^{\text{N}} \cdot \Delta q_i^T$ -$\phi_j^{\text{N}} \cdot \Delta q_j^T$	**-3.56**	**-3.94**
$\phi^{\text{N}} \cdot \Delta q^N$	**-3.25**	**-3.56**	$\phi_i^{\text{N}} \cdot \Delta q_i^N$ -$\phi_j^{\text{N}} \cdot \Delta q_j^N$	**-3.61**	**-3.73**
Critical values					
1%	-2.07	-2.69		-1.73	-2.37
5%	-1.90	-2.53		-1.67	-2.31
10%	-1.82	-2.45		-1.64	-2.28

Note 1 **Bold** (*italic*) numbers: The null hypothesis of a unit root can be rejected at a confidence level of 1% (5%).

Note 2 π_{CPI}: consumer price inflation; π_{GPI}: GDP deflator inflation; π^T_{PPI}: producer price inflation; π^T_{XPI}: export price inflation; ϕ^{N} share of value added in the non-traded goods sector; Δq^T productivity growth in the traded goods sector; Δq^N productivity growth in the non-traded goods sector.

	π^T=PPIT	π^T=XPI
A	1971,1972 1977,1994 (18)	1971,1972 1977,1994 (18)
BL	1976,1980 1983,1992 (13)	1971,1980 1983,1992 (18)
DK	1976,1995 (19)	1971,1995 (24)
FIN	1971,1995 (24)	1971,1995 (24)
FR	1978,1995 (17)	1971,1975 1978,1995 (21)
GE	1971,1993 (22)	1971,1993 (22)
IT	1982,1995 (13)	1971,1976 1979,1995 (21)
NL	1972,1995 (23)	1971,1995 (24)
PO	(0)	1987,1993 (6)
SP	1971,1971 1974,1975 1987,1992 (6)	1971,1971 1974,1975 1987,1992 (6)
SW	1971,1978 1981,1994 (20)	1971,1978 1981,1994 (20)
UK	1971,1990 (19)	1971,1990 (19)

As there are no missing observations for CPI and GPI–inflation, the samples only differ according to the proxy for traded goods inflation (PPI in manufacturing, or the XPI). The number in brackets is the number of observations for each country.

Samples for each country

References

Alberola, E. and Tyrväinen, T. (1998). Is there scope for inflation differentials in EMU? An empiricial evaluation of the Balassa–Samuelson model in EMU countries. Bank of Finland Discussion Papers,15/98.

Asea, P. and Mendoza, E. (1994). Do long–run productivity differentials explain long–run exchange rates? IMF Working Paper, WP 94/60.

Balassa, B. (1964). The PPP doctrine:A reappraisal. *Journal of Politicial Economy*, 584–596.

Bayoumi, T. and Alun, T. (1995). Relative price and economic adjustment in the United States and the European union: A real story about EMU. *IMF Staff Paper*, 42(1).

Campillo, M. and Miron, J. (1996). Why does inflation differ accross countries? NBER Working Paper 5540.

Canzoneri, M., Diba, B, and Eudey, G. (1996). Trends in European producitivity and real exchange rates: implications for the Maastricht convergence criteria and for inflation targets after EMU. CEPR Discussion Papers, 1417.

Canzoneri, M., Cumby, R. and Diba, B.(1999). Relative labour productivity and the real exchange rate in the long–run: evidence for a panel of OECD countries. *Journal of International Economics*, 47:245–266.

Chinn, M. and Johnston, L. (1997). Real exchange rate levels, productivity and demand shocks: Evidence froma panel of 14 countries. IMF Working Paper, WP 97/66.

De Gregorio, J. and Wolf, H. (1994). Terms of trade, productivity, and the real exchange rate. NBER Working Paper 4807.

De Gregorio, J., Giovannini, A. and Wolf, H. (1994). International evidence on tradables and nontradables inflation. *European Economic Review*, 38:1225–1244.

Froot, K. and Rogoff, K. (1991). The EMS, the EMU and the transition to a common currency. *NBER Macroeconomics Annual*, 269–327.

Froot, K. and Rogoff, K. (1991). Perspectives on PPP and long–run real exchange rates. NBER Working Paper 4952.

Hondroyiannis, G. and Papapetrou, E. (1998). Temporal causality and the inflation–productivity relationship: evidence from eight low inflation OECD countries. *International Review of Economics and Finance*, 7(1):117–135.

Hsieh, D. (1982). The determination of the realexchange rate: the productivity approach. *Journal of International Economics*, 12:355–362.

Im, K., Pesaran, H. and Shin, W. (1996). Testing for unit roots in heterogeneous panels. University of Cambridge, mimeo.

Levin, A. and Lin, C-F. (1993). Unit roots tests in panel data: New results. University of California at San Diego, Discussion Paper 93-56.

MacDonald, R. (1997). What determines real exchange rates? The long and short of it. IMF Working Paper, WP 97/21.

Marston, R. (1987). Real exchange rates and productivity growth in the United States and Japan. In Ardnt, S. and Richardson, J., editors, *Real Financial Linkages among Open Economies*. MIT Press, Cambridge.

Micossi, S. and Milesi–Ferretti, M. (1994). Real exchange rates and the price of non-tradable goods. IMF Working Paper, 94/19.

Obstfeld, M. and Rogoff, K. (1996). *Foundations of International Macroeconomics.* MIT Press.

Officier, L. (1976). The productivity bias in purchasing power parity: An econometric investigation. *IMF Staff Papers*, 23(3):545–580.

Oh, K. (1996). Purchasing power parity and unit root tests using panel data. *Journal of International Money and Finance*, 15(3):405–418.

Poloz, S. (1990). Real exchange rate adjustment between regions in a common currency area. Bank of Canada.

Rebelo, S. (1993). Inflation in fixed exchange rate regimes: The recent Portuguese experience. In Torres,F.and Giavazzi, F., editors, *The Transition to EMU in Europe.* CEPR, London.

Rogoff, K. (1992). Traded goods consumption smoothing and the random walk behavior of the real exchange rate. NBER Working Paper, 4119.

Samuleson, P. (1964). Theoretical notes on trade problems. *Review of Economics and Statistics*, 64:145–154.

Strauss, J. (1995). Real exchange rates, PPP and the relative price of nontraded goods. *Southern Economic Journal*, 61(4):991–1005.

Chapter 5: Open Market Shocks in a Business Cycle Model with Financial Intermediation.

Burkhard Heer
Department of Public Economics, University of Innsbruck, Austria & CESifo, Germany

Andreas Schabert
Department of Economics, University of Cologne, Germany

Abstract This paper presents a business cycle analysis of monetary policy shocks measured by disturbances to open market operations, *i.e.* the ratio of bonds to reserves. We develop a dynamic general equilibrium model with financial intermediation and staggered prices. In accordance with empirical evidence, a monetary tightening leads to a fall in output, monetary aggregates, and factor prices. In contrast to an alternative model specification with money growth shocks, our model with disturbances to open market operations generates a persistent decline in output as well as a rise of nominal and real interest rates on bonds in response to a monetary contraction. In addition, the model's ability to replicate second moments of empirical time series is superior to the one of a model with a money growth shock.

1. Introduction

Standard monetary business cycle models assume that money supply is exogenous. The growth rate of money supply is usually assumed to follow a stochastic process. Hence, monetary policy is identified by innovations to the growth rate of money, even if the latter is specified as a broad aggregate. Changes in money supply are injected lump-sum directly either to the households or to the financial intermediaries. Short-run effects on real activity driven by these nominal transfers are generated by an inflation tax, price or wage rigidities on the one hand,[1]

[1]Examples of this literature include models with i) an inflation tax, *e.g.* Cooley and Hansen, 1989, ii) cash-in advance constraints, *e.g.* Lucas and Stokey, 1987 or Cooley and Hansen, 1998, iii) price rigidities, *e.g.*, Hairault and Portier, 1993, Chari *et al.*, 1996, Rotemberg,

and trading frictions on asset markets on the other hand.[2] Contrary to these studies on monetary policy analysis, we construct a model where monetary policy is conducted via open market operations. Since open market operations are the most commonly used instrument of monetary authorities in developed countries, we identify innovations to open market trades as exogenous monetary policy measures. An alternative choice of the monetary policy instrument has been prominently applied in recent work on business cycle modeling. Following Taylor, 1993, the monetary authority is assumed to set the short-term nominal interest rate depending on the history of inflation, output, and the interest rate itself. We disregard this policy measure, as the introduction of an interest rate rule in a monetary business cycle model is often associated with real indeterminacy. As several studies have shown, the uniqueness of rational expectations equilibrium then crucially depends on the parameter of the interest rate rule and the corresponding fiscal policy (see, *e.g.*, Leeper, 1991, Rotemberg and Woodford, 1998, Christiano and Gust, 1999, Clarida *et al.*, 2000, and Benhabib *et al.*, 2001).

Our analysis presents a measure for monetary policy shocks which is already applied in long run analyses of monetary policy (Schreft and Smith, 1998, and 2000). When the monetary authority conducts monetary policy, it uses swaps of ownerships over securities. It provides reserves in exchange for open market instruments, typically in the form of government debt. The central bank receives orders for open market transactions from banks and, after that, decides on the amount of reserves and securities which are exchanged. Presuming that these securities, *i.e.*, treasury bills, are predominately held by banks for refinancing purposes, the monetary authority controls the ratio of short-run government bonds to reserves.

We develop a quantitative general equilibrium model of the US economy where money is introduced in the utility function. We also aim to add to the literature, *e.g.* Chari *et al.*, 1996, or Yun, 1996, which has discussed the effects of sticky prices on the propagation mechanism, and allow for price staggering in our model. As another distinguishing feature of our model, we incorporate a banking sector with costly financial intermediation. Banks take funds from households and lend these funds to firms with lending rates exceeding the rate of return on open

---

1996, Yun, 1996, and iv) wage rigidities, *e.g.* Cho and Cooley, 1995 or Jeanne 1998, to name but a few.

[2]1990, Fuerst, 1992, Cristiano and Eichenbaum, 1992, and Christiano *et al.*, 1997a, real effects of monetary injections are due to an unsyncronized participation of households and firms in financial markets.

market instruments, namely, bonds. In order to abstract from liquidity effects due to limited participation, households funds are deposited at banks and withdrawn within one period. When the monetary authority alters the ratio of bonds to reserves, it affects the liquidity of the entire financial system and the portfolio composition of banks and households in our model. Banks react to a contractionary monetary policy measure by adjusting their security holdings, their reserves, and their lending to firms. Accordingly, total reserves of the banking system are determined by both monetary policy measures and money demand by the banks. Interest rates are mainly determined by changes in the liquidity of the financial system. In response to a monetary tightening, nominal interest rates rise persistently. With higher lending rates, marginal costs rise as we assume that the factor remunerations has to be financed by loans. Consequently, factor demand and production decline.

The specification of monetary policy in the form of open market operations is contrasted with the standard approach to describe monetary policy by exogenous money growth. The performance of the business cycle models with these two specifications for monetary policy is assessed with regard to the ability to induce persistent responses of real activity which can be observed empirically. Furthermore, we compare the empirical correlations of various variables with the corresponding correlations as computed from the simulations of our theoretical models. In accordance with recent literature on monetary business cycles, we find that a business cycle model with exogenous monetary growth has various deficiencies in reproducing the empirical effects of monetary policy shocks.[3] Endogenizing money in our benchmark model where monetary policy is conducted by open market operations helps to overcome most of these deficiencies. In particular, nominal interest rates rise in response to tight money. In contrast to the monetary injection case, the impulse response function of output always displays persistence regardless of the degree of price stickiness. Furthermore, contemporaneous correlations of the monetary policy measures and output, different monetary aggregates, nominal assets, inflation, interest rates, and velocity implied by the simulation of our theoretical model accord well with empirical observations.

The organization of the paper is as follows. In section 2, our model is introduced and calibrated with regard to characteristics of the US economy. In section 3, the numerical results of the model are presented. First, we present impulse responses for the two monetary policy shocks considered in this paper, the open market operations shock and the

[3]See Christiano and Eichenbaum, 1997 and Cooley and Hansen, 1998.

money growth shock. Second, we study the effect of different model specifications on the persistence and the amplitude of the impulse response function of output. Finally, we present second moment properties for our theoretical models and compare them with the empirical counterparts. Section 4 concludes.

2. The model

In this section we present a dynamic general equilibrium model with a financial intermediary sector based upon Heer and Schabert, 2000. It distinguishes between two monetary aggregates, inside money and outside money. This feature, in particular, allows us to study the propagation of monetary shocks via the banking sector. Lending is assumed to be costly. We employ open market operations as exogenous monetary policy measures in our benchmark case. For comparison, we also consider monetary policy characterized by exogenous money growth. Price stickiness is introduced via monopolistic retailers who set their prices according to Calvo's, 1983 staggered price setting.

2.1 Households

We assume that households are identical, of measure one and maximize their expected sum of discounted instantaneous utility over an infinite horizon. The instantaneous utility function u is logarithmic in consumption c, real money balances $m = \frac{M}{p}$ and leisure $1 - l$.[4] Total assets of the households comprise nominal government bonds $B^h = Pb^h$ and cash $M = Pm$. Households are the owners of the firms and banks. Maximizing lifetime utility subject to a budget constraint with respect to consumption, leisure, bond holdings, and cash leads to the following first order conditions:

$$\lambda_t = \gamma / c_t \tag{1}$$

$$\lambda_t w_t = \eta / (1 - l_t) \tag{2}$$

$$\frac{1}{\beta} = E_t \left[\frac{\lambda_{t+1}}{\lambda_t} (1 + i_{t+1}) \frac{p_t}{p_{t+1}} \right] \tag{3}$$

$$\frac{\lambda_t}{\beta} = E_t \left[\left(\frac{1-\gamma}{m_{t+1}} + \lambda_{t+1} \right) \frac{p_t}{p_{t+1}} \right] \tag{4}$$

$$c_t + \frac{M_{t+1}}{P_t} + \frac{B^h_{t+1}}{P_t} = \frac{M_t}{P_t} + (1 + i_t) \frac{B^h_t}{P_t} + w_t l_t + \tau_t + \Omega^f_t + \Omega^b_t \tag{5}$$

[4] Instantaneous utility is given by: $u(c_t, m_t, l_t) = \gamma \ln c_t + (1 - \gamma) \ln m_t + \eta \ln (1 - l_t)$, with $\eta, \gamma > 0$.

where β, p, w, i, τ, Ω^f, Ω^b_t, and Ω^r_t denote the discount rate, the price level, the wage, the nominal rate of return on bonds, a lump-sum transfer from the government, and the dividends from firms, banks, and retailers, respectively. The households' debt holdings are managed by banks and the wage income is deposited into checking accounts. The Lagrangian multiplier λ is associated with the budget constraint (5). The first two equations guarantee that the households equate the marginal utilities of both goods (consumption and leisure) to the marginal utility of wealth times the price of the respective good. Equation (3) is the standard intertemporal allocation condition. Equation (4) governs the optimal allocation of cash over time.

2.2 Production

In the production sector, identical and monopolistically competitive firms produce differentiated goods. Each firm i uses a linear technology employing labor for its differentiated goods y_i, with $i \in (0,1)$. Firms' profits are distributed among the firm owners, the households. Labor is rented at perfectly competitive factor markets. It is assumed that firms have to use bank credits Z_{it} to pay the wage bill $p_t w_t l_{it}$. The funds Z_i a firm borrows from a bank are made available in form of checking accounts. At the end of the period, the firm repays the loan plus interest i^l, $(1+i^l)Z_i$. We consider a nominal stickiness in form of staggered price setting as developed by Calvo, 1983. Each period firms may reset their prices with the probability $1-\phi$ independent of the time elapsed since the last price setting. Firms maximize their profits by choosing optimal schedules for labor demand and for prices. In a symmetric equilibrium, optimal decisions of firms are identical, such that the production sector is characterized by the following equations in terms of aggregate variables:

$$y_t = a_t l_t \tag{6}$$

$$\log a_t = \rho^a \log a_{t-1} + \varepsilon^a_t \tag{7}$$

$$Z_t = p_t w_t l_t, \tag{8}$$

$$w_t = \frac{1}{x_t} a_t \left(1 + i^l_t\right)^{-1} \tag{9}$$

$$\Omega^f_t = \frac{1}{x_t} y_t - \left(1 + i^l_t\right) w_t l_t \tag{10}$$

$$-(1-\phi)(1-\beta\phi)\phi^{-1}\hat{x}_t = \widehat{\pi}_t - \beta E_t \widehat{\pi}_{t+1} \tag{11}$$

where x denotes the markup and a is the stochastic total factor productivity level generated by the AR1 process in (7). The autoregressive parameter ρ^a is less than one and the innovations ε^a are i.i.d., with

$\varepsilon^a \sim N(0, \sigma_a^2)$. The first equation describes the production technology which is affected by the realizations of the technology parameter following the stochastic process in (7). The equation (9) gives the labor demand schedule and equation (11) is the optimal pricing equation, which is also known as the New Keynesian Phillips curve. The derivation of this aggregate supply constraint can be found in the appendix.

2.3 Financial intermediation

Banking is assumed to be costly and is affected by monetary policy measures. Perfectly competitive banks take deposits from the households and provide loans Z to the firms at the rate i^l. Banks hold bonds B^b and high-powered money, *i.e.* reserves, to fulfill the reserve requirements imposed on deposit holdings. Since high-powered money is a non-interest bearing asset, banks do not hold excess reserves in equilibrium. The households are assumed to deposit their factor remunerations $p_t w_t l_t$ at the beginning of the period at the bank. As the households withdraw these funds at the end of the same period, they do not receive interest on these funds. We assume that lending is costly. These costs $\Psi(z)$ can be rationalized by screening and monitoring activities of banks and, therefore, are assumed to increase in real loans. Taken as given the time path of the interest rates and the monetary policy variable $\{\mu_t\}$ the banks maximize their profits subject to (12) and (13) with respect to loans and bonds. Thus, the behavior of the banking sector can be described by the following equations:

$$B_t^h + p_t w_t l_t = S_t + B_t + Z_t \tag{12}$$

$$S_t = \theta (p_t w_t l_t) \tag{13}$$

$$\Omega_t^b - i_t b_t^b + i_t^l z_t - \Psi(z_t) \tag{14}$$

$$i_t^l = i_t + \Psi_z(z_t) \tag{15}$$

where total bonds B equal $B^h + B^b$, and θ and $\Psi_z(z_t)$ denote the reserve requirement ratio and the first derivative of the lending cost function, respectively. Equation (12) is the balance sheet of the bank ensuring that the banks' liabilities equal their total assets. Equation (13) determines the reserve holdings of the banks. The first order condition (15) provides the efficient relation between the yield of bonds and the lending rate which depends on the amount of loans.

2.4 Government

The government, or equivalently the monetary authority, sets the reserve-requirement ratio θ and the monetary policy instrument μ. Further, the monetary authority is assumed to conduct open market operations. Monetary policy shocks are modelled as exogenous changes in the ratio μ^{omr} of the total amount of bonds B held by the agents in the economy to reserves S : $\mu_t^{omr} = B_{t+1}/S_t$. We do not consider optimal government policies and assume that monetary policy measure μ^{omr} is exogenously given. As an alternative measure of monetary policy, we consider exogenous growth of a monetary aggregate as it is common in the literature on monetary business cycle theory. For this case, the growth rate of the monetary base H_t, which consists of cash holdings of households and banks' reserves, is assumed to be stochastic: $\mu_t^{mgr} = H_{t+1}/H_t$. The government can be described by

$$(1 + i_t) B_t - B_{t+1} = H_{t+1} - H_t - p_t \tau_t \tag{16}$$

$$\log \mu_t^i = \rho^i \log \mu_{t-1}^i + (1 - \rho^i) \log \overline{\mu}^i + \varepsilon_t^i, \text{for } i = \text{omr}, \text{mgr} \tag{17}$$

The autoregressive parameters ρ^i are smaller than one and the innovations ε^i are i.i.d., with $\varepsilon^i \sim N(0, \sigma_i^2)$ for $i = omr, mgr$. According to the first equation, the government budget constraint, the increase in government debt, $B_{t+1} - B_t$, is equal to the interest payment on government debt, $i_t B_t$, minus the receipts from money creation, $H_{t+1} - H_t$, and transfers $p_t \tau_t$.

2.5 Competitive equilibrium

The state variables for the representative household are

$$s^e = (K, H, B, \pi) \text{ and } s^x = (a, \mu),$$

where s^e and s^x denote the vector of endogenous state variables and the vector of stochastic state variables, respectively. The competitive equilibrium then consists of a maximum value for the household's objective and a set of decision rules for the household's decision variables $c_t(s_t^x, s_t^e)$, $l_t(s_t^x, s_t^e)$, and $M_{t+1}(s_t^x, s_t^e)$,. Further, it consists of a corresponding set of aggregate per capita decision rules, the factor price functions $w_t(s_t^x, s_t^e)$, and $Z_t(s_t^x, s_t^e)$, and the nominal interest rate functions $i_t(s_t^x, s_t^e)$ and $i_t^l(s_t^x, s_t^e)$. These optimal decision rules and functions have to satisfy the following conditions:

1 Households maximize their lifetime utility taken prices as given, *i.e.* (1)-(5) hold.

2 The banks' and firms' profits are maximized, *i.e.* (12)-(15) and (6)-(11) hold.

3 The stochastic variables follow the processes described in (7) and (17).

4 The government's balanced budget constraint (16) is satisfied.

5 Individual and aggregate variables are consistent.

6 All factor, asset, goods, and money markets clear: $y_t^f = c_t + e_t + \psi(z_t)$; $B_t = B_t^h + B_t^b$; $H_t = S_t + M_t$.

2.6 Model parameterization

To calibrate the model we choose values for the preference and technology parameters which are fairly standard.[5] The discount factor of households β is set equal to $1.03^{-0.25}$. As total time available for the households is normalized to 1, steady state labor input is set equal to 0.3. The utility parameter γ is set equal to 0.996, implying an average velocity $GDP/M1$ of 6.79. The steady state value of total factor productivity a is set equal to 1. The marginal cost of loans Ψ_z equals the average historical spread between the prime bank loan rate and the treasury bill rate (0.006). We set the reserve requirement ratio θ equal to 0.1. The elasticity of the retail good production ϵ is assigned a value of 6, implying a mark-up x equal to 1.2.[6] The probability for a retailer to receive a price signal $1 - \phi$ is set equal to 0.25 for the benchmark case. This value leads to an average price fixity duration of 3 periods (3/4 years). Alternatively, we will also use a value of 1, implying flexible price adjustments of the retailers. The former value seems to be justified by the empirical price responses estimated in section 2 and is also used in related analyses of monetary policy effects in sticky price models.[7]

The parameters of the stochastic processes for both monetary policy measures are estimated for the period 1984:4–1994:4.[8] For the open market ratio (OMR), we applied the ratio of the time series of open market papers outstanding ($OMPAP$) and non-borrowed reserves ($NBRES$).[9] For the growth rate of high-powered money, we employed the growth rate of M1 ($M1GR$). The autoregressive parameter in (17) for the open market ratio (money growth) is estimated at 0.923 (0.469). The standard deviation of the respective residuals equals 0.058 (0.0129). The steady state inflation rate $\overline{\pi}$ which equals the steady state money growth rate $\overline{\mu}^{mgr}$ is estimated at 1.0189. The parameter ρ^a of the AR1 process for the technological level is assigned a value which is standard in the

[5]See, *e.g.*, Christiano and Eichenbaum, 1992.
[6]See Christiano *et al.*, 1997a.
[7]See, *e.g.*, Yun, 1996 and Jeanne, 1998.
[8]This period is characterized by a stable monetary regime (see, *e.g.*, Cooley and Hansen, 1998).
[9]The sources of the time series are given in Appendix B.

business cycle literature ($\rho^a = 0.95$). The standard deviation is set so that the simulation of our benchmark model approximately replicates the empirical standard deviation of output ($\sigma^a = 0.0035$).

3. Propagation of monetary policy shocks

In this section, we analyze the propagation of monetary policy shocks.[10] We contrast the effects of the monetary policy shocks for our benchmark case where the monetary authority conducts monetary policy via open market operations on the one hand, with the case where monetary policy is conducted by exogenous changes in the money growth rate on the other hand. We also perform a sensitivity analysis of our results with regard to the degree of price flexibility and by introducing physical capital in order to reveal the persistence of the output responses for both measures.

3.1 Real effects of alternative monetary policy measures

Figure 1 presents the responses of several variables to a contractionary shock of size 0.01 in the open market ratio (OMR). The responses are expressed as percentage deviation from the steady state values of the respective variables. In the course of an open market operation, the monetary authority imposes a higher relation of outstanding bonds to reserves and reduces the liquidity of the financial system.

In period 1, when the shock hits the economy, we observe a decline in reserves, whereas the predetermined variables households' bonds and high-powered money remain unchanged. The macroeconomic effects of a 1% innovation to the OMR are mainly driven by the increased amount of government bonds outstanding. An increase in the open market ratio b_{t+1}/s_t for given reserves s_t is associated with an increase in bond holdings b_{t+1} of private agents on the one hand and, by the assumption of a balanced budget (16), a decline in high-powered money h_t on the other hand. In order to induce agents to hold more bonds and less cash m, the market clearing interest rate on bonds i has to increase. Consequently, the portfolio structures of households and banks change. Households substitute their bond holdings b^h for cash holdings m as the opportunity costs of real balances increase with higher nominal rates i.

[10] In order to compute the model, we linearized the model at the steady state and used the algorithm of King *et al.*, 1987. The linearized version of the model can be found in the appendix.

Figure 1. Impulse Responses to an OMR Shock

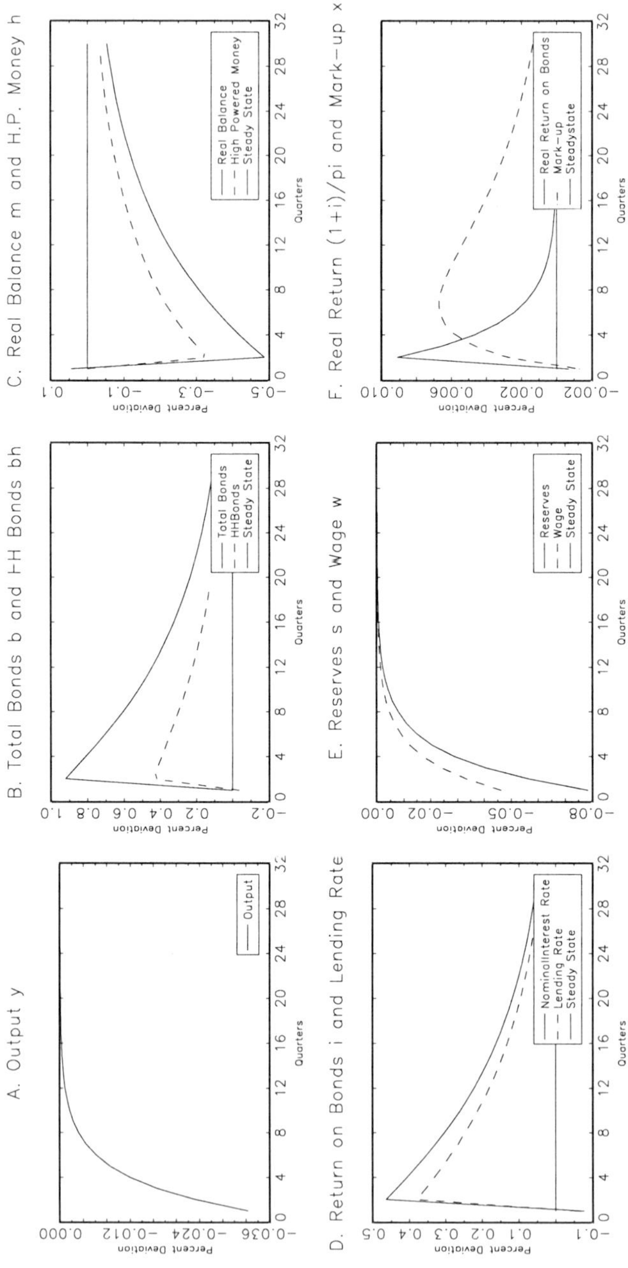

In order to understand the adjustments in the balance sheets of the banks, we need to study the behavior of firms' loan demand. Firms must obtain loans from banks in order to pay labor. An increasing interest rate i on bonds also translates into a higher lending rate i^l according to (15). By increasing the marginal costs of labor l, firms decrease their labor demand as can be seen from the inspection of the firms' labor demand schedule (9). As a consequence, equilibrium employment l falls and the real wage w declines as well. For constant productivity, the fall in labor input results in a fall of total loans z and output y. Consequently, real reserves s which are a constant fraction of loans decline as well, but to a smaller extent than government bonds rise. As implied by the forward looking pricing condition of firms (11) the decline in inflation is accompanied by an increased mark-up x. The rise of the mark-up ratio is associated with a downward pressure on factor remuneration, as the equilibrium real wage w is negatively related to the mark-up. Consequently, aggregate production exhibits a decline in period 1 in response to the contractionary monetary impulse. In sum, the responses of monetary aggregates, interest rates, and real variables to a monetary tightening are almost as expected and as found in empirical studies.[11]

The impulse responses to a MGR shock are different from the ones to an OMR shock. Figure 2 presents responses to a contractionary MGR shock. Following a contraction of nominal money supply H, households receive less transfers τ. Consequently, households' consumption demand falls. The price behavior of the firms is similar to the one in the model with OMR shocks. As demand falls, the flexible price firms cut their prices p and the sticky price retailers reduce their output. Consequently, inflation falls and the mark-up increases. The wage rate w declines with a higher mark-up x. As the supply of bonds $B = B^h + B^b$ is exogenous, the fall in the inflation rate results in a fall of the nominal interest rate i. The household adjusts its portfolio by reducing bond holdings B^h, while it even increases real cash holdings m. The most important difference between the model with an OMR shock and the model with a MGR shock is the counterfactual behavior of the nominal interest rate induced by a strong inflation rate effect in the latter model. The rate of return on bonds i and the lending rate i^l decrease in response

[11] See, *e.g.*, Christiano *et al.*, 1999. In contrast to empirical observations, though, consistent with related studies (see, *e.g.*, Christiano *et al.*, 1997b), profits of price setters (which equal the retailers' profits Ω^r) increase in our model as the mark-up increases during a monetary contraction and, in particular, the effect of the rise in the mark-up x is initially more pronounced than the effect of a fall in the output y. Bank profits $\Omega_t^b = (1/\theta - 1)i_t s_t$ (not illustrated), which are only a small fraction of total profits, display a persistent rise after a transitory contraction.

Figure 2. Impulse Responses to an MGR Shock

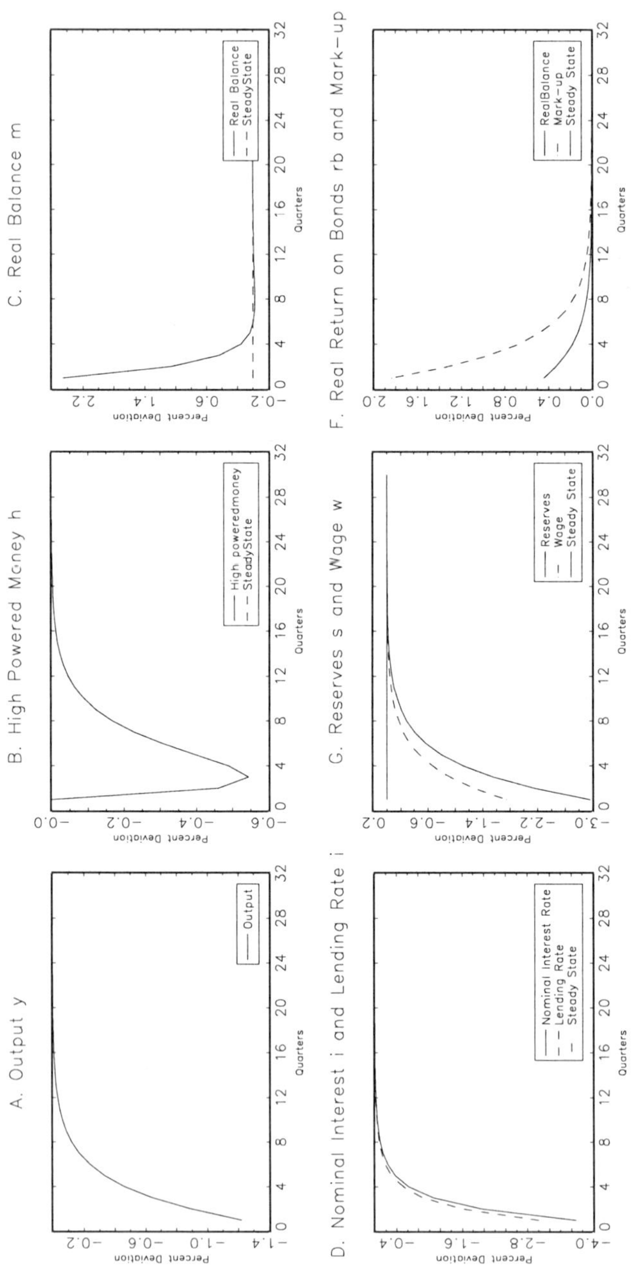

to a monetary contraction. This behavior of nominal interest rates is inconsistent with empirical evidence. Hence, the OMR specification of the monetary policy seems to be more appropriate for our model.[12]

3.2 Persistence and the amplitude of output responses

In this section, we perform an analysis of output responses concentrating on the effects of price rigidity and, in addition, the introduction of physical capital together with adjustment costs. As we allow physical capital to be accumulated, the households' first order conditions in the previous section must be supplemented by the following three equations:

$$q_t = \frac{1}{\Phi'\left(\frac{e_t}{k_t}\right)} \tag{18}$$

$$q_t = E_t\left\{r_{t+1} + q_{t+1}\left[\Phi\left(\frac{e_{t+1}}{k_{t+1}}\right) - \Phi'\left(\frac{e_{t+1}}{k_{t+1}}\right)\frac{e_{t+1}}{k_{t+1}} + 1 - \delta\right]\right\} \times \frac{1}{1+i_{t+1}}\frac{p_{t+1}}{p_t} \tag{19}$$

$$k_{t+1} = \Phi\left(\frac{e_t}{k_t}\right)k_t + (1-\delta)\,k_t \tag{20}$$

where δ denotes the depreciation rate. The adjustment cost function $\Phi\left(\frac{e_t}{k_t}\right)$ is increasing and concave.[13] The shadow price of physical capital q^*, which equals the Lagrangian multiplier associated with the law of motion for physical capital (20), can be derived by multiplying λ with the market price of capital q. The first equation determines the market price of capital, while the second equation is an arbitrage conditions relating the return on physical capital and the real return on bonds. As physical capital is also used in the production, the firms are now characterized by the following equations in a symmetric equilibrium:[14]

$$y_t = a_t k_t^{\alpha} l_t^{1-\alpha}, \text{ with } 0 < \alpha < 1 \text{ and } \log a_t = \rho^a \log a_{t-1} + \varepsilon_t^a \tag{21}$$

$$Z_t = p_t w_t l_t + p_t r_t k_t \tag{22}$$

$$w_t = \frac{1}{x_t}(1-\alpha)\,a_t k_t^{\alpha} l_t^{-\alpha}\left(1+i_t^l\right)^{-1} \tag{23}$$

[12] In models of limited participation, a decrease of money growth only results in a lasting rise of nominal interest rates if both financial markets are subject to frictions and households face adjustment costs of their asset portfolio (Chari *et al.*, 1995).

[13] The depreciation rate is set equal to 0.0212 and the benchmark value of the elasticity of Φ is -0.033 (see, Corriera *et al.*, 1995).

[14] The production elasticity of capital α equals 0.36. The complete model is presented in the appendix.

$$r_t = \frac{1}{x_t} \alpha a_t k_t^{\alpha-1} l_t^{1-\alpha} \left(1 + i_t^l\right)^{-1} \tag{24}$$

$$\Omega_t^f = \frac{1}{x_t} y_t - \left(1 + i_t^l\right) w_t l_t - \left(1 + i_t^l\right) r_t k_t \tag{25}$$

$$\hat{x}_t = \frac{-\phi}{(1-\phi)(1-\beta\phi)} \left(\widehat{\pi}_t - \beta E_t \widehat{\pi}_{t+1}\right) \tag{26}$$

Figure 3 displays the responses of output to an OMR shock and to a MGR shock of 1% for different degrees of price rigidity and for the specifications of the model without capital and with capital. Obviously, the amplitude of the output responses to an OMR shock declines with more flexible prices, whereas the persistence rises. The responses to MGR shocks are generally found to have a much stronger amplitude than the responses to OMR shocks. Regarding the persistence of the impulse responses, we find that the persistence of output responses to OMR shocks is robust. Neither the inclusion of capital nor varying degrees of the price rigidity induces output to return immediately to the steady state. This result does not hold in the case of money growth shocks. First, the introduction of capital reduces the persistence. This property is already analyzed in detail by Chari *et al.*, 1996, so we refrain from a further discussion of this point. Second, as also supported by the majority of the literature output persistence is strongly reduced when prices are more flexible. Figure 3 shows that, in case of a monetary injection, output immediately recovers for all degrees of price rigidity, whereas the output responses to OMR shocks display a marked persistence, especially for more flexible prices. As displayed in the first row of Figure 3, the output response to an OMR shock remains persistent, even if we allow for capital to be accumulated.

The findings in Figure 3 are supported by our estimated autocorrelations of simulated output series.[15] In the case with $\phi = 0.75$ and with physical capital, the autocorrelation of output is moderately positive amounting to $\rho^y = 0.296$. For comparison, the empirical autocorrelation of output amounts to $\widehat{\rho}^y = 0.86$ in the US economy.[16] Notice, however, that our model is only simulated for an isolated shock to monetary policy, whereas the additional consideration of a technology shock generally results in a higher first-order autocorrelation of output. In the case of a MGR shock, the estimate for output autocorrelation ($\rho^y = 0.07$) is much smaller than in the case of OMR shocks. With lower degrees of

[15] Autocorrelations are estimated from the simulated output series which have been logged and detrended using the Hodrick-Prescott filter.

[16] The statistics have been computed using logged and detrended time series of output (GDP92) during 1960-99.

Figure 3. Output Responses to OMR and MGR Shocks

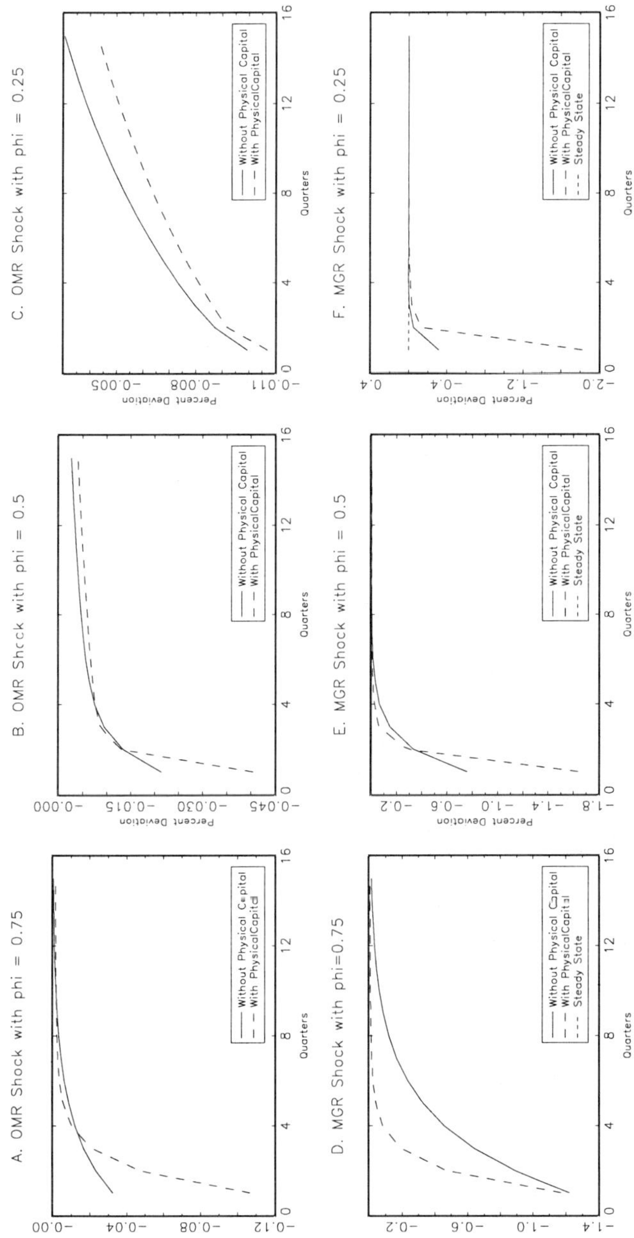

price rigidity, we find that the autocorrelation of output rises in the case of OMR shocks.

From this discussion, we conclude that there is a trade-off between the amplitude and the persistence of the output response depending on the degree of price rigidity in our model. Surprisingly, the response of output is less persistent when prices are more sticky. The reason for our result is simple. After period 2, the output response to an OMR shock is mainly driven by increased marginal costs due to the persistent rise in the lending rate. Therefore, the output response pattern to an OMR shock are almost identical after the 3nd period for all degrees of price stickiness. However, in the case of more rigid prices ($\phi = 0.75$), we also observe a strong decline of production in period 1, induced by a fall in aggregate demand. The initial output response is much lower if all retailers are able to adjust prices instantaneously. As a consequence, if prices are more sticky, the output response in the first period relative to the output response in later periods rises and we observe a jump in the output response function in period 2. For this reason, persistence as measured by the first-order autocorrelation of output declines.

3.3 Second-order moments of money-related series

In this subsection, we discuss the second moment properties of money-related series simulated with our theoretical model for both specifications of monetary policy and compare them with their empirical counterparts. We start the analysis of this simulation experiment with the discussion of selected correlations for the cases of pure monetary policy shocks in order to isolate the effects stemming from the particular specification of our monetary policy rule. We apply the standard treatment of data for the computation of the statistics in the real business cycle literature. In particular, the moments reported in tables 1 and 2 are computed from Hodrick-Prescott filtered quarterly time series.[17] The 5-7th columns of Table 1 present the contemporaneous correlations of variables with output and the monetary policy measures for our benchmark model with shocks to open market operations. The correlations as implied by our theoretical model are computed for the benchmark degree of price stickiness ($\phi = 0.75$). The 8-10th columns of Table 1 present the corresponding correlations for the economy with innovations to the technology level as an additional shock.

[17]The description and the sources of the time series can be found in Appendix B.

Table 1. Correlations for the model with the open market measure

	Moments of US Series (1960:1-1999:1)			Moments of Simulated Series $\sigma_a = 0$			$\sigma_a > 0$		
	Output	MGR	OMR	Output	MGR	OMR	Output	MGR	OMR
Financial series									
FFRATE	0.33	-0.44	0.58	0.08	-0.23	0.65	0.22	-0.26	0.58
PRLOAN	0.37	-0.40	0.49	-	-	-	-	-	-
TBILLR	0.32	-0.47	0.57	-	-	-	-	-	-
M1	0.11	0.20	-0.60	0.12	0.32	-0.78	-0.02	0.33	-0.72
M1GR	-0.11	1	-0.25	0.36	1	-0.33	0.18	0.18	-0.28
VELOC	0.24	-0.29	0.73	0.11	-0.22	0.62	0.26	-0.26	0.56
OMR	-0.04	-0.25	1	-0.69	-0.33	1	-0.44	-0.28	1
NBRES	-0.19	0.24	-0.78	0.99	0.40	-0.70	0.85	0.17	-0.53
OMPAP	-0.20	-0.18	0.86	-0.05	-0.25	0.74	0.12	-0.25	0.67
DEBT	0.49	-0.15	0.24	-	-	-	-	-	-
BLOANS	0.48	-0.10	0.13	0.99	0.40	-0.70	0.85	0.17	-0.53
Non-financial series									
GDP92	1	-0.11	-0.04	1	0.36	-0.69	1	0.18	-0.44
GDPDF	-0.68	-0.06	0.34	0.46	0.43	-0.61	-0.02	0.29	-0.55
EMPL	0.83	-0.23	0.22	1	0.35	-0.64	0.88	0.11	-0.43
INFL	0.36	-0.26	0.35	0.44	0.03	0.34	0.52	-0.11	0.2
PROF	0.65	-0.28	-0.08	-1	-0.33	0.62	-0.71	-0.07	0.39

Note: The moments are computed from logged and Hodrick-Prescott filtered data. Series not expressed in percentage terms have been logged first. The statistics for the theoretical models are computed as averages from 500 $\times$ 150 simulations.

In the subsequent analysis, we focus on correlations of financial variables, which are displayed in the upper part of each Table. The sign and the magnitude of all correlations, except for those of bank loans, are in good accordance with the empirical correlations presented in column 2-4. In the case of monetary injections, we find that the empirical correlations between various variables cannot be replicated (see Table 2). *e.g.*, instead of negative values, we find nearly perfect positive correlations between money growth on the one hand and interest rates, inflation, and the velocity on the other hand. Furthermore, contrary to empirical evidence, the model with monetary injections predicts a negative correlation of the money stock with both output and money growth.

Up to this point, we can conclude that our sticky price model generates reasonable values for most of the financial correlations in the case of an OMR shock. A closer look at the correlations between

Table 2. Correlations for the model with the money growth measure

	Moments of US Series (1960:1-1999:1)		Moments of Simulated Series $\sigma^a = 0$		$\sigma^a > 0$	
	Output	MGR	Output	MGR	Output	MGR
Financial series						
FFRATE	0.33	-0.44	1	1	1	0.99
PRLOAN	0.38	-0.40	-	-	-	-
TBILLR	0.32	-0.47	-	-	-	-
M1	0.11	0.20	-0.28	-0.27	-0.33	-0.31
M1GR	-0.11	1	0.99	1	0.99	1
VELOC	0.24	-0.29	1	0.99	1	0.99
OMR	-0.04	-0.25	-	-	-	-
NBRES	-0.19	0.24	-0.94	-0.95	-0.96	-0.95
OMPAP	-0.20	-0.18	-0.94	-0.95	-0.96	-0.95
DEBT	0.49	-0.15	-	-	-	-
BLOANS	0.48	-0.10	-0.94	-0.95	-0.96	-0.95
Non-financial series						
GDP92	1	-0.11	1	0.99	1	0.99
GDPDF	-0.68	-0.06	-0.27	-0.25	-0.32	-0.29
EMPL	0.83	-0.23	1	0.99	1	0.99
INFL	0.36	-0.26	1	1	0.99	0.99
PROF	0.65	-0.28	-0.93	-0.94	-0.99	-0.97

Note: The moments are computed from logged and Hodrick-Prescott filtered data. Series not expressed in percentage terms have been logged first. The statistics for the theoretical models are computed as averages from 500 × 150 simulations.

output on the one hand and the components of our shock measure $(NBRES, OMPAP, OMR)$ as well as the level and the growth rate of the monetary aggregate $(M1, M1GR)$ on the other hand suggests that some empirical moments cannot solely be replicated by monetary shocks. This conclusion is also supported by the correlations of the nonfinancial variables in the lower half of Table 1. With the exception of inflation, these variables exhibit correlations with output and the monetary policy measures which are inconsistent with the empirical ones. In order to reconcile the behavior of our model with theses observations, we also consider innovations to the technology level. As already mentioned, we assume that the innovations to the technology level and the innovations to the monetary policy measure are independently distributed. The standard deviation of the technology innovations is chosen to replicate the empirical standard deviation of output with our benchmark model.

The correlations for the series simulated with both shocks are presented in the last three columns of Table 1.

As can be seen in column 8 of Table 1, the additional consideration of technology shocks leads to a slight improvement concerning the correlations between the monetary aggregates and output. The reduced correlations between output on the one hand and money and the open market ratio on the other hand are more favorable than in the case of pure money shocks, whereas the output correlations with money growth, non-borrowed reserves and open market papers remain inconsistent with the empirical ones. Turning to the bottom half of Table 1, the correlations between the nonfinancial variables and output are in accordance with the empirical correlations except for total profits.[18] Furthermore, the addition of technology shocks leads to reduced correlations between money growth and the nonfinancial variables. Comparing these correlations with their empirical counterparts, the latter also being moderately negative, we find that the consideration of technology shocks helps to improve the model's performance. The corresponding values for the case of a MGR shock are presented in column 6 of Table 2. It is obvious looking at these values that the results in the case of MGR shocks remains unsatisfactory even after adding technological shocks.

Notice, however, that our model generates moderately negative correlations between our shock variable, the open market ratio, on the one hand and output, prices, and employment on the other hand. This result accords well with our previous finding that a monetary contraction leads to a decline in output, prices, and employment. Our empirical contemporaneous correlations, however, do not reflect this kind of causality. In particular, employment and prices are positively correlated with the open market ratio and negatively correlated with money growth. The lacking ability of standard monetary business cycle models to replicate these empirical observations has also been noticed by Cooley and Hansen, 1998, among others. One possible reason for the divergence of the simulated correlations from their empirical counterparts is our treatment of monetary policy. Like in many monetary business cycle models, monetary policy is exogenous, while in reality the monetary

[18] The behavior of profits has been attracting increasing attention in recent work on monetary business cycle analysis. *e.g.*, Christiano *et al.*, 1997a conclude that the counterfactual implication for profits is the key failure of sticky price models. In fact, for our benchmark calibration, both firms' profits and total profits (which simply equal firms' profits plus bank profits) are anticyclical, whereas firms' profits (and, similarly, total profits) become procyclical in the case of flexible prices ($\phi = 0$), and bank profits are procyclical independent of the degree of price stickiness.

authority changes its policy depending on the state of the economy.[19] In order to reconcile the model's behavior with empirical observations on the OMR (or, similarly, the money growth) correlations with non-financial variables, we consider the endogenization of monetary policy as a worthwhile area of future research.

In sum, our monetary model with OMR shocks cannot account for the empirical second moments of all money-related variables. Our results, however, indicate that the sticky price model with monetary policy specified as innovations to open market operations is able to reproduce most monetary features of the business cycle more successfully than the model with a monetary policy measure in the form of exogenous money growth. In our benchmark model with the OMR measure, private agents react to an open market operation by reducing aggregate demand and cash holdings. Money is endogenous and, as a consequence, the extremely high comovement between money growth and most financial and nonfinancial variables in the case of monetary injections breaks down. We therefore carefully conclude that monetary business cycle models with OMR shocks and endogenous monetary aggregates are a promising alternative to standard business cycle models with exogenous money growth.

4. Conclusion

In most industrialized countries, open market operations are the dominant instrument of monetary policy. What is more natural then than specifying monetary policy as the exchange of securities for reserves between the monetary authority and the banks? In this paper we examine a business cycle model where monetary policy is conducted by open market operations. We add several features which we consider being important aspects in order to enhance empirical relevance of the theoretical model. In particular we introduce price staggering and financial intermediation. The transmission of monetary policy shocks is mainly driven by portfolio adjustments of private agents who change the composition of real balances, bonds, and physical capital.

We assess the performance of the model to generate realistic impulse response functions and to reproduce second moment properties of US time series. First, we find that most impulse responses of our model to an open market operations' shock are consistent with empirical evidence on monetary policy effects. Particularly, real and nominal interest rates on

[19]See Christiano *et al.*, 1997b for a discussion of the appropriateness to specify monetary policy as an exogenous process rather than highly reactive to the state of the economy in the analysis of quantitative general equilibrium models.

bonds rise and output, aggregate demand, factor prices as well as monetary aggregates decline persistently in response to a monetary tightening. Second, we compare contemporaneous correlations of US time series with the correlations implied by simulations of our model. While the model generates reasonable contemporaneous correlations between various financial variables and monetary policy measures, it displays difficulties in replicating correlations of non-financial variables. The monetary policy measure presented in this paper is shown to be a promising alternative to traditional measures. For more ambitious simulation purposes, the latter deficiencies suggest the consideration of a monetary policy rule where the monetary authority also reacts to the state of the economy.

Appendix

Derivation of the New Keynesian Phillips curve

A monopolistically competitive firm i produces good y_i with a technology which is linear in labor. Entry and exit into the production sector is ruled out. The firms rent labor in a perfectly competitive labor market. The final good is an aggregate of a continuum of differentiated goods produced by the firms indexed with $i \in (0,1)$. The aggregator of differentiated goods is defined as follows:

$$y_t = \left[\int_0^1 y_{it}^{\frac{(\epsilon-1)}{\epsilon}} di\right]^{\frac{\epsilon}{\epsilon-1}}, \text{ with } \epsilon > 1, \tag{A.1}$$

where y is the number of units of the final good, y_i the amount produced by firm i, and ϵ the constant elasticity of substitution between these differentiated goods. Let P_i and P denote the price of good i set by firm i and the price index for the final good. The demand for each differentiated good is derived by minimizing the total costs of obtaining y subject to (A.1):

$$y_{it} = \left(\frac{P_{it}}{P_t}\right)^{-\epsilon} y_t. \tag{A.2}$$

Hence, the demand for good i increases with aggregate output and decreases in its relative price. Regarding the price index P of the final good, cost minimization implies:

$$P_t = \left[\int_0^1 P_{it}^{(1-\epsilon)} di\right]^{\frac{1}{1-\epsilon}}. \tag{A.3}$$

We introduce a nominal rigidity in form of staggered price setting as developed by Calvo, 1983. Each period firms may reset their prices with the probability $1-\phi$ independent of the time elapsed since the last price setting. The fraction ϕ of firms are assumed to adjust their previous period's prices according to the following simple rule:

$$P_{it} = \overline{\pi} P_{it-1}, \tag{A.4}$$

where $\overline{\pi}$ denotes the average of the inflation rate $\pi_t = P_t/P_{t-1}$. In each period the measure $1-\phi$ of randomly selected firms set new prices $\tilde{P}_{it}$ in order to maximize the value of their shares

$$\max_{\tilde{P}_{it}} E_t \left[\sum_{s=0}^{\infty} (\beta\phi)^s \vartheta_{t,t+s} \left(\overline{\pi}^s \tilde{P}_{it} y_{it+s} - P_{t+s} mc_{t+s} (y_{it+s} + \kappa) \right) \right], \quad \text{(A.5)}$$

$$\text{subject to } y_{it+s} = \left(\overline{\pi}^s \tilde{P}_{it} \right)^{-\epsilon} P^{\epsilon}_{t+s} y_{t+s}.$$

where mc denotes the real marginal costs with $mc = x^{-1}$. Since the firms are owned by the households, the kernel $\vartheta_{t,t+s}$ for dividend payments depends on the marginal utilities of consumption: $\vartheta_{t,t+s} = \frac{\lambda_{t+s}}{\lambda_t} \frac{P_t}{P_{t+s}}$. The first order condition for the optimal price setting of flex-price producers is given by

$$\tilde{P}_{it} = \frac{\epsilon}{\epsilon - 1} \frac{\sum_{s=0}^{\infty} (\beta\phi)^s E_t \left[\vartheta_{t,t+s} y_{t+s} P^{\epsilon+1}_{t+s} \overline{\pi}^{-\epsilon s} mc_{t+s} \right]}{\sum_{s=0}^{\infty} (\beta\phi)^s E_t \left[\vartheta_{t,t+s} y_{t+s} P^{\epsilon}_{t+s} \overline{\pi}^{(1-\epsilon)s} \right]}. \quad \text{(A.6)}$$

Using the simple price rule for the fraction ϕ of the firms (A.4), the price index for the final good as defined in (A.3) evolves according to the following first-order difference equation :

$$P_t = \left[\phi \left(\overline{\pi} P_{t-1} \right)^{1-\epsilon} + (1 - \phi) \tilde{P}_t^{1-\epsilon} \right]^{\frac{1}{1-\epsilon}}. \quad \text{(A.7)}$$

In the case of flexible prices ($\phi = 0$) we obtain: $P_{it} = P_t mc_t \epsilon / (\epsilon - 1)$. Hence, in a symmetric equilibrium real marginal costs mc are constant over time when prices are flexible ($mc_t = (\epsilon - 1)/\epsilon$), while they vary in the sticky price version of the model. Equation (A.7) can be stated in terms of stationary variables:

$$1 = \left[\phi \left(\overline{\pi} \pi_t^{-1} \right)^{1-\epsilon} + (1 - \phi) \tilde{P}_{qt}^{\,1-\epsilon} \right]^{\frac{1}{1-\epsilon}}, \text{with } \tilde{P}_{qt} = \frac{\tilde{P}_{it}}{P_t} \text{and } \pi_t = \frac{P_t}{P_{t-1}}, \quad \text{(A.8)}$$

where $\widehat{x}$ denotes the percent deviation of x from its steady state value $\overline{x}$. Linearization of this equation at the steady state leads to:

$$\frac{\phi}{1 - \phi} \widehat{\pi}_t = \widehat{\tilde{P}}_{qt}. \quad \text{(A.9)}$$

Further, we need to rewrite the first order condition for the firm's optimal price $\tilde{P}_{it}$ (A.6) in terms of stationary variables and linearize it at the steady state:

$$\begin{aligned} &\tilde{P}_{qt} \tfrac{\epsilon-1}{\epsilon} \textstyle\sum_{s=0}^{\infty} (\beta\phi)^s E_t \left[\vartheta_{t,t+s} y_{t+s} \pi^{\epsilon}_{t,t+s} \overline{\pi}^{(1-\epsilon)s} \right] \\ &= \textstyle\sum_{s=0}^{\infty} (\beta\phi)^s E_t \left[\vartheta_{t,t+s} y_{t+s} \pi^{\epsilon+1}_{t,t+s} mc_{t+s} \overline{\pi}^{-\epsilon s} \right], \end{aligned} \quad \text{(A.10)}$$

where $\pi_{t,t+s}$ denotes a cumulative inflation rate: $\pi_{t,t+s} = \frac{P_{t+s}}{P_t} = \prod_{k=1}^{s} \pi_{t+k}$. Linearizing equation (A.10) at the perfect foresight steady state using the condition that $\overline{\tilde{P}}_q \frac{\epsilon-1}{\epsilon} = \overline{mc}$ holds in the steady state and substituting $\overline{\tilde{P}}_q$, we obtain:

$$\frac{\phi}{(1 - \phi)} \left(\widehat{\pi}_t - \beta\phi E_t \left[\widehat{\pi}_{t+1} \right] \right) = (1 - \beta\phi) \left(\widehat{mc}_t - \beta\phi \sum_{s=0}^{\infty} (\beta\phi)^s E_t \left[-\widehat{\pi}_{t+1} \right] \right). \quad \text{(A.11)}$$

Equation (A.11) can then be simplified, leading to the 'New Keynesian Phillips Curve':

$$\widehat{\pi}_t = (1 - \phi) (1 - \beta\phi) \phi^{-1} \widehat{mc}_t + \beta E_t \left[\widehat{\pi}_{t+1} \right]. \quad \text{(A.12)}$$

Data sources

- Federal Reserve Board, flow of funds:
  - Total Open Market Papers Outstanding: FL893169175 (OMPAP),
  - Credit Market Instruments Holdings of the Monetary Authority: FL14002105 (DEBT_FR),
  - Debt Outstanding Total Nonfinancial Sectors: FL384104005 (DEBT_NF),
  - Debt Outstanding Domestic Financial Sector: FL794104005 (DEBT_F, with DEBT=DEBT_NF+DEBT_F),
  - Non-Borrowed Reserves (NBRES).
- IMF Financial Statistics:
  - Federal Funds Rate (FFRATE),
  - Treasury Bill Rate (TBILL_R),
  - Bank Prime Loan Rate (PRLOAN_R),
  - M1 Seasonally Adjusted (M1).
- OECD Main Indicators:
  - Corporate Profits: 421013NSA (PROF),
  - CPI All Items SA: 425241K (CPI),
  - GDP 1992 Prices SA: 421037NSA (GDP92),
  - GDP Implicit Price Level SA: 421051KSA (GDPDF),
  - Bank Loans + Investments SA: 426131DSA (BLOANS),
  - Employment Civilian SA: 424023KSA (EMPL).

Linearized model for open market operations' shocks

State variables: $\tilde{h}_t \equiv \frac{H_t}{p_{t-1}}$, $\tilde{b}_t \equiv \frac{B_t}{p_{t-1}}$; Co-states: π_t, λ_t; ; Exogenous states: a_t, μ_t^{omr};
Control variables: $c_t, l_t, w_t, x_t, i_t^l, i_t, z_t, s_t, b_t^b, b_t^h, m_t$.
The dynamic equations of the model are given by:

$$-\hat{x}_t = E\left[\frac{\phi}{(1-\phi)(1-\beta\phi)}\left(\widehat{\pi}_t - \beta\widehat{\pi}_{t+1}\right)\right]$$

$$\tilde{b}_{t+1} = \hat{s}_t + \hat{\mu}_t$$

$$\hat{\lambda}_t - \hat{\lambda}_{t+1} + \hat{\pi}_{t+1} = \frac{i}{1+i}\hat{i}_{t+1}$$

$$\tilde{h}\tilde{h}_{t+1} + \tilde{b}\tilde{b}_{t+1} - \frac{\tilde{h}}{\pi}\tilde{h}_t - (1+i)\frac{\tilde{b}}{\pi}\tilde{b}_t + \frac{\tilde{h}}{\pi}\hat{\pi}_t + (1+i)\frac{\tilde{b}}{\pi}\hat{\pi}_t = \frac{i\tilde{b}}{\pi}\hat{i}_t$$

The remaining contemporaneous equations are:

$$\hat{c}_t = -\hat{\lambda}_t$$

$$\hat{w}_t = -\hat{\lambda}_t$$

$$\hat{w}_t + \hat{x}_t + \hat{l}_t + \frac{i^l}{1+i^l}\hat{i}_t^l = \hat{a}_t$$
$$\hat{a}_t = \frac{c}{y}\hat{c}_t - \hat{l}_t$$
$$0 = -i^l\hat{i}_t^l + i\hat{i}_t + \psi_{zz}z\hat{z}_t$$
$$wl\left(\hat{w}_t + \hat{l}_t\right) - z\hat{z}_t = 0$$
$$0 = -s/\theta\hat{s}_t + z\hat{z}_t$$
$$b^b\hat{b}_t^b + s\hat{s}_t = 0$$
$$\frac{\tilde{b}}{\pi}\left(\tilde{b}_t - \hat{\pi}_t\right) = b^h\hat{b}_t^h + b^b\hat{b}_t^b$$
$$\frac{\tilde{h}}{\pi}\left(\tilde{h}_t - \hat{\pi}_t\right) = s\hat{s}_t + m\widehat{m}_t$$
$$-\hat{\lambda}_t = \widehat{m}_t + \hat{i}_t$$

Linearized model with physical capital

State variables: k_t, $\tilde{h}_t \equiv \frac{H_t}{p_{t-1}}$, $\tilde{b}_t \equiv \frac{B_t}{p_{t-1}}$; Co-states: π_t, λ_t, q_t; Exogenous states: a_t, μ_t^{omr};
Control variables: $c_t, l_t, e_t, w_t, r_t, x_t, i_t^l, i_t, z_t, s_t, b_t^b, b_t^h, m_t$.
Introducing physical capital, the set of dynamic equations of the model without capital (see above) is supplemented by the equations:

$$\hat{k}_{t+1} - (1-\phi'\frac{e}{k})\hat{k}_t = \phi'(.)\frac{e}{k}\hat{e}_t$$
$$-\hat{q}_t + \hat{\lambda}_{t+1} - \hat{\lambda}_t + \beta\left(1-\phi'\frac{e}{k}\right)\hat{q}_{t+1} + \beta\phi''\left(\frac{e}{k}\right)^2\hat{k}_{t+1} = -\frac{\beta}{q}r\hat{r}_{t+1} + \beta\phi''\left(\frac{e}{k}\right)^2\hat{e}_{t+1}$$

Furthermore, the set of contemporaneous equations in Appendix C is replaced by:

$$\hat{c}_t = -\hat{\lambda}_t$$
$$\hat{w}_t = -\hat{\lambda}_t$$
$$\hat{w}_t + \hat{x}_t + \alpha\hat{l}_t + \frac{i^l}{1+i^l}\hat{i}_t^l = \alpha\hat{k}_t + \hat{a}_t$$
$$\hat{r}_t + \hat{x}_t - (1-\alpha)\hat{l}_t + \frac{i^l}{1+i^l}\hat{i}_t^l = -(1-\alpha)\hat{k}_t + \hat{a}_t$$
$$\frac{\phi''}{\phi'}\frac{e}{k}\hat{e}_t = \frac{\phi''}{\phi'}\frac{e}{k}\hat{k}_t - \hat{q}_t$$
$$\hat{a}_t + \alpha k_t = \frac{c}{y}\hat{c}_t + \frac{e}{y}e_t - (1-\alpha)\hat{l}_t$$
$$0 = -i^l\hat{i}_t^l + i\hat{i}_t + \psi_{zz}z\hat{z}_t$$
$$wl\left(\hat{w}_t + \hat{l}_t\right) + rk\hat{r}_t - z\hat{z}_t = -rk\hat{k}_t$$
$$0 = -s/\theta\hat{s}_t + z\hat{z}_t$$
$$b^b\hat{b}_t^b + s\hat{s}_t = 0$$
$$\frac{\tilde{b}}{\pi}\left(\tilde{b}_t - \hat{\pi}_t\right) = b^h\hat{b}_t^h + b^b\hat{b}_t^b$$
$$\frac{\tilde{h}}{\pi}\left(\tilde{h}_t - \hat{\pi}_t\right) = s\hat{s}_t + m\widehat{m}_t$$
$$-\hat{\lambda}_t = \widehat{m}_t + \hat{i}_t$$

References

Benhabib, J., Schmidt-Grohe, S., and M. Uribe (2001). Monetary policy and multiple equilibria. *American Economic Review*, forthcoming.

Calvo, G. (1983). Staggered prices in a utility-maximizing framework. *Journal of Monetary Economics*, 12:383-398.

Chari, V.V., L.J. Christiano, and M. Eichenbaum (1995). Inside money, outside money, and short-term interest rates. *Journal of Money, Credit and Banking*, 27:1354-86.

Chari, V.V., P.J. Kehoe, and E.R. McGrattan (1996). Sticky price models of the business cycle: can the contract multiplier solve the persistence problem? Research Department Staff Report 217, Federal Reserve Bank of Minneapolis.

Cho, J.-O., and T. Cooley (1995). The business cycle with nominal contracts. *Economic Theory*, 6:13-33.

Christiano, J.L., and M. Eichenbaum (1992). Liquidity effects and the monetary transmission mechanism. *American Economic Review*, 82:346-53.

Christiano, J.L., M. Eichenbaum, and C.L. Evans (1997a). Sticky price and limited participation models of money: a comparison. *European Economic Review*, 41:1201-49.

Christiano, J.L., M. Eichenbaum, and C.L. Evans (1997b). Modeling money, paper presented at the Meeting of the Society for Economic Dynamics, Oxford, 1997.

Christiano, J.L., M. Eichenbaum, and C.L. Evans (1999). Monetary Policy Shocks: What Have We Learned and to What End? In M. Woodford and J.B. Taylor (eds.), *Handbook of Macroeconomics*, Amsterdam: North-Holland.

Christiano, J.L., and G. Gust (1999). Taylor Rules in a Limited Participation Model. In *Monetary Policy Rules*, edited by J.B. Taylor, University of Chicago Press.

Clarida, R., J. Gali, and M. Gertler (2000). Monetary policy rules and macroeconomic stability: evidence and some theory. *Quarterly Journal of Economics*, 140:147-180.

Cooley, T.F., and G.D. Hansen (1989). The inflation tax in a real business cycle model. *American Economic Review*, 79:733-48.

Cooley, T.F., and G.D. Hansen (1995). Money and the Business Cycle. In Cooley, T.F. (ed.), *Frontiers of Business Cycle Research*, Princeton University Press, Princeton, 175-216.

Cooley, T.F., and G.D. Hansen (1998). The role of monetary shocks in equilibrium business cycle theory: three examples. *European Economic Review*, 42:605-617.

Corriera, I., J. Neves, and S. Rebelo (1995). Business cycles in a small open economy. *European Economic Review*, 34:1275-1301.

Fuerst, T.S. (1992). Liquidity, loanable funds, and real activity. *Journal of Monetary Economics*, 29:3-24.

Hairault, J. and Portier, F. (1993). Money, new–Keynesian macroeconomics and the business cycle. *European Economic Review*, 37:1533–68.

Heer, B., and A. Schabert (2000). Open market operations as a monetary policy shock measure in a quantitative business cycle model. CESifo working paper No. 396.

Jeanne, O. (1998). Generating real persistent effects of monetary policy: how much nominal rigidity do we really need? *European Economic Review*, 42:1009-1032.

King, R.G., C. Plossser, and S. Rebelo (1987). Production growth and the business cycle: Technical Appendix. Working paper, University of Rochester, revised 1990.

Leeper, E.M. (1991). Equilibria under 'active' and 'passive' monetary and fiscal policies. *Journal of Monetary Economics*, 27:129-147.

Lucas, R.E. Jr. (1990). Liquidity and interest rates. *Journal of Economic Theory*, 50:237-264.

Lucas, R.E. Jr., and N.L. Stokey (1987). Money and interest in a cash-in-advance economy. *Econometrica*, 55:491-513.

Rotemberg, J. (1996). Prices, output and hours: an empirical analysis based on a sticky price model. *Journal of Monetary Economics*, 27:505-533.

Rotemberg, J., and M. Woodford (1998). Interest rate rules in an estimated sticky price model. NBER Working Paper, no. 6618.

Schreft, S., and B.D. Smith (1998). The effects of open market operations in a model of intermediation and growth. *Review of Economic Studies*, 65:519-550.

Schreft, S.L., and B.D. Smith (2000). The evolution of cash transactions: some implications for monetary policy. *Journal of Monetary Economics*, 46:97-120.

Taylor, J.B. (1993). Discretion versus policy rules in practice. *Carnegie-Rochester Conference series on Public Policy*, 39:195-214.

Yun, Tack (1996). nominal price rigidity, money supply endogeneity, and business cycles. *Journal of Monetary Economics*, 37:345-370.

Chapter 6: Optimal Monetary Policy in an Optimizing Stochastic Dynamic Model with Sticky Prices.

Michael Gail
Universität Siegen, Germany

Abstract Recently macroeconomic researchers have begun studying models of optimal monetary policy within the Real Business Cycle (RBC) framework. A standard RBC model is augmented by New Keynesian elements like sticky prices and monopolistically competitive firms. The monetary authority acts as a social planner maximizing the utility of a representative agent while at the same time taking care of the optimal price setting behavior of the firms via an implementation constraint. King and Wolman, 1999 analyze the outcome of such a model with respect to the appropriate monetary policy of the central bank. They conclude that the central bank achieves a complete stabilization of the price level. Inflation is not only constant at the steady state but also through time. It is shown that this very special result does not hold under alternative preference specifications that allow for a richer set of substitution effects between consumption and labor.

1. Introduction

In the last two or three years macroeconomists have intensified their interest in analyzing monetary policy. This is mainly due to the adoption of inflation targeting in several countries in the world, among them the United Kingdom and Sweden. These countries have been particular successful in driving down their inflation rates in the 1990s. Svensson, 1999 gives an excellent overview of the literature on that topic.

The task of the monetary authority in these models is to regulate aggregate demand to stabilize output and inflation. Output stabilization is necessary because sticky prices deteriorate aggregate demand causing "Okun gaps". High and variable inflation is generally viewed as resulting in increased relative price volatility and in other costs of production or exchange and thus has to be avoided. In order to determine how the central bank will balance the "Okun gaps" against the costs of inflation a loss function in these two arguments is assumed. The specific optimal monetary policy rule depends on the specific form of this loss function and on the detailed structure of the economy. In general the policy cannot completely eliminate fluctuations in output and inflation.

In the model analyzed here the central bank focuses just on the stabilization of the price level. This policy is optimal although the macroeconomic equilibrium is inefficient because firms have market power and "Okun gaps" can arise through price stickiness. The model combines two strands of research: the public finance approach to policy analysis and features of the "New Keynesian" macroeconomics. This combination is quite new to the macroeconomic literature.

In general the public finance approach concentrates on identifying distortions and on measuring the resulting costs to individuals, sometimes called "Harberger triangles". So far "Okun gaps" have not been analyzed using the public finance approach because they were considered not to be caused by microeconomic distortions.[1] This is fundamentally different here. Making use of two central New Keynesian features, namely the optimizing approach to sticky prices, as *e.g.* in Calvo, 1983, and the modeling of firms in an imperfect competition environment, as *e.g.* in Rotemberg, 1987, and embedding this into a dynamic general equilibrium model of the form used in the Real Business Cycle literature Okun gaps in fact arise from microeconomic distortions. This "New Neoclassical Synthesis" makes it possible to use Harberger-type analysis to identify distortions and to characterize optimal policy.

The model at hand cannot (yet) be used to answer questions like "What is the trade-off between inflation variability and output variability under alternative specifications of an interest rate rule?". For this purpose the structure of the model has to be improved upon. So far the only exogenous disturbances are productivity shocks. To produce a reasonable outcome some other shocks as energy or government spending shocks have to be included. What the model can answer are questions concerning the response of the optimal policy to a productivity disturbance and its influence on output, inflation and interest rates.

The result of King and Wolman, 1999 that the central bank can achieve a complete stabilization of the price level does not hold in this version of the model. Their result is mainly due to the assumed utility function which implies the absence of any substitution between consumption and leisure.

[1] See Tobin, 1977: "It takes a heap of 'Harberger triangles' to fill an 'Okun gap'."

The paper proceeds as follows: Section 2 describes the model and its underlying structure in detail. Section 3 discusses the policy problem as a social planner exercise of the central bank. Section 4 demonstrates on a theoretical basis why prices will not be constant here. The model is calibrated and impulse response functions will be analyzed focusing on the their optimal character. Section 5 concludes and gives some suggestions for future research.

2. The model

In the model monopolistically competitive firms are assumed to set final product prices optimally. Supply satisfies demand at theses prices. Firms do so in a staggered manner: each firm sets its price for two periods with half of the firms adjusting each period.[2] So far the model is in line with Taylor, 1980. Stickiness in individual prices causes stickiness in the price level and therefore there is room for monetary policy to combat this nonneutrality.

The model can be viewed as representative for a class of models in the spirit of the "New Neoclassical Synthesis" (see also Goodfriend and King, 1997 for a detailed description of this new approach). It combines the above mentioned New-Keynesian-style price stickiness with an otherwise neoclassical business cycle model in the tradition of the RBC literature. To facilitate the analysis the model abstracts from capital accumulation considerations. The production functions will therefore all be constant returns to scale in the single production factor labor. There will be no money demand distortions caused by positive nominal interest rates in order to focus the analysis completely on the effects of monetary policy (money supply side) that operate through sticky prices. This is justified here since empirically money nearly bears an interest equal to other assets so that there is no distortion from holding money for the representative household. The model does not consider fiscal policy. Changes in the money supply are thus offset by transfers to or lump-sum taxes from the household.

2.1 Consumers

Consumers are assumed to have preferences over consumption (c_t) and leisure ($1 - n_t$) given by the utility function

$$\sum_{t=0}^{\infty} \beta^t u\left(c_t, n_t, a_t\right) \tag{1}$$

[2]The analysis can be easily extended to multi-period price setting.

The momentary utility function used by King and Wolman, 1999 is given by

$$u(c_t, n_t, a_t) = \ln\left(c_t - \frac{a_t\theta}{1+\gamma} n_t^{1+\gamma}\right) \tag{2}$$

Here a_t is a preference shock that also acts like a productivity shock. θ and γ are positive parameters, β is the discount factor. This function is familiar from the analysis of Greenwood, Hercowitz and Huffman, 1988 and accordingly labelled GHH-preferences. It has the special property that hours worked only depend upon the real wage and not upon consumption.

The utility function analyzed in this paper is the standard CRRA function used in many Real Business Cycle models. σ governs the degree of risk aversion and ζ measures the relative weight of consumption for the representative agent.

$$u(c_t, n_t, a_t) = \frac{\left[a_t c_t^{\zeta}(1-n_t)^{1-\zeta}\right]^{1-\sigma} - 1}{1-\sigma} \tag{3}$$

It should be noted that in contrast to the standard use of this utility function there is a disturbance a_t acting like a preference shock.[3]

There is a *micro structure for consumption* as well as production of differentiated products that is derived explicitly in Blanchard and Kiyotaki, 1987. Every producer faces a downward-sloping demand curve with elasticity ϵ. When there is a continuum of firms the consumption aggregate c_t is an integral of differentiated products $c(\omega), \omega \in [0,1]$

$$c_t = \left(\int_0^1 c(\omega)^{(\epsilon-1)/\epsilon} d\omega\right)^{\epsilon/(\epsilon-1)} \tag{4}$$

as in Dixit and Stiglitz, 1977. In case that prices are fixed for just two periods and assuming that all price adjusting producers in a given period choose the same price the consumption aggregate can be written as

$$c_t = c(c_{0,t}, c_{1,t}) = \left(\frac{1}{2}c_{0,t}^{(\epsilon-1)/\epsilon} + \frac{1}{2}c_{1,t}^{(\epsilon-1)/\epsilon}\right)^{\epsilon/(\epsilon-1)} \tag{5}$$

[3]King and Wolman, 1999 argue that it is necessary in (2) to have a_t affecting equally production and preferences in order to achieve balanced growth. This is doubtful because the model does not explicitly account for growth aspects as, *e.g.*, in King, Plosser and Rebelo, 1988. The use of a_t in (3) affecting preferences is a new feature not analyzed in the literature in the context of optimal monetary policy before.

where $c_{j,t}$ is the quantity of a good consumed in period t whose price was set in period $t-j$. It can be shown that for this Dixit-Stiglitz aggregator the constant elasticity demands for each good take the form

$$c_{j,t} = \left(\frac{P_{j,t}}{P_t}\right)^{-\epsilon} c_t \tag{6}$$

$P_{j,t}$ is the nominal price at time t of any good whose price was set j periods ago and P_t is the price index at time t and is given by

$$P_t = \left(\int_0^1 P(\omega)^{(1-\epsilon)}\, d\omega\right)^{1/(1-\epsilon)} \tag{7}$$

Here firms set prices for two periods implying that half of them adjust their price in period t and half do not. Moreover all adjusting firms choose the same price. So the price index can be written as

$$P_t = \left(\frac{1}{2}P_{0,t}^{1-\epsilon} + \frac{1}{2}P_{1,t}^{1-\epsilon}\right)^{1/(1-\epsilon)} \tag{8}$$

The *intertemporal optimization* problem for the household is to maximize lifetime utility over aggregate consumption and leisure subject to an intertemporal budget constraint. The household is assumed to have access to a bond market and to hold money. Its budget constraint is therefore given by

$$\begin{aligned} &c_t + \tfrac{M_t}{P_t} + \tfrac{B_t}{P_t} + w_t h\left(\tfrac{M_t}{P_t c_t}\right) = \\ &w_t n_t + \left(1 + R_{t-1}^M\right)\tfrac{M_{t-1}}{P_t} + (1 + R_{t-1})\tfrac{B_{t-1}}{P_t} \end{aligned} \tag{9}$$

The uses of wealth are real consumption c_t, holdings of real money balances M_t/P_t and real bonds B_t/P_t. $h\left(\frac{M_t}{P_t c_t}\right)$ is the time spent on transactions activity, *i.e.* for purchasing goods while the real wage w_t is considered to be the opportunity cost of a unit of time spent shopping.[4] The household has several sources of his wealth. It earns money working in the market at the real wage rate $(w_t n_t)$. As money is assumed to be interest bearing it can spend its money holdings carried over from the previous period augmented by the interest on these real money balances $\left(1 + R_{t-1}^M\right)\frac{M_{t-1}}{P_t}$. Finally there are previous period bond holdings including the interest on them $(1 + R_{t-1})\frac{B_{t-1}}{P_t}$. The interest rate on

[4]For a detailed discussion of the shopping-time approach see King and Wolman, 1996.

bonds is endogenous while the one on money R^M_{t-1} is set exogenously by the monetary authority and is slightly below the bond rate.

The Lagrangian for the household (index H) can be written as follows:

$$
\begin{aligned}
L_H &= \sum_{t=0}^{\infty} \beta^t u(c_t, n_t, a_t) \\
&+ \sum_{t=0}^{\infty} \beta^t \lambda_t \Big[w_t n_t + \left(1 + R^M_{t-1}\right) \frac{P_{t-1}}{P_t} m_{t-1} \\
&\quad + (1 + R_{t-1}) \frac{P_{t-1}}{P_t} b_{t-1} - c_t - m_t - b_t - w_t h\left(\frac{m_t}{c_t}\right) \Big]
\end{aligned} \tag{10}
$$

Here small variables indicate real quantities, *i.e.* for example $b_t = B_t/P_t$. This function is maximized over c_t, n_t, m_t and b_t. The first order conditions will be important for the optimal policy of the central bank so they are reported below.

$$\frac{\partial L_H}{\partial c_t} = \beta^t \frac{\partial u(c_t, n_t, a_t)}{\partial c_t} - \beta^t \lambda_t + \beta^t \lambda_t w_t \frac{m_t}{c_t^2} h'\left(\frac{m_t}{c_t}\right) = 0 \tag{11}$$

$$\frac{\partial L_H}{\partial n_t} = \beta^t \frac{\partial u(c_t, n_t, a_t)}{\partial n_t} + \beta^t \lambda_t w_t = 0 \tag{12}$$

$$
\begin{aligned}
\tfrac{\partial L_H}{\partial m_t} &= -\beta^t \lambda_t \left[1 + \tfrac{w_t}{c_t} h'\left(\tfrac{m_t}{c_t}\right)\right] + E_t\left[\beta^{t+1} \lambda_{t+1} \left(1 + R^M_t\right) \tfrac{P_t}{P_{t+1}}\right] \\
&= 0
\end{aligned} \tag{13}
$$

$$\frac{\partial L_H}{\partial b_t} = -\beta^t \lambda_t + E_t\left[\beta^{t+1} \lambda_{t+1} (1 + R_t) \frac{P_t}{P_{t+1}}\right] = 0 \tag{14}$$

The third condition defines implicitly the money demand function. $h'(\cdot)$ is the derivative of h with respect to m/c. Combining this equation with (14) allows to analyze the nature of money demand in this model.

$$\lambda_t \left[\frac{w_t}{c_t} h'\left(\frac{m_t}{c_t}\right)\right] = \beta E_t \left[\lambda_{t+1} \left(R^M_t - R_t\right) \frac{P_t}{P_{t+1}}\right] \tag{15}$$

When the rate on money approaches the rate on bonds ($R^M_t \cong R_t$) real costs of holding money go to zero. This implies that $h'(\cdot)$ is zero. Since only the derivative of a constant is zero real money holdings per unit of consumption must be constant: $m_t/c_t = k$. Hence money demand is given by

$$m_t = k c_t \Leftrightarrow M_t = k P_t c_t \tag{16}$$

k represents the satiation level of cash balances. Money supply always satisfies the demand for cash. As there are lump-sum taxes and transfers available for the household they can be used to offset changes in the money supply. The efficiency condition for bond holdings establishes a relation between the nominal interest rate (on bonds) and the price level. Rearranging terms yields

$$(1+R_t) = E_t \left[\frac{\lambda_t}{\lambda_{t+1}} \frac{1}{\beta} \frac{P_{t+1}}{P_t} \right] \tag{17}$$

Supposing the Fisher equation is valid the real interest rate r_t is implicitly defined as

$$(1+r_t) = E_t \left[\frac{\lambda_t}{\lambda_{t+1}} \frac{1}{\beta} \right] \tag{18}$$

because $E_t [P_{t+1}/P_t]$ equals one plus the rate of expected inflation. Combining the first two efficiency conditions and remembering that $h'(\cdot) = 0$ reveals that the marginal rate of substitution between consumption and labor is equal to the real wage.

$$-\frac{\partial u(c_t, n_t, a_t)/\partial n_t}{\partial u(c_t, n_t, a_t)/\partial c_t} = \frac{dc_t}{dn_t} = w_t \tag{19}$$

2.2 Firms

Firms produce with a technology that is linear in labor $n_{j,t}$ and subject to random productivity shocks a_t.

$$y_{j,t} = c_{j,t} = a_t n_{j,t} \tag{20}$$

Here $n_{j,t}$ is the labor input employed in period t by a firm who set the price in period $t-j$. Firms always meet the demand for their product, that is $y_{j,t} = c_{j,t}$. Those who do not adjust their prices in a given period can be interpreted as passive while those who do adjust do so optimally.

Firms set their prices to maximize the present discounted value of their profits.[5] With a relative price defined by $p_{j,t} = P_{j,t}/P_t$ real profit $z_{j,t}$ for a firm of type j is given by

$$z_{j,t} = p_{j,t} a_t n_{j,t} - w_t n_{j,t} \tag{21}$$

w_t is the real wage rate. Firms minimize their costs which are given in this environment solely by wages. Thus minimizing $P_t w_t n_{j,t}$ subject to

[5]The model deviates in this respect from the standard textbook model in which profits are maximized over the quantity.

the production function implies for the total cost function $TC_{j,t}$[6]

$$TC_{j,t} = \frac{P_t w_t c_{j,t}}{a_t} \tag{22}$$

It is useful for further calculations to define real marginal cost as ψ_t which is equal to $(\partial TC_{j,t}/\partial c_{j,t})/P_t = w_t/a_t$. So the profit function can be rewritten as

$$z_{j,t} = z(p_{j,t}, c_t, \psi_t) = p_{j,t}^{-\epsilon} c_t (p_{j,t} - \psi_t) \tag{23}$$

making use of the fact that demand equals output $\left(c_{j,t} = p_{j,t}^{-\epsilon} c_t = a_t n_{j,t}\right)$.

In the case in which prices are not sticky the firm can just set prices on a period by period basis optimizing the profit function (23) with respect to $p_{j,t}$. The result of this exercise would be that relative prices will have to be set according to

$$p_{j,t} = p_t^* = \frac{\epsilon}{\epsilon - 1}\psi_t \tag{24}$$

But when prices are fixed for two periods the firm has to take into account the effect of the price chosen in period t on current and future profits. The price in period $t+1$ will be affected by the gross inflation rate Π_{t+1} between t and $t+1$ ($\Pi_{t+1} = P_{t+1}/P_t$).

$$p_{1,t+1} = \frac{p_{0,t}}{\Pi_{t+1}} \tag{25}$$

If there is positive inflation, $p_{1,t+1}$ will fall because nominal prices are fixed for two periods. As the nominal price in period t is defined by $P_{0,t}$ and in period $t+1$ by $P_{1,t+1}$, one has $P_{0,t} = P_{1,t+1}$, so that $p_{0,t} = P_{0,t}/P_t$ and $p_{1,t+1} = P_{1,t+1}/P_{t+1} = (P_{0,t}/P_t)(P_t/P_{t+1})$ which is what is stated in (25). So the optimal relative price has to balance the effects due to inflation between profits today and tomorrow. This intertemporal maximization problem is formally given by

$$\max_{p_{0,t}} E_t \left[z(p_{0,t}, c_t, \psi_t) + \beta \frac{\lambda_{t+1}}{\lambda_t} z(p_{1,t+1}, c_{t+1}, \psi_{t+1}) \right]$$
$$\text{s.t.} \quad p_{1,t+1} = \frac{p_{0,t}}{\Pi_{t+1}} \tag{26}$$

The term λ_{t+1}/λ_t is equal to the ratio of future to current marginal utility of consumption (derived in the household's optimization problem)

[6] It should be noticed that the wage is perfectly flexible in a competitive input market. So there is no index j for w_t and P_t which means that they are not firm-specific.

and considered to be – in conjunction with β – the appropriate discount factor for real profits. This is a consequence of the assumption that households own the production factor labor and rent it to the firms. They also own a diversified portfolio of claims to the profits earned by the firms. Although there will be no asset accumulation in equilibrium λ_t can be used to determine the present value of profits.[7] The efficiency condition for this problem is given by

$$0 = \frac{\partial z\left(p_{0,t}, c_t, \psi_t\right)}{\partial p_{0,t}} + \beta E_t \left(\frac{\lambda_{t+1}}{\lambda_t} \frac{\partial z\left(p_{1,t+1}, c_{t+1}, \psi_{t+1}\right)}{\partial p_{1,t+1}} \frac{1}{\Pi_{t+1}} \right) \tag{27}$$

Multiplying this equation by $p_{0,t}$ and λ_t produces a more symmetric form of the efficiency condition that will be more convenient to derive the optimal monetary policy later.

$$0 = \lambda_t p_{0,t} \frac{\partial z\left(p_{0,t}, c_t, \psi_t\right)}{\partial p_{0,t}} + \beta E_t \left(\lambda_{t+1} p_{1,t+1} \frac{\partial z\left(p_{1,t+1}, c_{t+1}, \psi_{t+1}\right)}{\partial p_{1,t+1}} \right) \tag{28}$$

Using (23) one can solve this condition for the optimal price to be set in period t which corresponds to the optimal price in case that prices are flexible derived before. This yields a forward-looking form of the price equation and is in that respect similar to the one in Taylor, 1980.

$$p_{0,t} = \frac{\epsilon}{\epsilon - 1} \frac{\lambda_t c_t \psi_t + \beta E_t \lambda_{t+1} \left(P_{t+1}/P_t\right)^{\epsilon} c_{t+1} \psi_{t+1}}{\lambda_t c_t + \beta E_t \lambda_{t+1} \left(P_{t+1}/P_t\right)^{\epsilon - 1} c_{t+1}} \tag{29}$$

The optimal price $p_{0,t}$ depends upon the current and future real marginal costs, the gross inflation rate, current and future consumption as well as today's and tomorrow's interest rates (through the influence of the λ-terms). It is thus fundamentally different from the one derived under fully flexible prices on a period-by-period basis (see (24)).

2.3 Constraints of the monetary authority

The objective of the monetary authority is to maximize welfare which means here maximizing the utility of the representative agent. In the absence of any distortions any rate of inflation would coincide with an optimal policy. But in this setup there are monopolistic competition and sticky prices. So the authority has to offset – in principle – the effects of these two frictions. It is constrained by technology and resource conditions as well as the price setting behavior of the firms.

[7] More details on this can be found in Dotsey, King and Wolman, 1999, p. 659-665 as well as in Dotsey, King and Wolman, 1997, p. 9-13.

It is assumed that the central bank follows an optimal plan under commitment. Fiscal policy instruments are not available so a first best allocation cannot be achieved. The purpose is to isolate the characteristics of an optimal monetary policy without a discussion of fiscal issues.

Three resource conditions have to be considered. Consumption of a good the price of which was set j periods ago cannot exceed production of that good.

$$c_{j,t} \leq a_t n_{j,t} \quad \text{for j} = 0, 1 \tag{30}$$

The consumption aggregator for a firm setting its price for two periods is given by (5) and repeated here.

$$c_t \leq \left(\frac{1}{2} c_{0,t}^{(\epsilon-1)/\epsilon} + \frac{1}{2} c_{1,t}^{(\epsilon-1)/\epsilon} \right)^{\epsilon/(\epsilon-1)} \tag{31}$$

The agent's time endowment is n_t and can be used for production of goods whose prices were set in period t and $t-1$.

$$n_t = \frac{1}{2} n_{0,t} + \frac{1}{2} n_{1,t} \leq 1 \tag{32}$$

The household equally splits his time for producing goods whose prices were set in the actual period and the period before.[8]

The quantities the monetary authority chooses must be consistent with those of the monopolistic price setting firms. Formally this is achieved via an implementation constraint. The central bank must make sure that the firms will in fact set their quantities as the optimal plan implies. It has to induce the firms to choose those quantities which are consistent with an optimal monetary policy. So it takes into account the optimality condition in (28) which is repeated here for convenience.

$$\lambda_t p_{0,t} \frac{\partial z_{0,t}}{\partial p_{0,t}} + \beta E_t \lambda_{t+1} p_{1,t+1} \frac{\partial z_{1,t+1}}{\partial p_{1,t+1}} = 0 \tag{33}$$

This condition can be expressed in a more compact way making use of the function x which only depends on real quantities.

$$x\left(c_{0,t}, c_t, n_t, a_t\right) + \beta E_t x\left(c_{1,t+1}, c_{t+1}, n_{t+1}, a_{t+1}\right) = 0 \tag{34}$$

Using the demand function $c_{j,t} = p_{j,t}^{-\epsilon} c_t$ one can eliminate relative prices. Real marginal costs are substituted by w_t/a_t and the real wage

[8]This seems to be an arbitrary assumption. It is used to make the outcome comparable to that of King and Wolman, 1999.

w_t is eliminated by use of the equality with the rate of substitution between consumption and leisure (see (19)). This yields:

$$x\left(c_{j,t}, c_t, n_t, a_t\right) = \lambda_t c_t \left[(1-\epsilon)\left(\tfrac{c_{j,t}}{c_t}\right)^{1-1/\epsilon} + \epsilon \tfrac{1-\zeta}{\zeta}\tfrac{1}{a_t}\tfrac{1}{1-n_t}\left(\tfrac{c_{j,t}}{c_t}\right) c_t\right] \quad (35)$$

As λ_t is equal to the marginal utility of consumption in period t it is in that respect also a function of c_t, n_t and a_t. This formula deviates from the one in King and Wolman, 1999 in that there is also a direct influence of a_t in the second term in the bracketed expression.

3. The policy problem

The determination of the optimal monetary policy is conducted in a two-step procedure. First, the optimal choices for the real variables in the model are derived by solving the policy problem of the monetary authority acting as a social planner. Second, the implications for the nominal variables such as prices and interest rates are determined by using these optimal decision functions and by combining them with those of the household's problem. While unusual in macroeconomics this practice is common in public finance and other areas of applied general equilibrium analysis and is getting more and more standard in dynamic macroeconomic models with distortions. Expectations are not considered here so that the solution is derived under a certainty equivalence perspective.

The Lagrangian of the central bank (index C) can be written as follows:

$$\begin{aligned} L_C = & \sum_{t=0}^{\infty} \beta^t u\left(c_t, n_t, a_t\right) \\ & + \sum_{t=0}^{\infty} \beta^t \phi_t \left[x\left(c_{0,t}, c_t, n_t, a_t\right) + \beta x\left(c_{1,t+1}, c_{t+1}, n_{t+1}, a_{t+1}\right)\right] \\ & + \sum_{t=0}^{\infty} \beta^t \Lambda_t \left[c\left(c_{0,t}, c_{1,t}\right) - c_t\right] \\ & + \sum_{t=0}^{\infty} \beta^t \Omega_t \left[n_t - \frac{1}{2} n_{0,t} - \frac{1}{2} n_{1,t}\right] \\ & + \sum_{t=0}^{\infty} \beta^t \left[\rho_{0,t}\left(a_t n_{0,t} - c_{0,t}\right) + \rho_{1,t}\left(a_t n_{1,t} - c_{1,t}\right)\right] \end{aligned} \quad (36)$$

This function is maximized over $c_{0,t}, c_{1,t}, c_t, n_{0,t}, n_{1,t}, n_t$ and of course with respect to the Lagrange multipliers $\phi_t, \Lambda_t, \Omega_t, \rho_{0,t}$ and $\rho_{1,t}$.

3.1 Optimality conditions

Defining an artificial multiplier ϕ_{-1} at date $t = 0$ the optimality conditions can be written in the time-invariant form below. The multiplier will be discussed more thoroughly in the next section.

The first order condition with respect to each firm's labor input is given by

$$\frac{\partial L_C}{\partial n_{j,t}} = \beta^t \left(-\frac{1}{2}\Omega_t + \rho_{j,t} a_t \right) = 0 \text{ for j} = 0, 1 \tag{37}$$

The optimal choice of consumption levels from each type of firm is determined by

$$\begin{aligned} \frac{\partial L_C}{\partial c_{j,t}} &= \beta^t \left(\phi_{t-j} \frac{\partial x(c_{j,t}, c_t, n_t, a_t)}{\partial c_{j,t}} + \Lambda_t \frac{\partial c(c_{0,t}, c_{1,t})}{\partial c_{j,t}} - \rho_{j,t} \right) \\ &= 0 \text{ for j} = 0, 1 \end{aligned} \tag{38}$$

Aggregate consumption must obey

$$\begin{aligned} \frac{\partial L_C}{\partial c_t} &= \beta^t \left(\frac{\partial u(c_t, n_t, a_t)}{\partial c_t} + \phi_t \frac{\partial x(c_{0,t}, c_t, n_t, a_t)}{\partial c_t} \right) \\ &+ \beta^t \left(\phi_{t-1} \frac{\partial x(c_{1,t}, c_t, n_t, a_t)}{\partial c_t} - \Lambda_t \right) = 0 \end{aligned} \tag{39}$$

whereas for aggregate labor the condition is

$$\begin{aligned} \frac{\partial L_C}{\partial n_t} &= \beta^t \left(\frac{\partial u(c_t, n_t, a_t)}{\partial n_t} + \phi_t \frac{\partial x(c_{0,t}, c_t, n_t, a_t)}{\partial n_t} \right) \\ &+ \beta^t \left(\phi_{t-1} \frac{\partial x(c_{1,t}, c_t, n_t, a_t)}{\partial n_t} + \Omega_t \right) = 0 \end{aligned} \tag{40}$$

In addition the constraints have to hold with equality, that is the derivatives of the Lagrangian with respect to the multipliers.

$$\frac{\partial L_C}{\partial \rho_{j,t}} = \beta^t \left(a_t n_{j,t} - c_{j,t} \right) = 0 \quad \text{for j} = 0, 1 \tag{41}$$

$$\frac{\partial L_C}{\partial \Lambda_t} = \beta^t \left[c\left(c_{0,t}, c_{1,t} \right) - c_t \right] = 0 \tag{42}$$

$$\frac{\partial L_C}{\partial \phi_t} = \beta^t \left[x\left(c_{0,t}, c_t, n_t, a_t \right) + \beta x\left(c_{1,t+1}, c_{t+1}, n_{t+1}, a_{t+1} \right) \right] = 0 \tag{43}$$

$$\frac{\partial L_C}{\partial \Omega_t} = \beta^t \left[n_t - \frac{1}{2} n_{0,t} - \frac{1}{2} n_{1,t} \right] = 0 \tag{44}$$

It should be noted that the multiplier ϕ_{-1} is not present in (36). It is introduced to have a simple representation of optimal policy in a world of commitment of the central bank. The multiplier guarantees that the efficiency conditions take the same form irrespective of the period the monetary authority is optimizing.

3.2 General implications of the optimality conditions

In most cases the optimality conditions differ from those of an unrestricted representative agent. This is due to the effect of the implementation constraint on the social planner's behavior.

The conditions for the firms' labor input $n_{j,t}$ just equate the utility-denominated price of a unit of each type of good $(\rho_{j,t})$ to the utility-denominated value of labor (Ω_t) divided by productivity (a_t) which is the same under purely flexible prices. But the efficiency conditions for aggregate consumption and labor differ from those of an unrestricted planner. ϕ_t is the shadow price of decreasing a price-settings firm's marginal present discounted profits with respect to relative price and it is negative here because the planner wants the firms to have positive marginal profits.[9] In comparison to the decentralized problem the central bank values a marginal unit of consumption, measured by Λ_t, higher. This is because the derivative of $x(c_{j,t}, c_t, n_t, a_t)$ with respect to aggregate consumption c_t is negative so that Λ_t is higher than marginal utility of consumption $(\partial u\,(c_t, n_t, a_t)\,/\partial c_t)$. For similar reasons a marginal unit of labor Ω_t is valued higher here than under perfect competition.

The first-order conditions for $c_{j,t}$ do not have such a straightforward analogue in the competitive model. But it can be shown that the monetary authority equates appropriately chosen marginal rates of substitution and transformation (see King and Wolman, 1999, p. 376).

The multiplier ϕ_t appears not only in the current period t, but also in lagged form ϕ_{t-1} as can be seen in the conditions for aggregate labor and consumption. This is a consequence of the fact that changes in future consumption affect the price-setting behavior of firms in period $t-1$. Recall that from (29) $p_{0,t}$ depends not only on current period consumption but also on future consumption c_{t+1}. (29) is a forward-looking constraint. It must be clear that the efficiency conditions are valid for all periods, including $t = 0$, whereas in the Lagrangian ϕ_{-1} is not present. This lagged multiplier in $t = 0$ is introduced to make sure that an optimal plan is feasible. It allows the use of standard fixed-coefficient linear rational expectations solution methods.

---

[9] This can be shown when introducing a zero bound on marginal profits which means rewriting the implementation constraint as:

$$-\sum_{t=0}^{\infty} \beta^t \phi_t \left[0 - x\left(c_{0,t}, c_t, n_t, a_t\right) - \beta x\left(c_{1,t+1}, c_{t+1}, n_{t+1}, a_{t+1}\right)\right].$$

If the monetary authority is allowed to reformulate its policy on a period-by-period basis, then a problem of time-inconsistency of the optimal plan will arise as in Kydland and Prescott, 1977 and Barro and Gordon, 1983. In that case the optimal policy problem cannot be formulated in the way just described. But here it is assumed that the central bank is required to commit to the state-contingent plan in the initial period and to stick to it through time. The introduction of ϕ_{-1} prohibits the study of an optimal policy dependent on the effects of an initial start-up period. Therefore ϕ_{-1} is set to the steady state value of ϕ and not to zero. The use of the steady state of ϕ reflects that the central bank has been following an optimal plan for a long time.

3.3 The steady state

Looking at (37) in the steady state reveals that $\rho_0 a = \rho_1 a = (1/2)\Omega$ so that $\rho_1 = \rho_0 = (1/2)(\Omega/a)$. A conjecture for the steady state values of consumption is that they are all equal which means $c_0 = c_1 = c$. In order to determine whether this is possible one has to check whether the other optimality conditions are consistent with the conjecture. For this end it is helpful to look at first at equations (38). Dividing (38) for $j = 0$ by (38) for $j = 1$ results in the following term:

$$\frac{\phi\frac{\partial x(c_0,c,n,a)}{\partial c_0} + \Lambda\frac{\partial c(c_0,c_1)}{\partial c_0}}{\phi\frac{\partial x(c_1,c,n,a)}{\partial c_1} + \Lambda\frac{\partial c(c_0,c_1)}{\partial c_1}} = \frac{\rho_0}{\rho_1} \tag{45}$$

As just shown the right hand side of this expression is unity in the steady state. For (45) to be satisfied the left hand side must also be equal to unity. Calculating the derivative of the consumption aggregator and imposing $c_0 = c_1$ reveals that $\partial c\,(c_0, c_1)\,/\partial c_0 - 1/2 = \partial c\,(c_0, c_1)\,/\partial c_1$. Moreover, the effect of consumption related to today's price-setting firms on today's implementation constraint $\partial x\,(c_0, c, n, a)\,/\partial c_0$ is just the same as the effect of consumption related to yesterday's price-setting firms on yesterday's implementation constraint $\partial x\,(c_1, c, n, a)\,/\partial c_1$. As $\phi_t = \phi_{t-1} = \phi$ in the steady state and as Λ is constant the left hand side is equal to unity. Along a similar line of argument the derivatives of $x\,(c_0, c, n, a)$ and $x\,(c_1, c, n, a)$ with respect to c are identical so that (39) can be written as

$$\frac{\partial u\,(c, n, a)}{\partial c} + 2\phi\frac{\partial x\,(c_0, c, n, a)}{\partial c} - \Lambda = 0 \tag{46}$$

The condition for aggregate labor (40) reduces to

$$\frac{\partial u\,(c, n, a)}{\partial n} + 2\phi\frac{\partial x\,(c_0, c, n, a)}{\partial n} + \Omega = 0 \tag{47}$$

Using the results for (38) it suffices to use one of the conditions of (37) to get

$$\phi \frac{\partial x\left(c_0, c, n, a\right)}{\partial c_0} + \frac{1}{2}\Lambda - \frac{1}{2}\frac{\Omega}{a} = 0 \tag{48}$$

These three equations form a linear system in the three remaining Lagrange multipliers. The solution determines uniquely steady state values for Λ, Ω and ϕ.

Closer inspection of (41) - (44) reveals that all labor inputs are equal ($n_0 = n_1 = n = c/a$), and that marginal profits should be zero in any period ($x\left(c_0, c, n, a\right) = x\left(c_1, c, n, a\right) = 0$).

The optimal steady state inflation rate is equal to zero. This can be seen by calculating (6) at the steady state. Since $c_j = c$ one gets $P_j = P$. The price of a firm setting the price in t is just equal to the overall price level and equal to the price firms set in period $t-1$. Accordingly the gross inflation rate $\Pi_t = P_t/P_{t-1}$ is equal to unity and inflation is zero.

4. Optimal monetary policy

In this section the solution to the policy problem is analyzed in detail. Having determined the steady state of all endogenous variables one can start taking linear approximations of the efficiency conditions around it. These equations are given in detail in the appendix. The model has still to be augmented by equations for the nominal variables (nominal interest rate, price level, inflation rate and money demand) to analyze the implications of optimal monetary policy.

The solution is conducted using an extended version of the algorithm of King, Plosser and Rebelo, 1990 which allows for singularities in the system matrix of the reduced model. The theoretical background of this algorithm is developed in King and Watson, 1999 whereas computational aspects and the implementation are discussed in King and Watson, 1997.

4.1 Implications of the model solution

One can use the resulting decision functions to calculate optimal responses to a productivity shock (impulse responses). In contrast to King and Wolman, 1999 prices and labor inputs fluctuate and are not constant. The equality result for all relative prices even in the dynamic context is a very special one and due to the specific utility function used by these authors which has very strong implications for the substitution effects at work. It will be demonstrated which mechanisms are at work to stimulate fluctuating prices.

According to King and Wolman, 1999 the labor input must not fluctuate in response to a productivity shock in order to make sure that marginal profits do not deviate form zero, that is $dx_{j,t}(\cdot) = 0$. This constancy is necessary to guarantee that a productivity shock does not induce optimal price variation. Under their preference specification labor does indeed not respond to a technology shock as long as the markup is constant. The markup μ_t is the reciprocal of real marginal cost and is given by $\mu_t = a_t/w_t = 1/\psi_t$. They prove this to be possible and consistent with the linearized first order conditions with the help of the conjecture that $\hat{\phi}_t$ does not respond to productivity either and show that this is in fact the case and that it is compatible with the solution of the model.

This result is very special and does not hold in the model considered here. The utility function used in this model specification features a much richer set of substitution effects between consumption and labor. Refer to (3) and analyze the relationship between c and n in the household's optimization problem. The first order conditions of this problem imply - as shown above - the equality of the real wage with the rate of substitution between consumption and leisure. In the steady state this relationship is given by

$$n = 1 - \frac{c}{w}\frac{1-\zeta}{\zeta} \tag{49}$$

Labor increases in the real wage as in case of utility function (2). But there is also a direct influence of consumption. With a positive technology shock, consumption will be increased while at the same time labor will be decreased. The impact of this favorable shock will be used completely to reduce working effort and to raise consumption. So the dynamics of consumption influence the dynamics of labor. Note that a does not appear in (49) as opposed to King and Wolman, 1999. The respective steady state relation in their model is

$$n = \left(\frac{w}{a\theta}\right)^{1/\gamma} \tag{50}$$

This is the reason why they have to show that the markup $\mu = a/w$ is constant. Constancy of the markup implies constancy of real marginal cost. Using this in (29) one can show that firms will not adjust their relative prices $p_{0,t}$ if the price level will be constant, *i.e.* $P_t = P_{t-1}$. This is because one can factor out ψ of the numerator. Then the remaining expression and the denominator cancel. To prove that a constant price level is really a consequence of the optimal monetary policy, a zero response of the shadow price of real marginal profits $\hat{\phi}_t$ to the technological shock and responses of consumption levels $\hat{c}_t$, $\hat{c}_{j,t}$ exactly equal to productivity dynamics are needed. This is proved by just imposing the conjecture of constancy on the linearized equations. But here $\hat{\phi}_t$ *does* respond to $\hat{a}_t$ as will be shown in the next subsection with the help of impulse responses.[10] In addition the symmetry of the responses of the consumption levels of the firms adjusting prices in t and $t-1$ vanishes. They also cease to be exactly the same as productivity dynamics.

4.2 Impulse response functions and optimal monetary policy

To compute impulse responses the parameters of the model have to be calibrated. Going back to section 3.3 one can see that a and either n or c have to be set exogenously. Because more information is available about hours worked, n is specified to be equal to 0.25 implying that agents work 25 % of their non-sleeping time. The steady state value of the productivity shock is arbitrarily chosen to be 10.[11] It is assumed that productivity follows an AR(1)-process with $\rho_a = 0.8$. The discount factor β will be 0.99 and σ, the parameter governing the degree of risk aversion, is set to 2.[12] The elasticity of demand ϵ is 4 causing the average static markup $\mu = \epsilon/(\epsilon - 1)$ to be 1.33.[13] All remaining parameters can be calculated with the help of these specified values: the steady state consumption levels $c = an$, the real wage $w = a/\mu$, the real and nominal interest rates $r = R = (1-\beta)/\beta$, and the preference parameter $\zeta = c/(w + c - wn)$. For ζ this implies 0.3077, a value that is reasonably in line with other studies.

Figure 1 shows the impulse responses of consumption and labor caused by a one percent productivity shock. As mentioned above the response of $\hat{c}$ does not exactly track the reaction of $\hat{a}$ as in King and Wolman, 1999. Aggregate consumption reacts a bit weaker than productivity. Moreover it is weakly influenced by $\hat{\phi}$ which is itself hit by $\hat{a}$. The shadow price of marginal profits as well as aggregate labor input fall but the fall in $\hat{\phi}$ is a persistent one whereas labor $\hat{n}$ shows an interesting cyclical movement that is not very long-lasting. Figure 2 gives some more detailed insight in the mechanisms at work. Here one can see

[10] It is not clear whether it is possible to show this analytically.

[11] In contrast to the well known basic neoclassical model of King, Plosser and Rebelo, 1988 there is no escape from specifying parameters such as a at the steady state. The system cannot be reduced until only deep parameters remain to be calibrated.

[12] Model results are qualitatively *not* sensitive to this value. Especially the result of a fluctuating price level also holds for log-linear preferences with $\sigma = 1$. Quantitative results for other values of σ will be discussed below.

[13] This formula can be deduced by combining (29) with the price index (8) evaluated at the steady state, *i.e.* for zero inflation.

that labor used by firms setting their price in period t ($\hat{n}_0$) rises slightly while at the same time firms who set prices one period earlier will reduce labor input $\hat{n}_1$. This reduction is more pronounced than the expansion so that overall aggregate labor decreases. In the following period the picture changes. Now $\hat{n}_1$ rises and $\hat{n}_0$ falls. The effect is due to the shadow price of real marginal profits. Its relatively strong decline in the initial period of the shock drops to about only half of this magnitude. It should be noted that the fluctuations in labor are small compared with the respective values for consumption and $\hat{\phi}$. In addition, there is also a different reaction of $\hat{c}_1$ and $\hat{c}_0$. Because the impulse responses look quite similar the differences of the respective functions are plotted. This reveals the stronger reaction of $\hat{c}_0$ so that the difference is negative. $\hat{c}_1$ responds a bit weaker causing a positive difference. Notice that both graphs are mirror images of each other.[14]

Figure 3 shows the reaction of prices. As the shadow price of real marginal profits falls the central bank as the social planner has to optimally induce firms to reduce their prices. The reaction of $\hat{P}_0$ resembles much the behavior of $\hat{\phi}$ but not that strong. Note that $\hat{P}_0$ falls only by -0.005 % whereas $\hat{\phi}$ drops by nearly -0.11 % . Firms who have set their prices one period before react with a lag of one period so that the impulse response for $\hat{P}_1$ is the same as the one for $\hat{P}_0$ just shifted one period ahead. This results in an overall variation in the price level. The central bank optimally induces a disinflation in order reach its goals: to maximize the utility of the representative agent in an environment of monopolistically competitive firms fixing nominal prices for two periods. Due to this two period price setting behavior there is a kink in $\hat{P}$ that translates into a small inflationary period beginning two periods after the initial productivity shock but lasting only for just ten quarters. Although there are substitution effects at work (see (49)) these are small and cause only a weak inflationary bias. But nevertheless the monetary authority does not succeed in stabilizing the price level completely.

Figure 4 gives a graphical impression of the nominal and real interest rate. They are no longer equal. Since the price level is not constant there is inflation resulting in a slightly stronger reaction of the nominal rate to a productivity shock. The fall in the interest rate is quite strong: about 1.8 % on an annual basis. It is more than four times the reaction in the King and Wolman, 1999 model version with preference specification (2). Because the coefficients are even closer in value than those of the consumption levels in Figure 2 again the difference between the nominal

[14]The respective coefficients in the decision functions for $\hat{c}_0$, $\hat{c}_1$ and $\hat{c}$ are 1.0052, 0.9851 and 0.9951.

and real rate is plotted. The nominal rate initially decreases stronger so that the difference is negative.[15] Note the interesting "cyclical" character of this curve. There is a highly nonlinear relation between the response of the two rates due to the richer internal dynamics of the model. The response of money demand is nearly equal to that of consumption. This is due to the fact that the price level - which is the difference between the cyclical components of money and consumption - does not react very strong to a productivity shock. (See the respective graphs in Figure 4 and refer to (A.19).)

The result that real and nominal rate differ can also be demonstrated analytically. A typical Taylor-rule would link the real and nominal rate according to[16]

$$R_t = r_t + f\left(lnP_t - ln\overline{P}\right) \tag{51}$$

where f would be a positive coefficient and $\overline{P}$ the target price level. r_t would be determined from the real interest rate $\hat{r}_t$ of the model solution. In King and Wolman, 1999 the price level is constant under optimal policy so they reach the strong result that the central bank should just set the nominal rate equal to the real rate: $R_t = r_t$, which also implies the equality of the cyclical components: $\hat{R}_t = \hat{r}_t$. Here P fluctuates so that the term in parentheses ceases to be zero. Hence f would be different from zero. In addition it is no longer possible to write down the policy rule as in (51) because the fact that $\hat{R}_t$ is different from the real rate makes it depend upon several state variables.

Varying the degree of risk aversion has no qualitative consequences for the model results regarding the fact that prices cannot be completely stabilized. But there are interesting quantitative effects. For small values of σ (smaller than 2) the reactions of prices, inflation, labor and consumption decline while for higher values the cyclical variation gets stronger. The higher the degree of relative risk aversion which corresponds to a lower degree of the elasticity of intertemporal substitution the stronger the effects of productivity shocks. The strengthening of the cyclical character is most probably due to the two-period-price setting of the firms. Because very risk averse households care more for today than for tomorrow they frequently change their demand for the differentiated consumption goods and their labor supply. So firms react stronger in setting their prices so that the central bank is less successful in stabilizing the price level and inflation. Figure 5 illustrates this result for prices and inflation.

---

[15] This is because the negative reaction of the nominal rate is stronger than that of the real rate so that the sign gets negative.

[16] This formulation ignores a term for the output gap.

A second important factor for the success of the central bank to stabilize prices is the length of the price setting period. To explore the consequences the model is solved assuming that every period a constant fraction of 20% of the firms can change their price with all adjusting firms choosing the same price (5-period price setting). As Figure 6 depicts this has the consequence of strengthening the persistence effects of the productivity shock. Optimal pricing now implies a very smooth development of $\widehat{P}_{0,t}$ which translates into an even smoother curve for the price level. Note that the intensity of the disinflation gets smaller compared to the case with a high degree of relative risk aversion (see Figure 5). The pronounced peak of the gross inflation rate in the sixth period is due to the assumption of equal fractions of firms adjusting every period. This causes the marginal adjustment probability to be zero all the time and one in every fifth period. Relaxing that assumption and using a vector of declining fractions gives the central bank the opportunity to smooth the productivity shock even more. Figure 7 is an example for the vector of fractions given by [0.30 0.25 0.20 0.15 0.10] meaning that in the first period 30% of the firms do adjust prices, in the second 25% and so on. This causes the inflationary period to start earlier but it also allows the monetary authority to dampen the peak and therefore to stabilize prices more efficiently.

The success of the central bank in stabilizing the price level depends also to a great degree upon the specific productivity process at work. So far an AR(1)-process has been assumed. The decision functions of the model change sharply when considering an AR(2)-process for productivity. In order to be able to compare results to those of King and Wolman, 1999 the structure of the process is assumed to be

$$\widehat{a}_t = \rho_{a_1}\widehat{a}_{t-1} + \rho_{a_2}\widehat{a}_{t-2} + \epsilon_{\widehat{a}_t} \tag{52}$$

Using $\rho_{a_1} = 1.3$ and $\rho_{a_2} = -0.3$ one in fact has an ARIMA(1,1,0)-process for productivity. With ρ_{a_1} unchanged and $\rho_{a_2} = -0.4$ it follows a stationary AR(2)-process. Figure 8 shows the impulse responses under this AR(2) specification. The graph for the nominal interest rate looks very much like that of King and Wolman, but the central bank has to raise this rate by more than twice the value of their study. Note that $\widehat{R}_t$ *rises* initially as opposed to the decline under the AR(1)-process for the productivity shock.[17] This also implies a longer lasting inflationary bias. For difference stationary productivity Figure 9 gives a graphical impression of the impact of a technology shock. Again the reaction of the

[17] It should be mentioned that the nominal rate also rises for very small degrees of risk aversion.

nominal rate is more than twice as large as in King and Wolman's study. Surprisingly the central bank can nearly completely eliminate the inflationary bias but not the initial disinflation. Prices decline permanently due the permanent character of the shock.

As has been shown prices are not constant in this model. Accordingly there is some room for the analysis of other policy rules. Even the optimal policy does not produce a constant price level. It may be that some other type of rule performs better. To evaluate the performance of alternative rules one has to add the rule under consideration to the model and compare the resulting life-time-utility (1) to the optimal one. Technically the rule would be a function for the nominal interest rate replacing the equation that derives R_t in the optimal policy from the household's optimality conditions (see (17)). Such calculations are conducted in Henderson and Kim, 1999. They analyze models with *one-period* wage and price contracts where exact solutions can be obtained so that it is also possible to derive exact welfare levels. The Pareto optimal welfare level can be reached in any situation so that all other policies focusing only on the stabilization of prices, the output gap or nominal income are suboptimal. This special result is due to the one-period contract structure. Erceg, Henderson and Levin, 2000 extend the framework to *staggered* price and wage contracts. They show that under these circumstances the Pareto optimal welfare level cannot be achieved so that the policymaker always faces a tradeoff between wage inflation, price inflation and the output gap. However their claim that an optimal stabilization of prices is feasible if only prices are staggered is not supported by the results in this paper. Their expectational Phillips curve depends on the utility function used which is additively separable in consumption and leisure. It would probably have a different form under CRRA preferences implying similar results to those obtained here.

5. Conclusion

This paper has considered a version of the King and Wolman model of optimal monetary policy in a "New Neoclassical Synthesis" environment. It has turned out that their result of complete price level stabilization is a very special one that depends – at least to a great extent – on the specific preference specification with zero substitution between consumption and labor. Prices fluctuate optimally under a more general utility function so that inflation will not be constant through time. Nevertheless these fluctuations are quite small.

Future research should focus on a richer production structure including capital accumulation considerations. Also the pricing structure can be extended to allow for state-dependent pricing, as opposed to time-dependent pricing assumed here. Dotsey, King and Wolman, 1999 have begun studying the implications.

It would also be interesting to consider welfare losses associated with the inflationary bias. This could be done by comparing the approximated expected life-time-utility under CRRA preferences with that under King and Wolman's GHH specification. The approximation method proposed by Erceg, Henderson and Levin, 2000 can be used to answer that question. Yet in a recent article Kim and Kim, 2000 have shown that sometimes the method of log-linearization around the steady state can lead to spurious welfare reversals.[18] Woodford, 2001 derives some conditions for the validity of this method in models like the one considered here. Whether the model at hand satisfies these conditions remains an open question since the price level fluctuates and is not constant through time.

Finally the model could also be used to analyze the business cycle implications of optimal monetary policy. It can answer, for example, questions about the variability of output and consumption as well as inflation and money. Further it implies certain correlation patterns between real and nominal variables. This line of research has not been pursued in this kind of literature on monetary policy.

Acknowledgments

Comments from Hans-E. Loef, Jürgen Ehlgen, Jinill Kim, Andreas Schabert, other participants of the 5th T2M Meeting in May 2000 and an anonymous referee are gratefully acknowledged. The usual disclaimer applies.

Appendix

The linearized equations — real variables

The linearized equations for the firms' labor inputs are given by

$$0 = -\widehat{\Omega}_t + \widehat{\rho}_{0,t} + \widehat{a}_t \tag{A.1}$$

$$0 = -\widehat{\Omega}_t + \widehat{\rho}_{1,t} + \widehat{a}_t \tag{A.2}$$

A hat ($\widehat{\ }$) represents the relative deviation of the respective variable from its steady state ($\hat{a}_t = (a_t - a)/a$). For the consumption levels one gets

$$\begin{aligned} 0 = \quad & \phi n D_{13} x(c_0, c, n, a)\, \widehat{n}_t + [\phi c_0 D_{11} x(c_0, c, n, a) + \Lambda c_0 D_{11} c(c_0, c_1)]\, \widehat{c}_{0,t} \\ & + \Lambda c_1 D_{12} c(c_0, c_1)\, \widehat{c}_{1,t} + \phi c D_{12} x(c_0, c, n, a)\, \widehat{c}_t + \Lambda D_1 c(c_0, c_1)\, \widehat{\Lambda}_t \end{aligned}$$

[18]They propose a quite complicated method very recently developed by Sims, 2000.

$$-\rho_0\widehat{\rho}_{0,t} + \phi D_1x\left(c_0,c,n,a\right)\widehat{\phi}_t + \phi a D_{14}x\left(c_0,c,n,a\right)\widehat{a}_t \tag{A.3}$$

$$\begin{aligned} 0 = \quad & \phi n D_{13}x\left(c_1,c,n,a\right)\widehat{n}_t + \Lambda c_0 D_{21}c\left(c_0,c_1\right)\widehat{c}_{0,t} \\ & + \left[\phi c_1 D_{11}x\left(c_1,c,n,a\right) + \Lambda c_1 D_{22}c\left(c_0,c_1\right)\right]\widehat{c}_{1,t} + \phi c D_{12}x\left(c_1,c,n,a\right)\widehat{c}_t \\ & + \Lambda D_2c\left(c_0,c_1\right)\widehat{\Lambda}_t - \rho_1\widehat{\rho}_{1,t} + \phi D_1x\left(c_1,c,n,a\right)\widehat{\phi}_{t-1} \\ & + \phi a D_{14}x\left(c_1,c,n,a\right)\widehat{a}_t \end{aligned} \tag{A.4}$$

It should be noted that the equality of c_0, c_1 and c is not yet considered here in order to make clear the different derivatives of the x-function with respect to c_0, c_1 and c.[19] The condition for aggregate consumption results in

$$\begin{aligned} 0 = \quad & \left[nD_{12}u\left(c,n,a\right) + \phi n D_{23}x\left(c_0,c,n,a\right) + \phi n D_{23}x\left(c_1,c,n,a\right)\right]\widehat{n}_t \\ & + \phi c_0 D_{21}x\left(c_0,c,n,a\right)\widehat{c}_{0,t} + \phi c_1 D_{21}x\left(c_1,c,n,a\right)\widehat{c}_{1,t} \\ & + \left[cD_{11}u\left(c,n,a\right) + \phi c D_{22}x\left(c_0,c,n,a\right) + \phi c D_{22}x\left(c_1,c,n,a\right)\right]\widehat{c}_t \\ & - \Lambda\widehat{\Lambda}_t + \phi D_2x\left(c_0,c,n,a\right)\widehat{\phi}_t + \phi D_2x\left(c_1,c,n,a\right)\widehat{\phi}_{t-1} \\ & + \left[aD_{13}u\left(c,n,a\right) + \phi a D_{24}x\left(c_0,c,n,a\right) + \phi a D_{24}x\left(c_1,c,n,a\right)\right]\widehat{a}_t \end{aligned} \tag{A.5}$$

whereas for aggregate labor the linearized equation is

$$\begin{aligned} 0 = \quad & \left[nD_{22}u\left(c,n,a\right) + \phi n D_{33}x\left(c_0,c,n,a\right) + \phi n D_{33}x\left(c_1,c,n,a\right)\right]\widehat{n}_t \\ & + \phi c_0 D_{31}x\left(c_0,c,n,a\right)\widehat{c}_{0,t} + \phi c_1 D_{31}x\left(c_1,c,n,a\right)\widehat{c}_{1,t} \\ & + \left[cD_{21}u\left(c,n,a\right) + \phi c D_{32}x\left(c_0,c,n,a\right) + \phi c D_{32}x\left(c_1,c,n,a\right)\right]\widehat{c}_t \\ & + \Omega\widehat{\Omega}_t + \phi D_3x\left(c_0,c,n,a\right)\widehat{\phi}_t + \phi D_3x\left(c_1,c,n,a\right)\widehat{\phi}_{t-1} \\ & + \left[aD_{23}u\left(c,n,a\right) + \phi a D_{34}x\left(c_0,c,n,a\right) + \phi a D_{34}x\left(c_1,c,n,a\right)\right]\widehat{a}_t \end{aligned} \tag{A.6}$$

The production functions (resource constraints) must obey

$$0 = \widehat{n}_{0,t} - \widehat{c}_{0,t} + \widehat{a}_t \tag{A.7}$$

$$0 = \widehat{n}_{1,t} - \widehat{c}_{1,t} + \widehat{a}_t \tag{A.8}$$

and for the consumption aggregator one arrives at

$$0 = \frac{1}{2}\widehat{c}_{0,t} + \frac{1}{2}\widehat{c}_{1,t} - \widehat{c}_t \tag{A.9}$$

A crucial condition for the dynamic responses is the linearized implementation constraint:

$$\begin{aligned} & \beta n D_3x\left(c_1,c,n,a\right)\widehat{n}_{t+1} + \beta c_1 D_1x\left(c_1,c,n,a\right)\widehat{c}_{1,t+1} + \beta c D_2x\left(c_1,c,n,a\right)\widehat{c}_{t+1} \\ & = -nD_3x\left(c_0,c,n,a\right)\widehat{n}_t - c_0 D_1x\left(c_0,c,n,a\right)\widehat{c}_{0,t} - cD_2x\left(c_0,c,n,a\right)\widehat{c}_t \\ & - aD_4x\left(c_0,c,n,a\right)\widehat{a}_t - \beta a D_4x\left(c_1,c,n,a\right)\widehat{a}_{t+1} \end{aligned} \tag{A.10}$$

The labor resource constraint results in

$$0 = \frac{1}{2}\widehat{n}_{0,t} + \frac{1}{2}\widehat{n}_{1,t} - \widehat{n}_t \tag{A.11}$$

[19] $D_ix\left(\cdot\right)$ denotes the first partial derivative of the x-function with respect to the i-th argument. Similarly $D_{ij}x(\cdot)$ denotes the partial derivative of $D_ix(\cdot)$ with respect to the j-th argument.

So far the system contains eleven equations and twelve variables.[20] To close the system one has to add one extra equation. This is the tautology $\phi = \phi$ which is given in linearized form by

$$\widehat{\phi}_t = \widehat{\phi}_t \tag{A.12}$$

The linearized equations — nominal variables

As is known from the main text the nominal interest rate R_t is determined from the efficiency condition for bond holdings in the household's optimization plan (14). The real rate r_t was deduced via the Fisher equation (see (18)) so that the approximated equation is given by

$$\widehat{\lambda}_{t+1} = -\frac{r}{1+r}\widehat{r}_t + \widehat{\lambda}_t \tag{A.13}$$

where λ_t is equal to the marginal utility of consumption $\partial u(c_t, n_t, a_t)/\partial c_t$. This implies for the Taylor approximation

$$\begin{aligned} 0 = \quad & nD_{12}u\,(c,n,a)\,\widehat{n}_t + cD_{11}u\,(c,n,a)\,\widehat{c}_t - D_1u\,(c,n,a)\,\widehat{\lambda}_t \\ & +aD_{13}u\,(c,n,a)\,\widehat{a}_t \end{aligned} \tag{A.14}$$

The nominal interest rate follows, according to (17),

$$-\widehat{P}_{t+1} + \widehat{\lambda}_{t+1} = -\widehat{P}_t - \frac{R}{1+R}\widehat{R}_t + \widehat{\lambda}_t \tag{A.15}$$

in the approximated form, with R (respective r for the real rate) as the steady state values. As discussed earlier firms are unable to change their prices for two periods so $P_{0,t-1} = P_{1,t}$. The Taylor approximation for this condition is given by

$$0 = -\widehat{P}_{0,t-1} + \widehat{P}_{1,t} \tag{A.16}$$

Using the demand function (6) allows to determine the relation between $P_{0,t}$, $P_{1,t}$ and consumption.

$$\widehat{P}_{0,t} = -\frac{1}{\epsilon}\widehat{c}_{0,t} + \frac{1}{\epsilon}\widehat{c}_{1,t} + \widehat{P}_{1,t} \tag{A.17}$$

The price level is uniquely determined since $P_{1,t}$ is predetermined and $P_{0,t}$ is given by (A.17). Using (8) one gets

$$0 = \frac{1}{2}\widehat{P}_{0,t} + \frac{1}{2}\widehat{P}_{1,t} - \widehat{P}_t \tag{A.18}$$

The cyclical behavior of money demand can be deduced from (16).

$$0 = \widehat{c}_t + \widehat{P}_t - \widehat{M}_t \tag{A.19}$$

Since there are now eight new variables $\left(\hat{\lambda}_t, \hat{r}_t, \hat{R}_t, \hat{P}_t, \hat{P}_{0,t}, \hat{P}_{0,t-1}, \hat{P}_{1,t}, \hat{M}_t\right)$ but only seven equations another tautology must be added to the model. This is

$$\widehat{P}_{0,t} = \widehat{P}_{0,t} \tag{A.20}$$

Impulse response functions

[20] The twelfth variable is $\widehat{\phi}_{t-1}$.

Figure A.1. Impulse Response Functions for $\widehat{a}_t, \widehat{c}_t, \widehat{\phi}_t, \widehat{n}_t$

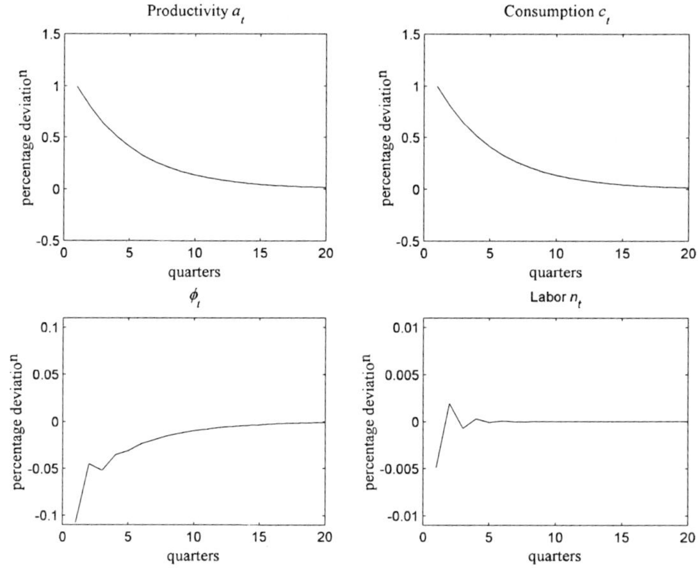

Figure A.2. Impulse Response Functions for $\widehat{n}_{0,t}, \widehat{n}_{1,t}, \widehat{c}_{0,t}, \widehat{c}_{1,t}$

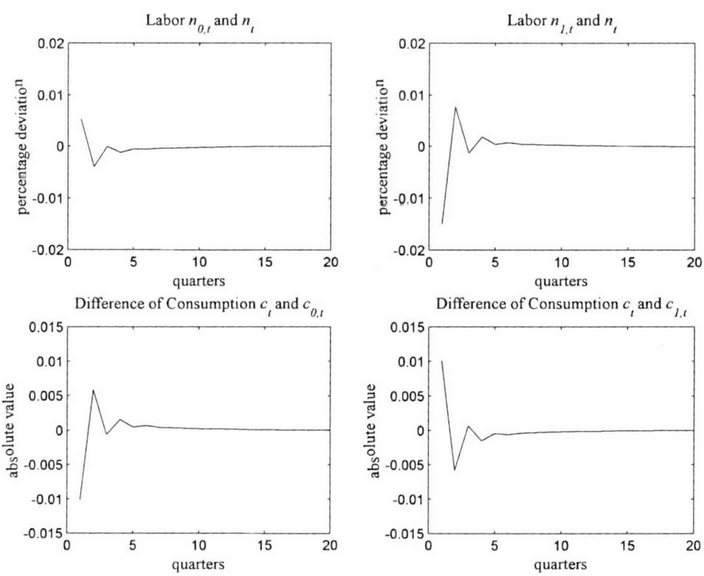

Figure A.3. Impulse Response Functions for $\widehat{P}_{0,t}, \widehat{P}_{1,t}, \widehat{P}_t, \widehat{\Pi}_t$

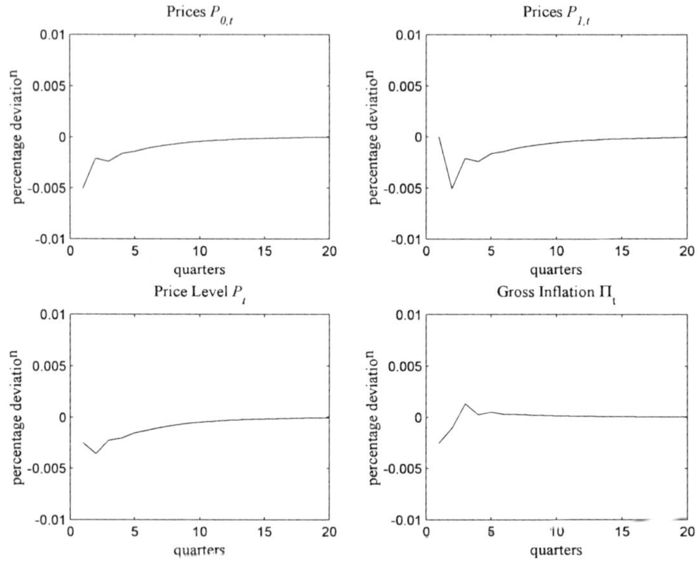

Figure A.4. Impulse Response Functions for $\widehat{R}_t, \widehat{r}_t, \widehat{M_t}$

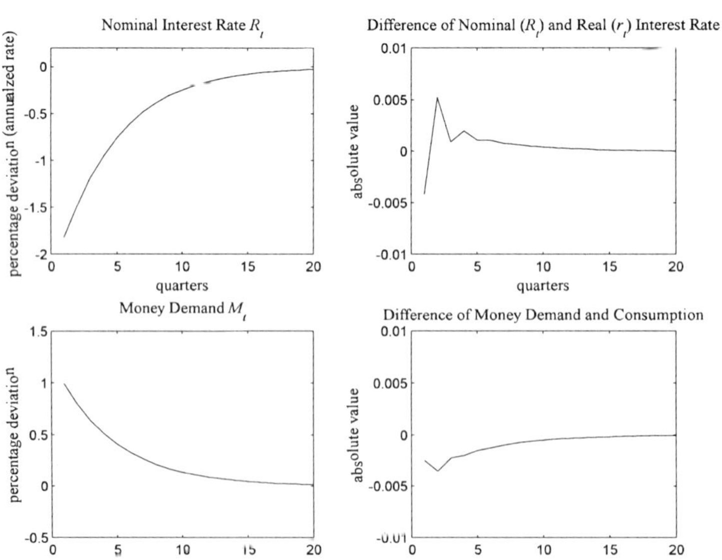

Figure A.5. Impulse Response Functions for $\widehat{P}_{0,t}, \widehat{P}_{1,t}, \widehat{P}_t, \widehat{\Pi}_t$, σ=10

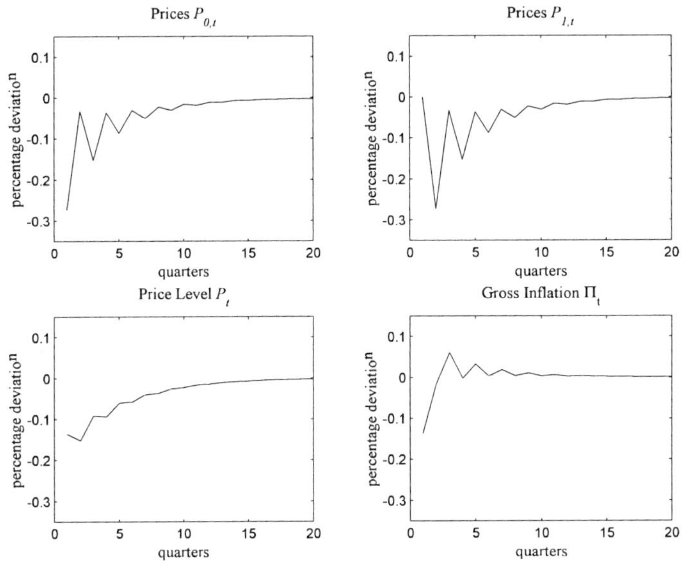

Figure A.6. Impulse Response Functions for $\widehat{P}_{0,t}, \widehat{P}_{1,t}, \widehat{P}_t, \widehat{\Pi}_t$, 5-period price setting, equal fractions

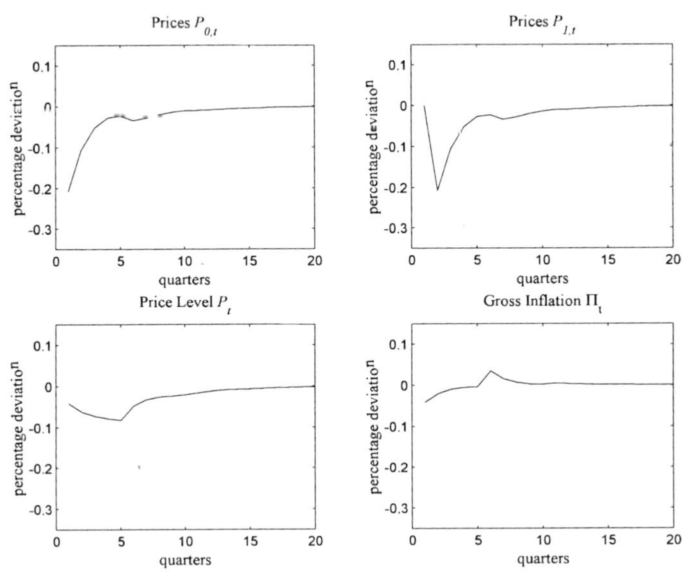

Figure A.7. Impulse Response Functions for $\widehat{P}_{0,t}, \widehat{P}_{1,t}, \widehat{P}_t, \widehat{\Pi}_t$, 5-period price setting, different fractions

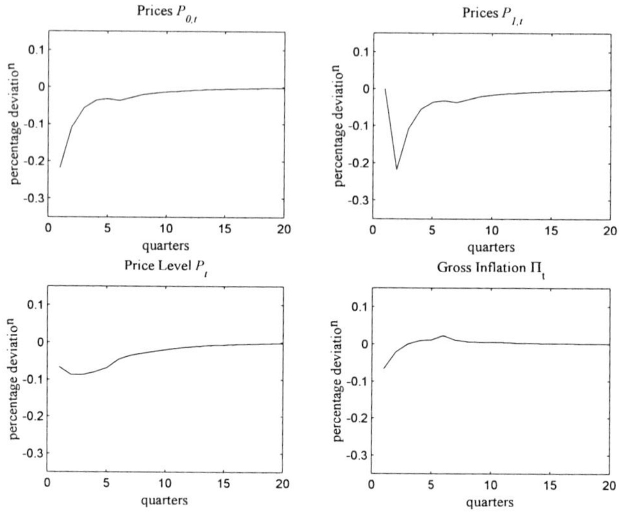

Figure A.8. Impulse Response Functions for $\widehat{R}_t, \widehat{P}_{0,t}, \widehat{P}_t, \widehat{\Pi}_t$, AR(2) productivity shock

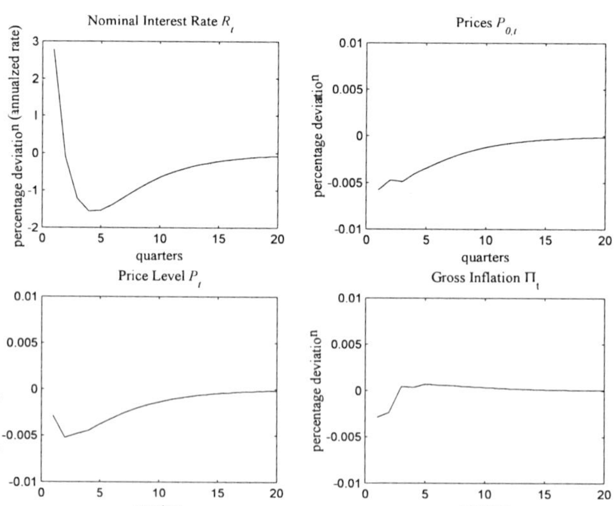

Figure A.9. Impulse Response Functions for $\widehat{R}_t, \widehat{P}_{0,t}, \widehat{P}_t, \widehat{\Pi}_t$, ARIMA(1,1,0) productivity shock

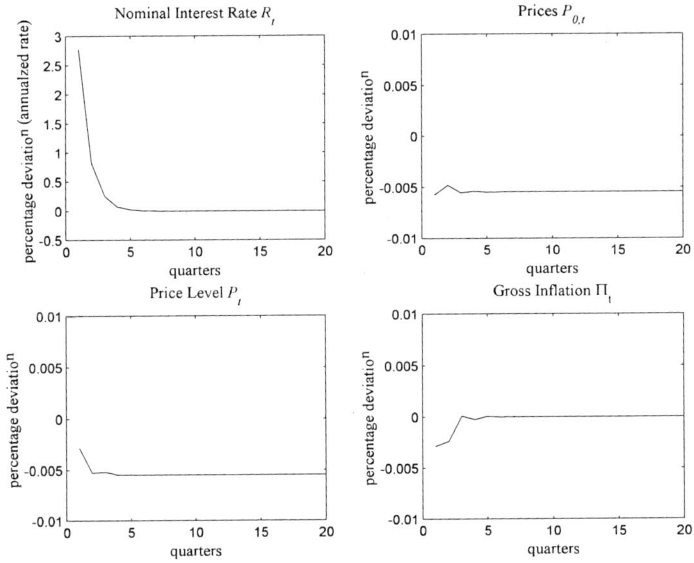

References

Blanchard, Olivier J. and Nobuhiro Kiyotaki (1987). Monopolistic competition and the effects of aggregate demand. *American Economic Review*, 77:647-666.

Barro, Robert J. and David B. Gordon (1983). Rules, discretion and reputation in a model of monetary policy. *Journal of Monetary Economics*, 12:101-121.

Calvo, Guillermo A. (1983). Staggered prices in a utility-maximizing framework. *Journal of Monetary Economics*, 12:383-398.

Dixit, Avinash and Joseph Stiglitz (1977). Monopolistic competition and optimum product diversity. *American Economic Review*, 67:297-308.

Dotsey, Michael, Robert G. King and Alexander L. Wolman (1997). State dependent pricing and the dynamics of business cycles. Federal Reserve Bank of Richmond, Working Paper 97-2. February.

Dotsey, Michael, Robert G. King and Alexander L. Wolman (1999). State dependent pricing and the general equilibrium dynamics of money and output. *Quarterly Journal of Economics*, 114:655-690.

Erceg, Christopher J., Dale W. Henderson and Andrew T. Lewin (2000). Optimal monetary policy with staggered wage and price contracts. *Journal of Monetary Economics*, 46:281-313.

Goodfriend, Marvin and Robert G. King (1997). The New Neoclassical synthesis and the role of monetary policy, in: Bernanke, Ben S. and Julio J. Rotemberg (eds.), *NBER Macroeconomics Annual 1997*. MIT Press. Cambridge, MA.

Greenwood, Jeremy, Zvi Hercowitz and Gregory W. Huffman (1988). Investment, capacity utilization and the real business cycle. *American Economic Review*, 78:402-417.

Henderson, Dale W. and Jinill Kim (1999). Exact utilities under alternative monetary rules in a simple macro model with optimizing agents. *International Tax and Public Finance*, 6:507-535.

Kim, Jinill and Sunghyun Henry Kim (2000). Spurious welfare reversals in international business cycle models. Working Paper, University of Virginia and Brandeis University. December. Revised Version.

King, Robert G., Charles I. Plosser and Sergio T. Rebelo (1988). Production, growth and business cycles i: the basic neoclassical model. *Journal of Monetary Economics*, 21:195-232.

King, Robert G., Charles I. Plosser and Sergio T. Rebelo (1990). Production, growth and business cycles. Technical Appendix. University of Rochester. May. Revised Version.

King, Robert G. and Mark W. Watson (1997). System reduction and solution algorithms for singular linear difference systems under rational expectations. Working Paper, University of Virginia and Princeton University. October. Revised Version.

King, Robert G. and Mark W. Watson (1999). The solution of singular linear difference systems under rational expectations. *International Economic Review*, 39:1015-1026.

King, Robert G. and Alexander L. Wolman (1996). Inflation targeting in a St. Louis Model of the 21st Century. *Federal Reserve Bank of St. Louis Review*, 78:83-107.

King, Robert G. and Alexander L. Wolman (1999). What should the monetary authority do when prices are sticky? in: Taylor, John B. (ed.), *Monetary Policy Rules.* University of Chicago Press. Chicago and London.

Kydland, Finn E. and Edward C. Prescott (1977). Rules rather than discretion: the inconsistency of optimal plans. *Journal of Political Economy*, 85:473-491.

Rotemberg, Julio J. (1987). The New Keynesian Microfoundations, in: Blanchard, Olivier J. and Stanley Fischer (eds.), *NBER Macroeconomics Annual 1987.* MIT Press. Cambridge, MA.

Sims, Christopher A. (2000). Second order accurate solution of discrete time dynamic equilibrium models. Working Paper, Princeton University. December.

Svensson, Lars E. O. (1999). Inflation targeting as a monetary policy rule. *Journal of Monetary Economics*, 43:607-654.

Taylor, John B. (1980). Aggregate dynamics and staggered contracts. *Journal of Political Economy*, 88:1-24.

Tobin, James (1977). How dead is Keynes? *Economic Inquiry*, 15:459-468.

Woodford, Michael (2001). Inflation stabilization and welfare, NBER Working Paper No. 8071. January.

III

Indeterminacy and Irreversibility

Chapter 7: Real Indeterminacy in a Cash–In–Advance Economy.

Stéphane Auray
LEN-C3E, Université de Nantes & GREMAQ, Université de Toulouse I, France

Fabrice Collard
GREMAQ, Université de Toulouse I & CNRS, France

Patrick Fève
GREMAQ, Université de Toulouse I & IDEI, France

Abstract This paper studies the dynamic properties of a highly stylized monetary economy in which an infinitely–lived representative household can transfer wealth from one period to another relying on money and is cash–constrained on the good market. We show that a low intertemporal substitution resulting from preferences can generate real indeterminacy. This result is illustrated by four showcases: isoelastic utility function, minimum consumption, internal habit and external habit. We further show that real indeterminacy is not sufficient *per se* to obtain an empirically relevant representation of the effects of monetary policy. The form of the beliefs matters.

1. Introduction

Modern macroeconomics largely builds on explicitly dynamic models, which — in some cases — yield multiplicity of equilibria. The existence of real indeterminacy in dynamic models means that there exist an infinite number of arbitrarily close equilibria which all converge to the same steady state. After having long been considered as a theoretical curiosity, this property is now perceived to constitute a route worth pursuing to account for aggregate fluctuations (see Benhabib and Farmer, 1999 for a survey in macroeconomics).

Benhabib and Farmer, 1999 pointed out that most of monetary business cycles models relying on cash–in–advance (CIA hereafter) or money–

in–the–utility–function specifications exhibit a unique rational expectations equilibrium (see Cooley and Hansen, 1989 and Hairault and Portier, 1993a, 1993b, among others). One possible reason for these calibrated models of money to produce determinacy is that they rely on too simple — or too restrictive — specifications for preferences and technology. Once some assumptions are relaxed, monetary models are not immune to real indeterminacy (see Matsuyama, 1990, Woodford, 1988, 1994, Benhabib and Farmer, 1996, Farmer, 1997 and Bloise et al., 1999, among others). The present paper follows this route and attempts to show that real indeterminacy can occur in a dynamic monetary model where simple mechanisms that lower intertemporal substitution are taken into account.

The paper introduces four showcases (isoelastic utility function, minimum consumption, internal and external habit persistence) and characterizes the local dynamics properties of a CIA model.[1] Our main contribution is to show that it is not necessary to strongly depart from standard assumptions on preferences and technology to generate real indeterminacy. For each considered CIA model, real indeterminacy occurs for plausible values of the structural parameters. In order to illustrate this phenomenon, we first propose an highly stylized CIA model. In each showcase, the level of intertemporal substitution in consumption decisions is ruled by a single parameter. This allows us to easily determine the local dynamic properties of the economy and to make clear the main mechanisms that generate real indeterminacy. We first show that low enough intertemporal substitution generates real indeterminacy. When individuals face the same positive belief on future inflation, higher expected inflation leads them to substitute current for future consumption. This translates into higher money demand for tomorrow when intertemporal complementarity is strong enough, putting upward pressure on prices. Then inflation expectations become self–fulfilling. Nevertheless we show that real indeterminacy is not sufficient *per se* to generate a positive effect of the monetary policy, the form of the beliefs matters a lot. Indeed when beliefs are not correlated with money injection, the model generates perfect price flexibility and money is neutral. Conversely when beliefs are correlated with money injections, the model displays endogenous price stickiness associated with a positive and persistent response of output.

The paper is organized as follows. A first section presents a simple monetary economy. Section 2 characterizes the conditions for real in-

[1]Our specification nests the standard specifications of time separable utility function used in business cycles models with money.

determinacy for alternative representations of the preferences. Section 3 presents some quantitative implications of real indeterminacy. A last section offers some concluding remarks.

2. A simple monetary economy

The economy is comprised of a unit mass continuum of identical infinitely lived agents. Each household has preferences over consumption and leisure represented by the following intertemporal utility function:

$$\max E_t \sum_{\tau=0}^{\infty} \beta^{\tau} u\left(c^{\star}_{t+\tau}, h_{t+\tau}\right)$$

where $\beta \in (0,1)$ is the discount factor, h_t denotes hours supplied by the household, and $c^{\star}_t$ is the flow of consumption services in period t which is assumed to take the following linear form:

$$c^{\star}_t = c_t - \theta c_{t-1} - x_t - c \tag{1}$$

where the parameter $\theta \in (0,1)$ denotes the internal habit persistence parameter, $x_t > 0$ an external habit and $c \geqslant 0$ a constant minimum consumption. In what follows, we assume that external habit is a linear function of past aggregate consumption,

$$x_t = aC_{t-1}$$

where $a \in (0,1)$ is the external habit parameter and C_t denotes the aggregate consumption. The habit stock x_t is taken as given by households and therefore acts as an externality. Equation (1) nests several representations of the preferences. For instance, when $\theta = a = c = 0$, we recover the usual time separable utility function. When $a = c = 0$, but $0 < \theta < 1$, current consumption decisions display complementarities with past consumption decisions, which corresponds to internal habit formation. Intertemporal complementarities are still present in the case of minimum consumption ($c > 0$) or external habit ($a > 0$).

The household's preferences are represented by the following utility function:

$$\begin{aligned} u\left(c^{\star}_t, h_t\right) &= \frac{c^{\star\,1-\sigma}_t}{1-\sigma} - h_t \quad \text{if } \sigma \in]0,1[\cup]1,\infty[\qquad (2) \\ &= \log(c^{\star}_t) - h_t \quad \text{if } \sigma = 1 \end{aligned}$$

The linearity of the utility function in h_t amounts to the Hansen's, 1985, assumption of labor indivisibility.[2] We introduce here an additional parameter σ that allows to large (small σ) or small (large σ) intertemporal substitution. Given the specification of the utility function and flow of consumption services, we will characterize the implications of changes in σ, c, θ and a on the dynamic properties of the economy.

The household enters period t with real balances m_t/P_t carried from the previous period, as a mean to transfer wealth from one period to another. The household supplies hours on the labor market at the real wage W_t. During the period the household receives a lump–sum transfer of cash equal to N_t/P_t. These revenues are then used to purchase the consumption bundle c_t and money balances m_{t+1}/P_t for the next period. Therefore, the budget constraint is given by:

$$\frac{m_{t+1}}{P_t} + c_t \leq \frac{m_t + N_t}{P_t} + w_t h_t \tag{3}$$

Money is held because the household must carry cash – money acquired in the previous period and the money lump sum transfert – in order to purchase goods. It therefore faces a standard cash–in–advance constraint of the form:

$$c_t \leq \frac{m_t + N_t}{P_t} \tag{4}$$

Note that below, we will focus on equilibria in which the constraint binds. Implicit in this is that we will consider equilibria where the gross nominal interest rate exceeds unity or equivalently where the inflation rate is strictly positive, which will turn out to be the case for the specification of the shock we will consider.

The household then determines its optimal consumption/money holdings and labor supply plans maximizing (2) subject to the budget (3) and cash–in–advance (4) constraints. Consumption behavior together with labor supply yield

$$\begin{aligned} \tfrac{1}{W_t} = \beta E_t \tfrac{P_t}{P_{t+1}} \Big[& (c_{t+1} - \theta c_t - aC_t - c)^{-\sigma} \\ & -\beta\theta \left(c_{t+2} - \theta c_{t+1} - aC_{t+1} - c\right)^{-\sigma} \Big] \end{aligned}$$

The technology is simply described by a constant return to scale production function $y_t = h_t$, such that in equilibrium the real wage is

[2]We choose this specification of hours supplied in order to simplify the analytical results. Nevertheless, the qualitative dynamic properties of the monetary economy are left unaffected when this assumption is relaxed.

$W_t = 1$. Money is exogenously supplied by the central bank according to the following money growth rule:

$$M_{t+1} = g_t M_t$$

where $g_t \geqslant 1$ is the gross rate of growth of money such that $N_t = M_{t+1} - M_t = (g_t - 1)M_t$. The good and labor markets clearing conditions imply $y_t = c_t = h_t$ and market clearing requires $m_{t+1} = M_{t+1} = M_t + N_t$. Finally in equilibrium, we have $c_t = C_t$ for every period. Since the cash constraint is binding, using the money growth rule the equilibrium reduces to the following finite difference equation:

$$\begin{aligned} y_t = \beta E_t \tfrac{y_{t+1}}{g_{t+1}} \Big[& (y_{t+1} - (\theta + a)y_t - c)^{-\sigma} \\ & -\beta\theta \left(y_{t+2} - (\theta + a)y_{t+1} - c\right)^{-\sigma} \Big] \end{aligned} \tag{5}$$

Equation (5) defines the dynamic properties of output and therefore constitutes the key relation that we will be dealing with in the sequel.

3. Four tales for real indeterminacy

We now study the dynamic properties of the monetary model about the deterministic steady state[3] y. Four cases are successively analyzed and compared. We choose to restrict our attention to a unique mechanism of intertemporal substitution that can be summarized in each case by a single parameter. This allows us to clarify the presentation of the analytical results and to isolate the main mechanisms that generate real indeterminacy.

Case 1. Isoelastic utility function ($\sigma \neq 1$, $c = 0$, $\theta = 0$ and $a = 0$) In this case, the utility is time separable and intertemporal substitution stems only from the values of σ as established by the following proposition.

Proposition 1 *If $\sigma > 2$, then the equilibrium is locally indeterminate.*

Proposition 1 shows that indeterminacy occurs for σ sufficiently large, *i.e.* when intertemporal substitution is low enough (see *e.g.* Woodford, 1994, Carlstrom and Fuerst, 1998, Farmer, 1999, Bloise et al., 1999). Figure 1 illustrates proposition 1. The solid line represents the values of the root of the characteristic equation associated with equation (5) with respect to σ. The shaded area corresponds to values of $\sigma \in]0, 1[\cup]1, 2]$ for which the equilibrium is totally determinate.

[3]It is straightforward to verify the existence and uniqueness of the steady state.

Figure 1. Regions of Determinacy and Indeterminacy (σ, λ)

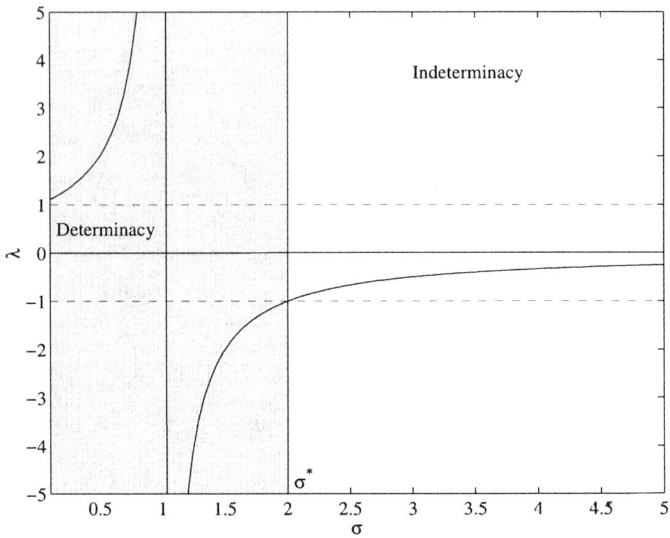

Note : The figure of the root is drawn for $\sigma \neq 1$, $c = 0$, $\theta = 0$ and $a = 0$

The threshold value of θ that allows for indeterminacy is equal to 2. This value is close to the usual calibrated value in business cycle models (see Kydland and Prescott, 1991). It follows that it is not necessary to strongly depart from standard calibration of σ to obtain real indeterminacy. The root is always negative when the condition for indeterminacy is fulfilled (see Figure 1). In this case, the model cannot generate persistent fluctuations in aggregate data. At the limit (when $\sigma \to \infty$), the root is zero.

Case 2. Minimum consumption ($\sigma = 1$, $c > 0$, $\theta = 0$ and $a = 0$)
We now study the effect of a minimum consumption $c > 0$. There exists strong evidence for minimum consumption requirement. For instance, using panel data on Indian villagers, Atkeson and Ogaki, 1996 and Rosenzweig and Wolpin, 1993 report minimum consumption requirements estimates that amount to a significant fraction of total consumption expenditures of the average household. We model this consumption requirements as a fraction, $\alpha \in (0, 1)$, of the steady state consumption.

Proposition 2 *The equilibrium is locally indeterminate when* $\alpha > 1/2$.

Proposition 2 shows that real indeterminacy occurs for α sufficiently large — *i.e.* when minimum consumption is large enough. This large minimum consumption induces an intertemporal complementarity in consumption choices, thus breaking the intertemporal substitution mechanism. It is worth noting that real indeterminacy occurs for a reasonable value of minimum consumption. Indeed, the threshold value 1/2 of α is below the values estimated reported by Atkeson and Ogaki, 1996, which is equal to 58%, and Rosenzweig and Wolpin, 1993, which is equal to 80%. The root is always negative, whatever the value of $\alpha \in (0, 1)$ (see

Figure 2. Regions of Determinacy and Indeterminacy (α, λ)

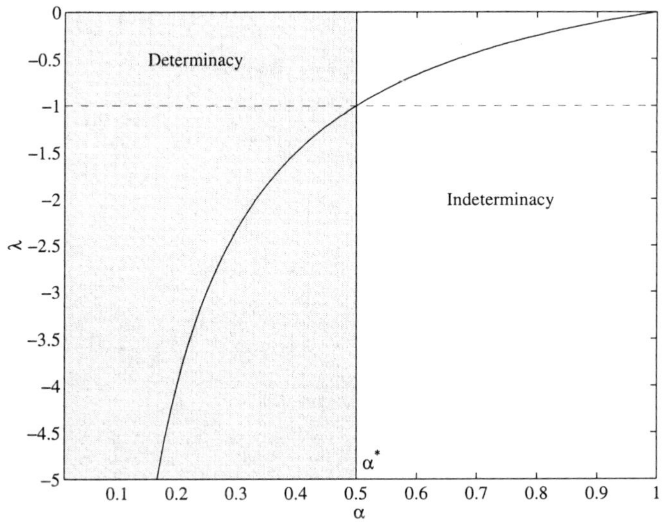

Note : The figure of the root is drawn for $\sigma = 1$, $c > 0$, $\theta = 0$ and $a = 0$

Figure 2). As in the previous case, the model cannot produce persistent fluctuations in aggregate data. In the limiting case of a minimum consumption equal to steady state consumption ($\alpha = 1$), the root is equal to zero. It is worth noting that these two first cases display very similar dynamic properties: the root is always negative and real indeterminacy emerges when intertemporal motives in consumption decisions are low enough.

Case 3. Internal habit ($\sigma = 1$, $c = 0$, $\theta > 0$ and $a = 0$)
We now study the dynamic effect of internal habit. This case is a little bit more complicated as it involves a second order difference equation and an additional predetermined variable (past consumption). It follows that the dynamics properties depend on the position of two eigenvalues

with respect to the unit circle. In this case, real indeterminacy occurs when one of the two roots lies inside the unit circle.

Proposition 3 *There exists a unique $0 < \theta^\star < 1$, such that the equilibrium is locally indeterminate when $\theta > \theta^\star$.*

Proposition 3 establishes that, for a given value of the discount factor (β), there exists a value of the habit persistence parameter above which prophecies become self–fulfilling, yielding real indeterminacy. Figure 3 illustrates this phenomenon.

Figure 3. Regions of Determinacy and Indeterminacy (θ, λ)

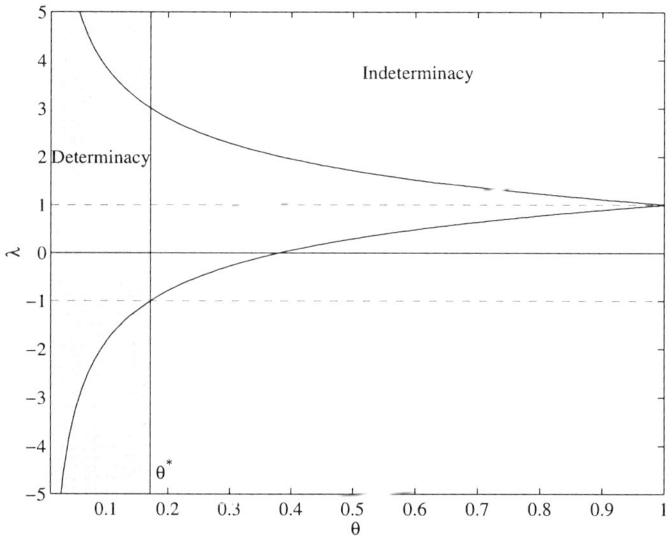

Note : The figure of the two roots is drawn for $\beta = 0.99$, $\sigma = 1$, $c = 0$, $\theta > 0$ and $a = 0$.

The two curves are the roots of the characteristic polynomial and the shaded area corresponds to values of $\theta \in (0, 1)$ for which the equilibrium is totally determinate. Then above $\theta^\star$ the equilibrium becomes indeterminate as one of the two roots of the characteristic polynomial lies inside the unit circle. The threshold value for real indeterminacy $\theta^\star$ of θ is given by:

$$\theta^\star = \frac{3(1+\beta) - \sqrt{9(1+\beta)^2 - 4\beta}}{2\beta}$$

for which it is easy to verify that $0 < \theta^\star < 1$. It is worth noting that contrary to the previous cases, there exist a value $\tilde{\theta}$ of θ such that the stable root is positive. The value of $\tilde{\theta}$ is given by:

$$\tilde{\theta} = \frac{2 + \beta - \sqrt{\beta^2 + 4}}{2\beta}$$

and verifies $0 < \theta^* < \tilde{\theta} < 1$. For instance, when $\beta = 0.99$, the stable root is positive if $\theta > \tilde{\theta} = 0.38$ and the model with internal habit produces persistence in aggregate data. Interestingly, real indeterminacy and aggregate persistence occur for reasonable values of the internal habit parameter. Empirical studies suggest parameter estimates for θ that exceed significantly the minimal value of θ that yields indeterminacy ($\theta^\star = 0.17$ when $\beta = 0.99$). For instance, Constantidines and Ferson, 1991 or Braun et al., 1993 obtain on macro data a value of θ that lies within the range [0.5,0.9]. On micro data, habit persistence appears to be lower but still significant. Naik and Moore, 1996 report estimates for habit persistence on food consumption data of 0.486, which is far both above the threshold value yielding indeterminacy ($\theta^\star = 0.17$ when $\beta = 0.99$) and persistence ($\tilde{\theta} = 0.38$ when $\beta = 0.99$) in our economy.

Case 4. External habit ($\sigma = 1$, $c = 0$, $\theta = 0$ and $a > 0$)
We present the dynamic property of the monetary model with external habit.

Proposition 4 *If $a > 1/3$, then the equilibrium is locally indeterminate.*

Proposition 4 shows that there exists a value of the external habit parameter above which real indeterminacy occurs (see Figure 4). As in the case of internal habit, there also exists a value $\tilde{a} = 1/2$ of a for which the root is positive. The threshold value of the external habit parameter for real indeterminacy exceeds the value of the internal one. Moreover, a similar result holds for a stable positive root, because $\tilde{\theta} < 1/2$ for all positive value of β. As in the previous case, indeterminacy and persistence occur for reasonable values of the habit formation parameter.

4. Quantitative implications of real indeterminacy

We discuss some quantitative implications of our simple model which illustrate its ability to account for persistent real positive effects of monetary policy and potential beliefs based price stickiness. Among the four showcase, we present here the quantitative implications of a stochastic version of the internal habit model. The output dynamics is then

Figure 4. Regions of Determinacy and Indeterminacy (a, λ)

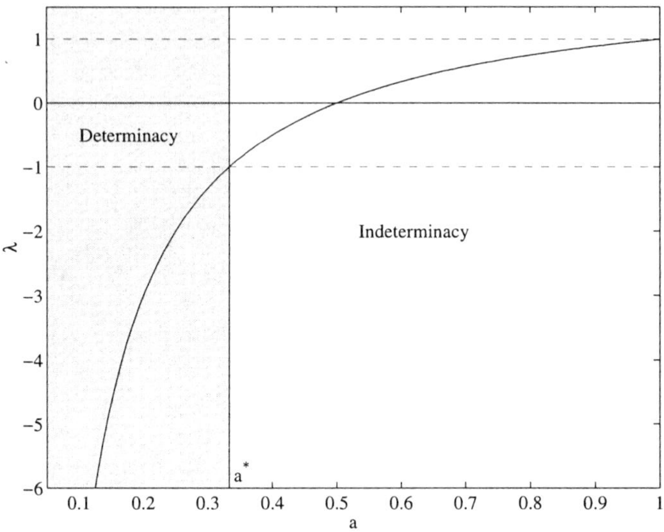

Note : The figure of the root is drawn for $\sigma = 1$, $c = 0$, $\theta = 0$ and $a > 0$

described by the second–order finite difference equation

$$E_t\widehat{y}_{t+2} - \frac{1+\beta}{\beta}E_t\widehat{y}_{t+1} + \left[\frac{1}{\beta} - \frac{(1-\theta)(1-\theta\beta)}{\beta\theta}\right]\widehat{y}_t$$
$$= \frac{(1-\theta)(1-\theta\beta)}{\beta\theta}E_t\widehat{g}_{t+1}$$

where E_t denotes the expectation operator conditional on the information set available in period t. $\widehat{g}_t$ is the percent change in the money supply. For simplicity, we assume that g_t evolves as an exogenous AR(1) process $\widehat{g}_{t+1} = \rho_g\widehat{g}_t + \varepsilon^g_{t+1}$ where $|\rho_g| < 1$ and ε^g is a white noise with variance σ^2_ε. We focus on solutions associated with indeterminate equilibrium. In such cases, we have

$$\widehat{y}_t = \mu\widehat{y}_{t-1} - \frac{\rho_g}{\lambda - \rho_g}\frac{(1-\theta)(1-\theta\beta)}{\beta\theta}\widehat{g}_{t-1} + \varepsilon^y_t$$

where ε^y_t denotes a martingale difference sequence that can be related to fundamental shocks (money shocks), depending on individuals beliefs about monetary policy. In others, the random variable ε^y_t writes

$$\varepsilon^y_t = b\varepsilon^g_t + \nu_t \tag{6}$$

with $E_{t-1}\nu_t = 0$ and $|b| < \infty$. ν_t denotes pure extrinsic beliefs that are unrelated to fundamentals. The parameter b rules the dependency of agents beliefs to fundamentals. This parameter is an extrinsic characteristic of agents beliefs and its value is critical for the properties of the equilibrium.[4] Let us consider the case where $\rho_g = 0$ and $\nu_t = 0$. Given (6), inflation and output dynamics are given by

$$\begin{aligned}
\widehat{y}_t &= \mu\widehat{y}_{t-1} + b\varepsilon_t^g \\
\widehat{\pi}_t &= (1-\mu)\widehat{y}_{t-1} + (1-b)\varepsilon_t^g = \mu\widehat{\pi}_{t-1} + (1-b)\varepsilon_t^g + (b-\mu)\varepsilon_{t-1}^g
\end{aligned}$$

The model can generate persistence, provided $\mu > 0$. However, real indeterminacy is not *per se* sufficient to generate the monetary transmission mechanism (output increases in face of a positive money injection), additional assumptions have to be placed on individuals' beliefs. Let us first consider the case where b=0, such that the above system reduces to $\widehat{y}_t = \mu\widehat{y}_{t-1}$ and $\widehat{\pi}_t = \varepsilon_t^g$. Money is neutral and the inflation rate responds one for one to a money injection. This case corresponds to a full price flexibility situation and we retrieve the quantitative theory of money, which can then be associated with a particular form of beliefs where agents do not trust in money. We now investigate a situation where individuals' beliefs are positively correlated with the money supply shock — agents trust in money — such that b=1. The output/inflation dynamics then rewrites $\widehat{y}_t = \mu\widehat{y}_{t-1} + \varepsilon_t^g$ and $\widehat{\pi}_t = (1-\mu)\widehat{y}_{t-1} = \mu\widehat{\pi}_{t-1} + (1-\mu)\varepsilon_{t-1}^g$ Then, output responds instantaneously one for one to a one percent change in money supply. The model generates price stickiness, as the inflation rate does not respond instantaneously to the current money supply shock, but rather takes one lag to adjust partially. Price stickiness does not result from any assumptions on the good market (like predetermined price setting, or nominal price contracts), but rather derives from particular individual beliefs concerning the monetary policy.

Figure 5 reports the impulse response functions of output and the inflation rate with respect to a one percent money supply shock, for several levels of habit persistence. The model possesses internal propagation mechanisms provided that θ is high enough ($\theta > \tilde{\theta} \approx 0.38$). Although $\rho_g = 0$, output and inflation remain above their steady state value for more than one period. After their initial shift, they go back steadily to their long–run value. Further, the higher θ is, the longer it takes to output and inflation to go back to their steady state. Conversely, when θ is small, the model generates negative serial correlation both in output and the inflation rate.

[4] See Benhabib and Farmer, 2000 and Matheny, 1998.

Figure 5. Impulse Response Functions (1% money growth shock)

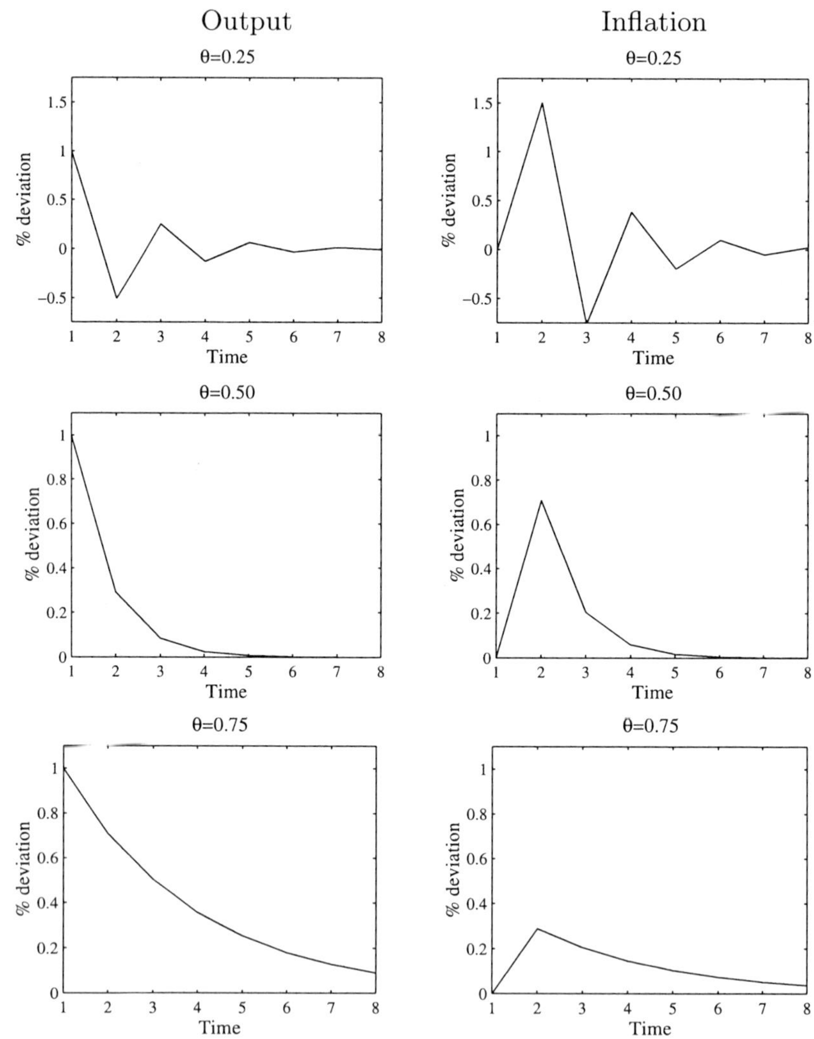

Note : These figures are drawn for $\beta = 0.99$, $\rho_g = 0$ and $b = 1$.

Table 1 reports the first order autocorrelation of output and inflation rate for the two polar views of price flexibility in the economy and various levels of monetary persistence and habit persistence.

Table 1. First–order autocorrelation

	b=0				b=1			
	ρ_g=0		ρ_g=0.5		ρ_g=0		ρ_g=0.5	
θ	(y)	(π)	(y)	(π)	(y)	(π)	(y)	(π)
0.25	–	0.00	-0.01	0.26	-0.50	-0.50	-0.62	-0.45
0.50	–	0.00	0.69	0.56	0.29	0.29	0.08	0.29
0.75	–	0.00	0.89	0.53	0.71	0.71	0.66	0.56

Note: These numbers were obtained for $\beta = 0.99$, $\sigma_g = 0.009$ and $\nu_t = 0 \ \forall t$.

A first implication of our model is that under the flexible price regime ($b = 0$) output does not respond to money injection and inflation does not display any persistence, when money growth is i.i.d. Conversely, under sticky price beliefs ($b = 1$), both output and the inflation rate display persistence. In particular, when θ=0.75, output persistence is of about 0.70 and the inflation rate displays the same high degree of persistence. If we now have a look at the implications of a persistent money growth, things changes significantly as the sticky price economy experiments less persistence than the flexible price economy. Indeed, in the flexible price economy, agents have no confidence in money, so that a persistent money injection leads them to cut down their consumption. Habit persistence only reinforces this effect. In the sticky price economy, individuals respond positively to a money injection as they trust in money. In the subsequent periods, this effect does not play anymore and individuals expect a persistent inflation tax effect, which leads them to reduce their consumption, even though they have habit persistence. The persistent inflation tax weakens the habit persistence mechanism.

5. Concluding remarks

The paper introduces various specifications of the utility function as a device to obtain real indeterminacy in an infinitely–lived agents monetary model with cash–in–advance constraint. Using a simple model where fiat money is the only disposable asset to allocate wealth intertemporally, we provide conditions on preferences to obtain self–fulfilling prophecies. These conditions essentially state that real indeterminacy occurs when intertemporal complementarity in consumption choices is sufficiently pronounced. However real indeterminacy is not sufficient *per se* to generate the monetary transmission mechanism. Two conditions have to be fullfilled: *(i)* beliefs should matter and *(ii)* beliefs should be positively related to money injection.

Several issues may then be worth considering. The robustness of our results may be checked against other monetary arrangements, such as money–in–the–utility–functions, shopping time endowment or introducing other assets (see Auray et al., 2001), or alternative specifications for preferences and technology (see Benhabib and Farmer, 2000 and Matheny, 1998). Finally one may assess the ability of monetary policy to rule out real indeterminacy.

Acknowledgments

We wish to thank J.P. Benassy, S. Bosi, R. Farmer, M. Guillard, P-Y. Hénin, F. Langot and D. Laskar for helpful comments. This paper has also benefited from discussions during presentation at Cepremap seminar and 5th T2M Meeting (Nanterre, 2000). All remaining errors are our own.

Appendix

Proof of Proposition 1. The log–linearization of (5) around $\bar{y}$ yields the following linear first order finite difference equation:

$$\widehat{y}_{t+1} = \frac{1}{1-\sigma}\widehat{y}_t$$

The root is positive and exceeds one if $\sigma \in (0,1)$. Conversely, the root is negative if $\sigma > 1$ and its modulus less than one if $\sigma > 2$.

□

Proof of Proposition 2. The log–linearization of (5) around $\bar{y}$ yields the following linear first order finite difference equation:

$$\widehat{y}_{t+1} = -\frac{1-\alpha}{\alpha}\widehat{y}_t$$

The root is always negative for $\alpha \in (0,1)$ and its modulus less than one if $\alpha > 1/2$.

□

Proof of Proposition 3. The log–linearization of (5) around $\bar{y}$ yields the following linear second order finite difference equation:

$$\widehat{y}_{t+2} - \frac{1+\beta}{\beta}\widehat{y}_{t+1} + \left[\frac{1}{\beta} - \frac{(1-\theta)(1-\theta\beta)}{\theta\beta}\right]\widehat{y}_t = 0$$

The characteristic polynomial associated to the above equation is given by:

$$P(\lambda) = \lambda^2 - \frac{1+\beta}{\beta}\lambda + \left[\frac{1}{\beta} - \frac{(1-\theta)(1-\theta\beta)}{\theta}\right]$$

First note that the two eigenvalues are real because the discriminant of $P(.)$ is strictly positive. Moreover, the characteristic polynomial verifies:

$$\begin{aligned} P(1) &= -\frac{(1-\theta)(1-\theta\beta)}{\theta\beta} \\ P(-1) &= \frac{2(1+\beta)}{\beta} - \frac{(1-\theta)(1-\theta\beta)}{\theta\beta} \\ P'(\lambda) &\lesseqqgtr 0 \text{ for } \lambda \lesseqqgtr \lambda^\star, \text{ with } \lambda^\star = \frac{1+\beta}{2\beta} \end{aligned}$$

As $\beta \in (0,1)$, $\lambda^\star > 1$ such that $P(.)$ is strictly decreasing for $\lambda \in (-\infty, \lambda^\star)$.

Sunspot equilibria occur when $|\lambda| \leqslant 1$ such that we first need to characterize situations for which $|\lambda| = 1$ is a solution of the characteristic polynomial. We first investigate what are the conditions for the positive eigenvalue to be equal to 1: as can be seen from the form of $P(1) = 0$, only two cases are of interest for this situation to occur $\theta = 1$ or $\theta = 1/\beta$. As we are interested in situations where $\theta \in (0,1)$ neither of them is relevant for our purpose. In others, multiple equilibria can only occur for $\theta = 1$, as far as the positive eigenvalue is concerned.

We now study the possibility of multiple equilibria originating from the negative eigenvalue. The limiting case being $P(-1) = 0$, this is equivalent to study:

$$Q(\theta) = \theta^2 - 3\frac{1+\beta}{\beta}\theta + \frac{1}{\beta}$$

First note that:

$$Q'(\theta) < 0 \text{ for } \theta < \tilde{\theta} = \frac{3}{2}\frac{1+\beta}{\beta}$$

Then, as $\beta \in (0,1)$, $\tilde{\theta} > 1$. This implies that $Q(\theta)$ is strictly decreasing for $\theta \in (0,1)$.

Further, $Q(0) = 1/\beta > 0$ and $Q(1) = -2(1+\beta)/\beta < 0$ such that there exists a unique value $\theta^\star \in (0,1)$ such that $Q(\theta) = 0$.

Finally, as $Q(\theta)$ is strictly decreasing, $Q(\theta) < 0$ (identically $P(-1) > 0$) for all $\theta > \theta^\star$.

□

Proof of Proposition 4. The log linearization of (5) around $\bar{y}$ yields the following linear first order finite difference equation:

$$\widehat{y}_{t+1} = \frac{2a-1}{a}\widehat{y}_t$$

The root has a modulus less than one if $1/3 < a < 1$

□

References

Atkeson, A. and Ogaki, M. (1996). Wealth–varying intertemporal elasticities of substitution: Evidence from panel and aggregate data. *Journal of Monetary Economics*, 38:507–534.

Auray, S., Collard, F., and Fève, P. (2001). Habit persistence and beliefs: Lessons for the effects of monetary policy. Discussion paper, IDEI.

Benhabib, J. and Farmer, R. (1996). The monetary transmission mechanism. Working Paper 96–13, C. V. Starr Center of Applied Economics, New-York University.

Benhabib, J. and Farmer, R. (1999). Indeterminacy and sunspots in macroeconomics. In Woodford, M. and Taylor, J., editors, *Handbook of Macroeconomics*, chapter 6. North-Holland.

Benhabib, J. and Farmer, R. (2000). The monetary transmission mechanism. *Review of Economic Dynamics*, 3(3):523–550.

Bloise, G., Bosi, S., and Magris, F. (1999). Sunspots, money and capital. working paper 99–07, EPEE, Université Evry.

Braun, P., Constantidines, G., and Ferson, W. E. (1993). Time nonseparability in aggregate consumption. *European Economic Review*, 37:897–920.

Carlstrom, C. and Fuerst, T. (1998). Real indeterminacy in monetary models with nominal interest rate distortions: The problem with inflation targets. Working Paper 9818, Federal Reserve Bank of Cleveland.

Constantidines, G. and Ferson, W. E. (1991). Habit persistence and durability in aggregate consumption. *Journal of Financial Economics*, 29:199–240.

Cooley, T. and Hansen, G. (1989). The inflation tax in a real business cycle model. *American Economic Review*, 79(4):733–748.

Farmer, R. (1997). Money in a real business cycle model. *Journal of Money Credit and Banking*, 29(4):568–611.

Farmer, R. (1999). *The Macroeconomics of Self-Fulfilling Prophecies.* MIT Press, Cambridge (MA).

Hairault, J. and Portier, F. (1993a). Monnaie et inflation dans un modèle de cycles réels. *Recherches Economiques de Louvain*, 59(4):427–61.

Hairault, J. and Portier, F. (1993b). Money, new–Keynesian macroeconomics and the business cycle. *European Economic Review*, 37:1533–68.

Hansen, G. (1985). Indivisible labor and the business cycles. *Journal of Monetary Economics*, 16(3):309–27.

Kydland, F. and Prescott, E. (1991). The econometrics of the general equilibrium approach to business cycles. *Scandinavian Journal of Economics*, 93:161–178.

Matheny, K. (1998). Non–neutral responses to money supply shocks when consumption and leisure are pareto substitutes. *Economic Theory*, 11:379–402.

Matsuyama, K. (1990). Sunspot equilibria (rational bubbles) in a model of money–in the–utility function. *Journal of Monetary Economics*, 25:137–144.

Naik, N. and Moore, M. (1996). Habit formation and intertemporal substitution in individual food consumption. *The Review of Economics and Statistics*, 78(2):321–328.

Rosenzweig, M. and Wolpin, K. (1993). Credit market constraints, consumption smoothing and the accumulation of durable production assets in low–income countries: Investments in bullocks in india. *Journal of Political Economy*, 101:223–44.

Woodford, M. (1988). Expectations, finance constraints and aggregate instability. In Kohn, M. and Tsiang, S., editors, *Finance Constraints, Expectations and Macroeconomics.* Oxford University Press, New–York.

Woodford, M. (1994). Monetary policy and price level determinacy in a cash–in–advance economy. *Economic Theory*, 4:345–80.

Chapter 8: Borrowing Constraint and Indeterminacy with Arbitrarily low Returns to Scale.

Jean-Paul Barinci
EPEE, Université d'Evry - Val d'Essonne & EUREQua, Université de Paris I, France

Arnaud Chéron
GAINS, Université du Maine & EUREQua, Université de Paris I, France

Abstract This paper argues that a finance constrained economy populated by two classes of households with heterogeneous preferences, workers and capitalists, allows to overcome two traditional puzzles that feature the link between indeterminacy and macroeconomics. It will be shown that, according to the elasticity of substitution between the productive factors and the intertemporal elasticity of substitution of capitalists, the model can exhibit indeterminacy with degrees of increasing returns-to-scale consistent with the more recent estimates. In addition, it will be established that, in opposition to conventional endogenous business cycle models, fluctuations driven by sunspots are consistent with procyclical movements of aggregate consumption.

1. Introduction

Recent research in macroeconomics has focused on models in which business cycles are driven by self-fulfilling prophecies. In these models, the resulting possibility of indeterminacy arises because of some market imperfections. These market imperfections may come from increasing returns-to-scale in production, often driven by external effects. Such models traditionally face two types of criticisms. On the one hand, the degree of increasing returns required for indeterminacy is inconsistent with recent estimates. For instance, Aiyagari, 1995 calls into question the upward-sloping labor demand curve required for the Benhabib and Farmer's, 1994, economy to exhibit indeterminacy. On the other hand, these models are unable to replicate major business cycles regularities. In particular, with a downward-sloping labor demand schedule, optimistic beliefs generally cause countercyclical movements of aggregate consumption (see, *e.g.*, Benhabib and Farmer, 1996, Bennett and Farmer, 2000 and Schmitt-Grohé, 2001).

These two lines of criticisms cast some doubt on the empirical plausibility of sunspots models. The relevance of expectations driven business cycles is then an open agenda and the purpose of the present contribution is precisely to provide some insight into this issue. We examine a finance constrained model with heterogenous households. More precisely, we consider an increasing returns to scale version of the Woodford's, 1986, one-sector model with heterogeneous agents and borrowing constraint. Briefly, the model features two classes of infinitely lived agents labelled "workers" and "capitalists". Workers supply variable units of labor time while facing in every period a liquidity constraint, whereas capitalists do not work. The model has two assets — money and capital. Under some mild assumptions, along equilibria close enough to the steady state, workers save their end-of-period wage earnings only in the form of money while capitalists never wish to accumulate money.

Barinci and Chéron, 2001, using a standard parameterization, have established that in this aggregate model indeterminacy is consistent with a downward-sloping labor demand schedule. The needed scale economies remain however slightly higher than the upper bound of the recent estimates range provided by Basu and Fernald, 1997. Yet, Barinci and Chéron, 2001 assume a standard Cobb-Douglas production function and retain the simplifying assumption that capitalists have logarithmic static preferences. These assumptions are indeed equivalent to setting the elasticity of substitution between capital and labor and the capitalists' intertemporal elasticity of substitution in consumption both equal to one. In the present contribution, we relax these assumptions by using generic forms. In this way, we can analyze the indeterminacy and dynamic properties of the model when these important parameters are allowed to vary.

Allowing these flexibilities, we demonstrate that indeterminacy occurs for *arbitrarily low* degrees of increasing returns to scale. In addition, we show that the fluctuations driven by sunspots are consistent with the data on US business cycles. In particular, and in opposition to available results, the model generates a strong *procyclical* behavior of aggregate consumption.

The rest of this paper is organized as follows. Section 2 presents the model and characterizes the intertemporal equilibrium. Section 3 analyzes its indeterminacy. Section 4 examines the cyclical properties of the model. Section 5 concludes.

2. The model

We consider a *monetary* one-sector economy inhabited by two classes of households, labeled workers and capitalists, in which a liquidity constraint prevents individuals from borrowing against future labor income.

2.1 Capitalists

The intertemporal preferences of capitalists are represented by the standard functional:

$$\sum_{t=0}^{\infty} \beta^t h(c_t^c), \tag{1}$$

for $\beta \in]0,1]$ and c_t^c respectively their positive rate of marginal impatience and their consumption at date $t \geq 0$. The instantaneous utility function $h(\cdot) : R_+ \to R$ is C^k, $k \geq 3$, on R_{++}, with $h' > 0, h'' < 0$ and $\lim_{c^c \to 0} h'(c^c) = \infty$.

Capitalists maximise (1) subject to:

$$c_t^c + K_{t+1}^c + \frac{m_{t+1}^c}{p_t} = (r_t + 1 - \delta)K_t^c + \frac{m_t^c}{p_t}$$

for $m_t^c \geq 0$ and $K_t^c \geq 0$ the nominal money balances and capital stock held by capitalists at the beginning of period t, p_t the nominal price of the produced good, r_t the real return on capital, and $\delta \in [0,1]$ the depreciation rate of the capital stock.

Necessary first order conditions write as follows:

$$h'(c_t^c) \geq \beta R_{t+1} h'(c_{t+1}^c), \tag{2}$$

$$h'(c_t^c) \geq \beta(p_t/p_{t+1}) h'(c_{t+1}^c), \tag{3}$$

for $R_t \equiv r_t + 1 - \delta$ and where the two conditions respectively bind for $K_t^c > 0$ and $m_t^c > 0$.

2.2 Workers

Workers' instantaneous preferences are represented by a separable utility function $u(c^w) - \alpha v(\ell)$, where $\alpha \in]0,1]$ denotes their common positive marginal rate of impatience; c^w and ℓ label their amounts of consumption and worked hours, respectively. It is assumed that both $u(\cdot)$ and $v(\cdot)$ are increasing maps from R_+ into R, of class C^k, $k \geq 3$, over R_{++}, $u(\cdot)$ and $v(\cdot)$ being respectively concave and convex over that set. Workers maximize:

$$\sum_{t=0}^{\infty} \alpha^t \{u(c_t^w) - \alpha v(\ell_t)\}$$

subject to the constraints:

$$\begin{aligned} K_{t+1}^w + \frac{m_{t+1}^w}{p_t} + c_t^w &= (r_t + 1 - \delta)K_t^w + w_t\ell_t + \frac{m_t^w}{P_t}, \\ K_{t+1}^w + c_t^w &\leq (r_t + 1 - \delta)K_t^w + \frac{m_t^w}{p_t}, \end{aligned}$$

for $m_t^w \geq 0$ and $K_t^w \geq 0$ the nominal money balances and the physical capital held by workers at the beginning of period t, and w_t the real wage.

Necessary first-order conditions state as:

$$u'(c_t^w) \geq \alpha(r_{t+1} + 1 - \delta)u'(c_{t+1}^w), \quad (4)$$

$$w_t u'(C_t^w) \geq \alpha v'(\ell_t), \quad (5)$$

$$w_t \left[\frac{p_t}{p_{t+1}} u'(c_{t+1}^w)\right] \leq v'(\ell_t). \quad (6)$$

Relations (4) and (6) respectively bind for $K_t^w > 0$ and $m_t^w > 0$; relation (5) binds whenever the liquidity constraint is slack.

2.3 Firms

The unique good to be consumed or accumulated is produced by a continuum of firms acting competitively through a common aggregate production function augmented by external effects:

$$\mathcal{F}(K_t, L_t; K_t, L_t) = F(K_t, L_t)(K_t)^\gamma (L_t)^\phi,$$

where K_t and L_t respectively denote the average amounts of capital and labor at date $t \geq 0$, for $\gamma, \phi \in R_+$. $F(\cdot, \cdot) : R_+ \times R_+ \to R_+$ is of class C^3 over $R_{++} \times R_{++}$, homogeneous of degree one (constant returns at the private level), and satisfies the Inada conditions. The first order condition of the firms problem provide the private forms of the rates of return on labor and capital:

$$w_t = F_L'(K_t, L_t)(K_t)^\gamma (L_t)^\phi, \quad (7)$$

$$r_t = F_K'(K_t, L_t)(K_t)^\gamma (L_t)^\phi. \quad (8)$$

2.4 Equilibrium

We turn now to the local characterization of the equilibrium under the assumption that workers are more impatient than capitalists, that is $\alpha < \beta$. Since capitalists positively discount the future, *i.e.*, $\beta < 1$, relations

(2) and (3) together imply that at an interior steady state the real return on capital is higher than that on money. Consequently, $K^{c\star} > 0$ and $m^{c\star} = 0$ (star indicates steady state values). Next, from $\beta(r^\star + 1 - \delta) = 1$ and (4), one sees that, under the assumption $\alpha < \beta$, workers choose not to hold capital: $K^{w\star} = 0$. But since capital dominates money, they are unwilling to hold money as well. As a matter of fact, they only hold money to finance their consumption expenditures in the subsequent period. It follows that the borrowing constraint, which is now a standard cash-in-advance constraint since $K^{w\star} = 0$, is binding: $m^{w\star} = p^\star c^{w\star} > 0$ (this can be seen by manipulating (5)-(6)). To sum up, at any steady states, $K^{c\star} > 0$, $m^{c\star} = 0$, $K^{w\star} = 0$ and $m^{w\star} > 0$ implying that relations (4), (5) and (3) are slack while relations (6) and (2) hold with equality.

The key remark is that, by continuity, the previous properties will extend to a small neighborhood of any stationary position. Therefore, nearby a steady state, all relevant information about households' optimal behavior is summarized by the following set of relations:

$$w_t \frac{p_t}{p_{t+1}} u'(c^w_{t+1}) = v'(\ell_t), \tag{9}$$

$$\frac{p_{t+1}}{p_t} c^w_{t+1} = w_t \ell_t, \tag{10}$$

$$h'(c^c_t) = \beta(r_{t+1} + 1 - \delta) h'(c^c_{t+1}), \tag{11}$$

$$c^c_t + K^c_{t+1} = (r_{t+1} + 1 - \delta) K^c_t, \tag{12}$$

where (10) and (12) are the workers and capitalists budget constraints, respectively. Combining (9) and (10) one gets the workers' *offer curve*:

$$c^w_{t+1} = \psi(\ell_t) \equiv (\mathcal{U}^{-1} \circ \mathcal{V})(\ell_t),$$

for $\mathcal{U}(c^w) = c^w u'(c^w)$ and $\mathcal{V}(\ell) = \ell v'(\ell)$.

Finally, noticing that the money market equilibrium condition writes as:

$$w_t l_t = \frac{M}{p_t} = c^w_t, \tag{13}$$

for M the constant level of money supply, it is straightforward to show that an intertemporal equilibrium is a sequence $\{c^c_t, K_t, L_t\}$ which satisfies:

$$h'(c^c_t) - \beta[F'_K(K_{t+1}, L_{t+1})(K_{t+1})^\gamma (L_{t+1})^\phi + 1 - \delta] h'(c^c_{t+1}) = 0 \tag{14}$$

$$K_{t+1} - [F'_K(K_t, L_t)(K_t)^\gamma (L_t)^\phi + 1 - \delta] K_t + c^c_t = 0 \tag{15}$$

$$F'_L(K_{t+1}, L_{t+1})(K_{t+1})^\gamma (L_{t+1})^{\phi+1} - \psi(L_t) = 0 \tag{16}$$

3. Empirical plausibility of indeterminacy

This section examines the indeterminacy properties of the model. More specifically, we wonder whether indeterminacy arises for empirically realistic levels of returns to scale. To do this, we study the first order Taylor expansion of (14)-(16) evaluated at the interior steady state.[1]

Let

$$\sigma \equiv \frac{F'_K F'_L}{F F''_{KL}},\ 1 - s \equiv \frac{F'_L L}{F},\ s \equiv \frac{F'_K K}{F},\ \eta \equiv -\frac{h'(c)}{h''(c)c},\ \varepsilon \equiv \frac{\psi'(L)L}{\psi(L)},$$

be respectively the elasticity of substitution between the productive factors, the share of wages, the share of profits, the capitalists' intertemporal elasticity of substitution in consumption and the elasticity of the workers' offer curve, all these values being considered at the steady state. Now, introducing $\varrho \equiv \beta^{-1} - 1 + \delta$, the polynomial characteristic of the Jacobian matrix writes as follows:

$$\mathcal{Q}(z) = -z^3 + \mathcal{T} z^2 - \Sigma z + \mathcal{D} = 0,$$

where

$$\begin{aligned}
\mathcal{T} &= 1 + \beta^{-1} - \frac{1 - s + (1-\sigma)\gamma + \phi}{\sigma - s + \phi\sigma}[1 - \eta(1-\beta)]\varrho + \frac{\sigma}{\sigma - s + \sigma\phi}\varepsilon, \\
\Sigma &= (1 + \beta^{-1})\frac{\sigma\varepsilon}{\sigma - s + \phi\sigma} + \beta^{-1} - \frac{\varrho[1 - s + (1-\sigma)\gamma + \phi]}{\sigma - s + \phi\sigma} \\
&\quad - \frac{1 - s - \gamma\sigma}{\sigma - s + \phi\sigma}\left(1 - \eta(1-\beta)\right)\varrho\varepsilon, \\
\mathcal{D} &= \frac{\varrho[\gamma - ((1-s)/\sigma) + (1/\beta\varrho)]}{\sigma - s + \phi\sigma}\sigma\varepsilon.
\end{aligned}$$

Since there is one historical variable, namely the stock of capital, and two forward variables, indeterminacy results whenever the characteristic polynomial possesses at *least* two roots located inside the unit circle.

In this section, we use the following benchmark annual parameterization: $s = 0.3, \delta = 0.1, \beta = 0.92$, $\varepsilon = 1$.[2] In addition, drawing on Barinci

[1] The existence of an interior steady state is ensured by usual boundary assumptions. Its uniqueness is trivial if the technology is Cobb-Douglas. Otherwise, some additional assumptions about the size of external effects are called for. In fact, it can be shown that if the *equilibrium* marginal product of labor is decreasing in labor and the *equilibrium* marginal product of capital is decreasing in capital, the interior steady state is bound to be unique.

[2] Note that as in Hansen, 1985 setting $\varepsilon = 1$ is equivalent to assuming a flat labor supply schedule.

and Chéron, 2001, we fix $\gamma = 0$.[3] It should be noticed that we do not calibrate the technology and preferences parameters σ and η. In this way, we can analyze the indeterminacy properties of the model when these key parameters are allowed to vary.

In order to evaluate how the specific features of the model alter the result of Benhabib and Farmer, 1994 regarding the needed size of scale economies, in a first step, we use their specifications for the utility and production functions, by setting $\eta = 1$ and $\sigma = 1$. Let ϕ_{min} denotes the minimum labor external effect above which indeterminacy results.[4] At the benchmark parameterization given above, $\phi_{min} = 0.18$. This shows that indeterminacy occurs with returns to scale much lower than in Benhabib and Farmer, 1994 and in accordance with the earlier empirical evidence provided by Burnside, 1996. In addition, noticing that the slope of the equilibrium labor demand is equal to $\phi - \frac{s}{\sigma}$, one sees that indeterminacy does not require the labor demand and supply curves should cross with the wrong slopes. We conclude that in our finance constrained economy, indeterminacy is more likely to be empirically relevant than in standard aggregate real models.

Because recent empirical estimates suggest that an upper bound of the degree of returns to scale in U.S. manufacturing is 1.09 (see for instance Basu and Fernald, 1997), the Cobb-Douglas - logarithmic utility case requires an implausibly high degree of returns-to-scale. However, as there is some uncertainty about the empirical value of the capital-labor elasticity of substitution (see, *e.g.*, Hamermesh, 1993), we find pertinent to relax the restriction $\sigma = 1$. We then examine the indeterminacy properties of the model under different parameterizations for σ, keeping temporarily the capitalists' intertemporal elasticity of substitution fixed at one. The outcome of this analysis, depicted in Figure 1, indicates that the size of the labor externality needed for indeterminacy is a decreasing function of the elasticity of substitution in production.[5] For example, drawing on the empirical estimates provided by Duffy and Papageorgiou, 2000, for $\sigma = 2$, $\phi_{min} = 9\%$. This is well within the empirical relevant range according to the estimates of Basu and Fernald.

---

[3]In fact, as the capital externality increases, the size of the labor externality, hence the overall returns to scale, needed for indeterminacy increases. This result has been analytically established in Barinci and Chéron, 2001 and numerical experiments demonstrate its robustness.

[4]More precisely, at $\phi = \phi_{min}$, the economy undergoes a Hopf bifurcation whereby the modulus of two nonreal conjugate eigenvalues is equal to one and the other lies outside the unit circle. See Barinci and Drugeon, 1999 for more details.

[5]This result corroborates the one obtained by Cazzavillan et al., 1998 in a two-dimensional version of the current model.

Figure 1. Sensitivity of ϕ_{min} with respect to σ

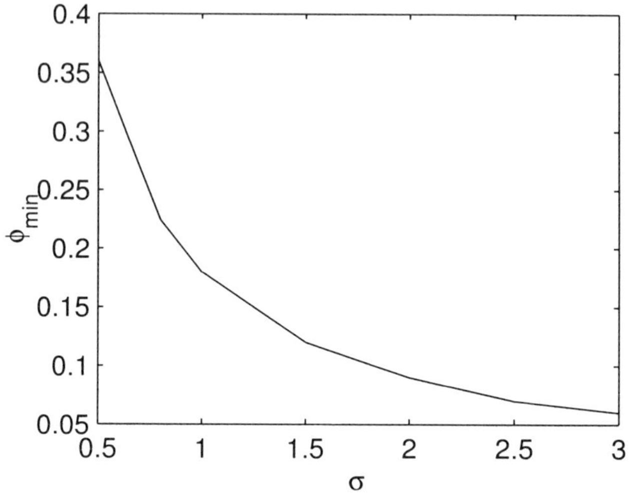

If there is some uncertainty about σ, the one about the (capitalists') intertemporal elasticity of substitution in consumption is perhaps much more stringent. Thus, relaxing the restriction $\eta = 1$, we now examine how the indeterminacy properties change with the shape of the capitalists' utility function. More precisely, for various values of σ and ϕ, we have computed the minimum value of η, denoted η_{min}, above which indeterminacy occurs (see Figure 2).

Figure 2. Sensitivity of η_{min} with respect to ϕ and σ

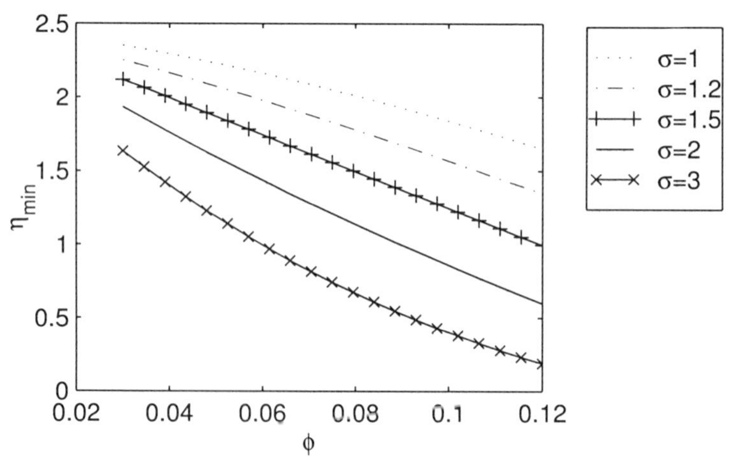

Figure 2 shows that, whatever the degree of increasing returns-to-scale, indeterminacy can emerge provided that η is sufficiently high. For example, setting $\sigma = 1.5$ and $\phi = 10\%$, the model exhibits indeterminacy for η greater than 1.25 (see Table 1).[6] We conclude that by modifying the shape of the capitalists' utility function to allow for varying degrees of intertemporal substitution, one is able to generate indeterminacy with *arbitrarily low increasing returns-to-scale.*

Table 1. $\sigma = 1.5$, $\phi = 10\%$

η	Roots 1 and 2	Root 3	Modulus of roots 1 and 2
0.5	1.0291±0.1254i	1.0334	1.0747
1	1.0046±0.1128i	1.0870	1.0219
1.2	0.9957±0.1116i	1.1066	1.0038
1.25	0.9936±0.1115i	1.1111	0.9996
1.5	0.9845±0.1113i	1.1316	0.9816
2	0.9701±0.1120i	1.1649	0.9536
5	0.9213±0.1139i	1.289	0.8617

4. Sunspots and the business cycle

Although we have established that in this model indeterminacy is empirically plausible, this does not means that it is able to mimic the data. The aim of the present section is precisely to assess the empirical relevance of this model on the basis of its ability to quantitatively reproduce business cycle stylized facts. It is well known that there exists discrepancies between actual data and those predicted by conventional endogenous business cycles models. For example, for reasonable values of the externality parameters, sunspots models produce a cross correlation between consumption and output with a wrong sign. This has been documented by various authors, including Benhabib and Farmer, 1996, Wen, 1998 Bennett and Farmer, 2000 and Schmitt-Grohé, 2001. We shall see that our model overcomes this weakness.

In order to evaluate the quantitative properties of the model, we use the following fairly standard parameterization: $\beta = 0.98$, $\delta = 0.025$, $s = 0.3$, $\gamma = 0$, and $\varepsilon = 1$. In addition, drawing on King and Rebelo, 1999 and Duffy and Papageorgiou, 2000, we set $\eta = 1/3$ and $\sigma = 2$. As

[6] Bennett and Farmer, 2000 find a similar negative relationship between the "plausibility" of indeterminacy and the relative degree of risk aversion.

usual in the literature (see *e.g.*, Benhabib and Farmer, 1996 and Schmitt-Grohé, 2001), we fix the labor externality parameter at 0.1. Lastly, the standard deviation of the sunspot shocks is chosen to reproduce the observed volatility of real per capita output.

Table 2. Cyclical Properties

	US		FCIR		BF	
x	(1)	(2)	(1)	(2)	(1)	(2)
C	0.74	0.83	0.75	0.99	0.72	-0.62
I	4.79	0.91	2.37	0.98	3.91	0.84
N	0.94	0.74	1.23	0.99	1.56	0.93

Note: (1): $\sigma(x)/\sigma(y)$, (2): $corr(x, y)$.

Table 2 shows the cyclical properties of US data (see Cooley and Prescott, 1995) and those of our finance constrained economy with increasing returns (FCIR). For comparison purposes, we also report those derived from the two-sector model of Benhabib and Farmer, 1996 (BF). Table 2 illustrates that the FCIR model is able to generate realistic comovements of output, hours, investment and consumption. In particular, it exhibits a strong *procyclical* aggregate consumption.[7]

To understand the intuition for these results it seems useful to remember why standard models produce a time series for consumption that is countercyclical.[8] Indeed, in models in which the labor demand schedule slopes downward (low increasing returns), a spontaneous increase in consumption, which shifts inward the labor supply schedule, leads to a decrease in hours and output. Hence consumption is countercyclical. This merely relies on the fact that, as long as consumption and leisure are normal goods, the household's intratemporal first-order condition, which equates the marginal value of leisure with the value of labor productivity in terms of utility, forces consumption and labor to move in opposite direction. The key feature of our model (FCIR) is that the intratemporal marginal efficiency condition does not hold with equality (see the first-order condition (5)). It follows that consumption and labor are not forced to move in opposite directions. Hence, optimistic beliefs

[7]Even though Barinci and Chéron, 2001 find analogous results with a logarithmic utility function, a Cobb-Douglas technology and a degree of returns to scale equal to 1.30, the flexibilities incorporated is the present paper allow to obtain consistent properties with a realistic magnitude of increasing returns.

[8]This has been documented by Benhabib and Farmer, 1996, Bennett and Farmer, 2000 and Schmitt-Grohé, 2001.

that shift outward the labor supply curve lead to an increase in hours. As a matter of fact, in the current model, workers consume their current real labor income (see the money market equilibrium condition (13)). Therefore, the increase in the wage bill (due to the rise of hours) entails a raise in workers' consumption and allows the aggregate consumption to be procyclical.

5. Conclusion

This paper has provided insight into the mechanisms by which indeterminacy results in dynamic models. It suggests that a model incorporating heterogenous agents and limited borrowing abilities allows to resolve two traditional puzzles faced by conventional endogenous business cycle models. It has been established that indeterminacy results for arbitrarily low degrees of increasing returns. Given empirical evidence on the size of external effects, indeterminacy is much more likely empirically plausible in this model than in real (aggregate or two-sectors) models. In addition, and in opposition to more recent works (see, *e.g.*, Benhabib and Farmer, 1996 and Schmitt-Grohé, 2001), we have shown that, even for reasonable values for the externality parameters, the propagation of sunspot disturbances is consistent with procyclical consumption.

References

Aiyagari, R. (1995). The econometrics of indeterminacy: an apply study: a comment. *Carnergie Rochester Series in Public Policy*, 43:273–284.

Barinci, J. and Chéron, A. (2001). Sunspots and the business cycle in a finance constrained economy. *Journal of Economic Theory*, 97:30–49.

Barinci, J. and Drugeon, J. (1999). A geometric approach to local indeterminacy and local bifurcations in three-dimensional dynamic systems. working-paper 1999.40, EUREQUA-Université de Paris 1.

Basu, S. and Fernald, J. (1997). Returns to scale in us production: estimates and implications. *Journal of Political Economy*, 105:249–283.

Benhabib, J. and Farmer, R. (1994). Indeterminacy and increasing returns. *Journal of Economic Theory*, 63:19–41.

Benhabib, J. and Farmer, R. (1996). Indeterminacy and sector specific externalities. *Journal of Monetary Economics*, 37:397–419.

Bennett, R. and Farmer, R. (2000). Indeterminacy with non-separable utility. *Journal of Economic Theory*, 93:118–143.

Burnside, C. (1996). Production function regressions, returns to scale, and externalities. *Journal of Monetary Economics*, 37:177–201.

Cazzavillan, G., Lloyd-Braga, T., and Pintus, P. (1998). Multiple steady state and endogenous fluctuations with increasing returns to scale in production. *Journal of Economic Theory*, 80:60–107.

Cooley, T. and Prescott, E. (1995). Economic growth and business cycles. In Cooley, T., editor, *Frontiers of Business Cycle Research*, pages 1–38. Princeton University Press, Princeton.

Duffy, J. and Papageorgiou, C. (2000). A cross-country empirical investigation of the aggregate production function specification. *Journal of Economic Growth*, 5:87–120.

Hamermesh, D. (1993). *Labor Demand.* Princeton University Press.

Hansen, G. (1985). Indivisible labor and the business cycles. *Journal of Monetary Economics*, 16(3):309–327.

King, R. and Rebelo, S. (1999). Resuscitating real business cycles. In Taylor, J.B., W. M., editor, *Handbook of Macroeconomics.* North-Holland, Amsterdam.

Schmitt-Grohé, S. (2001). Endogenous business cycles and the dynamics of output, hours and consumption. *American Economic Review*, 90(5):1136–1160.

Wen, Y. (1998). Capacity utilization under increasing returns to scale. *Journal of Economic Theory*, 81:7–36.

Chapter 9: Irreversible Investment Under Uncertainty in General Equilibrium.

Aude Pommeret

IRES, Université Catholique de Louvain, Belgium & EUREQua, Université de Paris I, France

Abstract This paper considers the decision of irreversible investment under macroeconomic uncertainty in a general equilibrium framework. Uncertainty thus affects the optimal decision through two different transmission channels. The first one is the irreversibility and the second one is the agents' preferences. The partial equilibrium counterpart of our model would have exhibited the standard negative relationship between uncertainty and the desired level of capital. We show that extending the analysis to a general equilibrium framework may reverse this relationship.

1. Introduction

This paper considers the decision of irreversible investment under uncertainty in a general equilibrium framework. Uncertainty thus affects the optimal decision through two different transmission channels. The first one is the irreversibility and the second one is the agents' preferences.

The effect of uncertainty on irreversible decisions has been widely studied. It has been shown (Arrow and Fisher, 1974, and Henry, 1974) that uncertainty and irreversibility may generate an option value to decide later which arises from the value of waiting for new information. The investment decision generally implies some irreversibility (capital may be specific, information asymmetries may exist...) and Mac Donald and Siegel, 1986 have proposed the first irreversible investment model under uncertainty. The idea is rather intuitive: since the world is stochastic, the firm may prefer to wait for new information before committing itself to investing. This has been extended to some other macroeconomic concerns. Indeed Brennan and Schwartz, 1985 show in a partial equilibrium framework that the optimal exploitation of a natural non-renewable resource is subject to hysteresis effects which delay the decision to exploit this resource, assuming that its price follows a geometric Brownian motion. This latter assumption is frequently used in the literature.[1] It is also the case in this paper in which the combination of the energy price uncertainty and of the irreversibility of macroeconomic investment is studied.

In the absence of irreversibility, uncertainty may also be transmitted to the economic variables through agents' preferences. In the case of the consumption/saving trade-off, the concept of precautionary saving (Kimball, 1990) which is linked to (but different from) the risk aversion and which measures the agent's propensity to save more when facing uncertainty is the most famous one. Considering the portfolio choice and consumption/saving model (Merton, 1969, 1971), uncertainty will favor savings as soon as the relative risk aversion coefficient is greater than unity.

Therefore, uncertainty seems to affect savings in opposite ways depending on the transmission channel considered. While the two transmission channels (irreversibility and agents' preferences) have often been separately studied, they barely have been considered simultaneously. Some studies based on numerical simulations (Bertola, 1994, Dow and Olson, 1992, Coleman, 1997) show that irreversibility may increase aggregate investment. Analytical models are very rare. Gilchrist and Williams, 1998 propose a general equilibrium model with a non persistent idiosyncratic uncertainty and irreversible investment; in such a framework, uncertainty reduces idiosyncratic investment but encourages aggregate investment. This paper focuses on the effect of persistent macroeconomic uncertainty. The partial equilibrium counterpart under monopolistic competition of our model would have exhibited the standard negative relationship between uncertainty and the desired level of capital. We show that extending the analysis to a general equilibrium framework may reverse this relationship.

In the next section, we present the model. The resolution framework is similar to that of standard partial equilibrium models of irreversible investment under uncertainty except that now, the cost of investment is no more a given acquisition cost a firm has to pay but a required reduction in consumption. Since we consider a stochastic model, we obtain short term optimal expressions for the key economic variables, depending on the observed realization of the uncertain variable and only expected

[1] See for instance Pindyck, 1981, Slade, 1988, or Lund, 1992; Epaulard and Pommeret, 1998, have constructed a general equilibrium model leading to a price of a non-renewable resource following a geometric Brownian motion

long term values for these key economic variables may be then derived. Indeed, we start by deriving the value of the program when there is no investment in the economy (section 2). In section 3, by comparing the various current and expected gains and losses in this value that are generated by a marginal investment, we obtain the analytical expression for the desired capital stock, from which we deduce the long term expected values of the key variables in the economy. Section 5 provides an analysis of the effect of uncertainty on the optimal capital stock and section 6 concludes.

2. Presentation of the model

We consider a stochastic world in which uncertainty appears through the energy resources size which in turn makes the energy price uncertain. It is assumed that the energy price follows a geometric Brownian motion[2] with no trend.

$$dP_E(t) = \sigma P_E(t) dz_t \tag{1}$$

Random shocks perturb the energy price rate of growth. dz_t is the increment of a standard Wiener process z_t ($dz_t = \epsilon(t)\sqrt{dt}$ where $\epsilon(t)$ is a white noise). σ gives the strength at which exogenous random shocks react on the price rate of growth. The absence of trend does not affect the qualitative results and allows to isolate the effect of uncertainty.

The production function exhibits constant returns:

$$y(t) = ak(t)^{\beta} e(t)^{\alpha} l(t)^{1-\alpha-\beta}$$

with $\alpha + \beta < 1$. The amount of labor corresponds to the population size which is assumed to be constant. In what follows, we consider per head variables, with $Y(t) = y(t)/l(t)$, $E(t) = e(t)/l(t)$, and $K(t) = k(t)/l(t)$. The production function becomes then:

$$Y(t) = aK(t)^{\beta} E(t)^{\alpha}$$

with $\alpha + \beta < 1$. The production provides a consumption good $c(t)$ ($C(t)$ stands for per head consumption), investment $i(t)$ ($I(t)$ stands for per head investment) and is also used to acquire energy $P_E(t)e(t)$ (per head energy is noted $E(t)$).

Investment is irreversible: the central planner cannot reduce the installed capital stock. In order to simplify (and without affecting the

[2]For a justification, see Epaulard and Pommeret, 1998.

nature of the results) the problem, the depreciation rate of capital is assumed to be null. The accumulation equation is thus:

$$PY(t) = PC(t) + P(dK(t)/dt) + P_e(t)E(t)$$
$$\Leftrightarrow dK(t) = (Y(t) - C(t) - P_E(t)E(t))dt \tag{2}$$

where $P_E(t) = Pe(t)/P$ and P is the price of the good which is produced, consumed and invested.

The central planner maximizes the standard utility function:

$$U(0) = \left(\int_{t=0}^{\infty} u(C(t))e^{-\delta t}dt\right) \quad \text{with} \quad u(C(t)) = \frac{C(t)^{1-\gamma}}{1-\gamma} \tag{3}$$

where γ is the relative risk aversion coefficient while $1/\gamma$ is the intertemporal elasticity of substitution, and δ is the time preference rate.

The central planner program may thus be written:

$$\left\{\begin{array}{l} \max U(t) = \left(\int_{t=0}^{\infty} u(C(t))e^{-\delta t}dt\right) \\ \text{sc.} \left| \begin{array}{l} dK(t) = (Y(t) - C(t) - P_E(t)E(t))dt \\ Y(t) = aK(t)^{\beta}E(t)^{\alpha} \\ C(t) \geq 0 \\ dK(t) \geq 0 \\ dP_E(t) = \sigma P_E(t)dz_t \\ \lim_{t\to\infty} E_0\left[V(K(t), P_E(t))e^{-\delta t}\right] = 0 \\ K(0) \text{ and } P_E(0) \text{ given} \end{array}\right. \end{array}\right. \tag{4}$$

where $V(K(t), P_E(t))$ gives the value of the program and the sixth condition is thus the transversality condition. Whatever the assumption on the reversible or irreversible nature of investment, energy is an input which may be adjusted immediately and without cost. The optimal use of energy at each time is thus:

$$E^*(t) = \left[\frac{a\alpha}{P_E(t)}K(t)^{\beta}\right]^{\frac{1}{1-\alpha}} \tag{5}$$

$E^*(t)$ may then be eliminated from the program which becomes:

$$\left\{\begin{array}{l} \max U(t) = \left(\int_{t=0}^{\infty} u(C(t))e^{-\delta t}dt\right) \\ \text{sc.} \left| \begin{array}{l} dK(t) = (CF(t) - C(t))dt \\ CF(t) = AK^{\frac{\beta}{1-\alpha}}P_E(t)^{\frac{\alpha}{\alpha-1}} \\ C(t) \geq 0 \\ dK(t) \geq 0 \\ dP_E(t) = \sigma P_E(t)dz_t \\ \lim_{t\to\infty} E_0\left[V(K(t), P_E(t))e^{-\delta t}\right] = 0 \\ K(0) \text{ and } P_E(0) \text{ given} \end{array}\right. \end{array}\right. \tag{6}$$

with $A = (1-\alpha)a^{\frac{1}{1-\alpha}}\alpha^{\frac{\alpha}{1-\alpha}}$. $CF(t)$ is thus the cash-flow. To solve this model, we first consider the value of the program when no investment occurs. Starting from this value, we can derive the variations in current and future values generated by a marginal investment. Comparisons between these variations allow in turn to obtain the desired level of capital.

3. Value of the program when there is no investment

Since investment is irreversible, the capital stock along the optimal growth path is the level of capital for which it is optimal not to invest given the observed energy price and *the already installed capital stock*. Once the effective capital stock has reached the optimal path given the observed energy price, it follows this path which moves according to the energy price fluctuations: when the energy price goes below its historically lowest level, the optimal capital stock corresponds to the desired capital stock; when the energy price exceeds this level, the optimal capital stock remains greater than the desired capital stock.

Given the recursive utility function that has been chosen, the value function is a solution of the following Bellman equation:

$$V(t) = \left\{ \frac{A^{1-\gamma}}{1-\gamma} K(t)^{\frac{\beta(1-\gamma)}{(1-\alpha)}} P_E(t)^{\frac{\alpha(1-\gamma)}{(\alpha-1)}} dt + e^{-\delta dt} \left[E_t \left(V(t+dt) \right) \right] \right\} \tag{7}$$

where $V(t)$ is the value function of the program.

Because of the irreversible nature of investment, the solution of the homogeneous part of this differential equation cannot be ignored; it is postulatod of the form:

$$W(P_E(t), K(t)) = B_1(K(t))P_E(t)^{\nu_1} + B_2(K(t))P_E(t)^{\nu_2}$$

Replacing $V(t)$ by $B(K(t))P_E(t)^{\nu}$ in the value function allows to identify parameters ν_1 and ν_2. Then, we get (see Dixit and Pindyck, 1994):

$$\nu_1 = \left[\frac{1}{2} - \sqrt{\frac{1}{4} + \frac{2\delta}{\sigma^2}} \right] < 0 \tag{8}$$

$$\nu_2 = \left[\frac{1}{2} + \sqrt{\frac{1}{4} + \frac{2\delta}{\sigma^2}} \right] > 0 \tag{9}$$

If the energy price tends towards infinity, it is never interesting to invest because more capital would not lead to more consumption (recall that after having invested, consumption becomes: $C(t) = CF(t) =$

$AK(t)^{\frac{\beta}{1-\alpha}}P_E(t)^{\frac{\alpha}{\alpha-1}}$); then, there is a condition on the value of the option to invest in the future:

$$\lim_{P_E(t)\to\infty} W(K(t), P_E(t)) = 0$$

Thus we only keep the part of the option value which corresponds to the negative root of the characteristic equation associated with the differential equation (7). Eventually the solution of the homogeneous equation is:

$$W(P_E(t), K(t)) = B_1(K(t))P_E(t)^{\nu_1} \tag{10}$$

One may easily show that $\partial\nu_1/\partial\sigma^2 > 0$. Thus, uncertainty increases the option value to invest in the future.

After having identified (see appendix 1) the particular solution of the differential equation (7), which is simply the present value of the sum of the instantaneous utilities (PVU), the general solution is:

$$V(P_E(t), K(t)) = \underbrace{\frac{A^{1-\gamma}}{(1-\gamma)\delta^*}K(t)^{\frac{(1-\gamma)\beta}{(1-\alpha)}}P_E(t)^{\frac{(1-\gamma)\alpha}{(\alpha-1)}}}_{PVU} + B_1(K(t))P_E(t)^{\nu_1} \tag{11}$$

with $\delta^* = \delta - \frac{1}{2}\frac{\alpha(1-\gamma)(1-\alpha\gamma)}{(\alpha-1)^2}\sigma^2$. δ^* is assumed to be positive to ensure that the sign of the present value of the sum of the instantaneous utilities is the same as that of $(1-\gamma)$. The effects of uncertainty are summarized in the following proposition:

Proposition 1 *If $\gamma < 1/\alpha$ (resp. $\gamma > 1/\alpha$), the concavity effect of uncertainty prevails on its convexity effect and therefore, the stronger the uncertainty the larger the value of the program.*

Indeed the effect of uncertainty on PVU depends on the relative values of technological and preferences parameters. The certainty equivalent of the energy price rate of growth EC defined as

$$EC = PVU^{-1}\left(E_t\left[PVU(dP_E/P_E)\right]\right),$$

may be written:

$$EC = -\frac{1}{2}\left(1 - \frac{\alpha(1-\gamma)}{(\alpha-1)}\right)\sigma^2.$$

We then have: $(1-\gamma)\delta^* = \delta - \alpha(1-\gamma)^2/(\alpha-1)EC$.

Uncertainty affects the present value of the sum of the instantaneous utilities in two different ways:

- If uncertainty is stronger, the convexity of the cash-flow (*via* parameter α) with respect to the uncertain variable generates a convexity effect which reduces this certainty equivalent.

- On the contrary, uncertainty increases this certainty equivalent through the agent's risk aversion, because of a concavity effect.

Thus the total effect on EC depends on the relative strength of these concavity and convexity effects. If $\gamma > 1/\alpha$ (*resp.* $\gamma < 1/\alpha$), the concavity effect (*resp.* convexity effect) prevails and it increases (*resp.* reduces) the certainty equivalent of the energy price rate of growth. Of course if the certainty equivalent of the energy price rate of growth becomes larger (*resp.* smaller), it reduces (*resp.* increases) the present value of the sum of the instantaneous utilities and also the value of the program $(\partial((1-\gamma)\delta^*)/\partial EC > 0)$.

The use of a time-additive utility function prevents from identifying which preferences parameter affects the certainty equivalent of the energy price rate of growth: we do not know whether it is the risk aversion or the intertemporal elasticity of substitution which has to be compared with α.

4. Determination of the optimal capital stock

Once the optimal growth path has been reached, the desired capital stock is such that the central planner is indifferent between investing one more unit or doing nothing: a marginal investment would generate an intertemporal utility variation which would exactly compensate for the loss in current utility. Since these variations are rather complex as investment is irreversible and the world is stochastic, we first derive expressions for these variations using the value function we determined in the previous function. A comparison between them allows then to obtain the desired capital stock.

The value function when there is no investment (*cf.* equation (11)) may be rewritten:

$$\begin{aligned} V(P_E(t),K(t)) &= B_1(K(t))P_E(t)^{\nu_1} \\ &+\frac{A^{(1-\gamma)}}{(1-\gamma)}K(t)^{\frac{(1-\gamma)\beta}{(1-\alpha)}}P_E(t)^{\frac{(1-\gamma)\alpha}{(\alpha-1)}}dt \\ &+\frac{e^{-\delta^* dt}}{\delta^*}\frac{A^{(1-\gamma)}}{(1-\gamma)}K(t)^{\frac{(1-\gamma)\beta}{(1-\alpha)}}P_E(t)^{\frac{(1-\gamma)\alpha}{(\alpha-1)}} \end{aligned} \qquad (12)$$

4.1 Variation in the future value generated by the marginal investment

From equation (12) we deduce that $\Delta V^f(K(t), P_E(t))_{\Delta K(t)\neq 0}$, which is the variation in future value due to the investment $\Delta K(t)$ during dt, is:

$$\begin{aligned}&\Delta V^f(P_E(t), K(t))_{\Delta K(t)\neq 0} = \\ &[B_1(K(t)+\Delta K(t)dt) - B_1(K(t))]\, P_E(t)^{\nu_1} + \frac{e^{-\delta^* dt}}{\delta^*}\frac{A^{(1-\gamma)}}{(1-\gamma)} \\ &\times \left((K(t)+\Delta K(t)dt)^{\frac{(1-\gamma)\beta}{(1-\alpha)}} - K(t)^{\frac{(1-\gamma)\beta}{(1-\alpha)}} \right) P_E(t)^{\frac{(1-\gamma)\alpha}{(\alpha-1)}}\end{aligned} \tag{13}$$

It is not simply a gain because if the present value of the sum of the instantaneous utilities increases with the stock of capital, the option value to invest $B_1(K(t)+\Delta K(t)dt)P_E(t)^{\nu_1}$ is a decreasing function of the capital stock (this is checked below with the identification of $B_1'(K(t))$).

If investment is marginal, $dK(t) \to 0$, and the limit of equation (13) may be written as:

$$\begin{aligned}&dV^f(K(t), P_E(t)) = \lim_{dK(t)\to 0}\left[\Delta V^f(K(t), P_E(t))_{dK(t)\neq 0}\right] \\ &= B_1'(K(t))P_E(t)^{\nu 1} dK(t)dt \\ &+ A^{(1-\gamma)}\frac{e^{-\delta^* dt}}{\delta^*}\frac{\beta}{1-\alpha}P_E(t)^{\frac{\alpha(1-\gamma)}{\alpha-1}} K(t)^{\frac{\beta(1-\gamma)}{1-\alpha}-1} dK(t)dt\end{aligned} \tag{14}$$

4.2 Loss of current value due to the marginal investment

As in the determinist world, investment requires a reduction in current consumption and subsequently in instantaneous utility. The loss in current valuc ΔV^c is thus:

$$\begin{aligned}&\Delta V^c(P_E(t), K(t))_{\Delta K(t)\neq 0} = \\ &\frac{1}{(1-\gamma)}\left[AK(t)^{\frac{\beta}{1-\alpha}}P_E(t)^{\frac{\alpha}{\alpha-1}} - \Delta K(t)\right]^{(1-\gamma)} dt \\ &-\frac{1}{(1-\gamma)}\left[AK(t)^{\frac{\beta}{1-\alpha}}P_E(t)^{\frac{\alpha}{\alpha-1}}\right]^{(1-\gamma)} dt < 0\end{aligned} \tag{15}$$

$$\begin{aligned}&\Rightarrow dV^c(K(t), P_E(t)) = \lim_{dK(t)\to 0}\left[\Delta V^c(K(t), P_E(t))_{dK(t)\neq 0}\right] \\ &= -\left[AK(t)^{\frac{\beta}{1-\alpha}}P_E(t)^{\frac{\alpha}{\alpha-1}}\right]^{(-\gamma)} dK(t)dt\end{aligned} \tag{16}$$

4.3 The desired capital stock

Since investment is irreversible, the desired capital stock $K^*(t)$ must satisfy the value matching and smooth pasting conditions (introduced in the investment literature by McDonald and Siegel, 1986).

The value matching condition ensures that if the installed capital is $K^*(t)$, the central planner is indifferent between investing $dK(t)$ during the period dt or doing nothing:

$$dV = dV^c + dV^f = 0 \Leftrightarrow$$

$$\begin{aligned} &\tfrac{A^{(1-\gamma)}}{\delta^*}\tfrac{\beta}{1-\alpha} P_E(t)^{\frac{\alpha(1-\gamma)}{\alpha-1}} K^*(t)^{\frac{\beta(1-\gamma)}{1-\alpha}-1} \\ &+B_1'(K^*(t))P_E(t)^{\nu_1} = \left[AK^*(t)^{\frac{\beta}{1-\alpha}} P_E(t)^{\frac{\alpha}{\alpha-1}}\right]^{(-\gamma)} \end{aligned} \tag{17}$$

Moreover the smooth pasting condition implies that the central planner invests $dK(t)$ during the period dt for an energy price level such that the variation in the value of the economy is smooth:

$$\frac{\partial(dV)}{\partial(P_E)} = \frac{\partial(dV^c)}{\partial(P_E)} + \frac{\partial(dV^f)}{\partial(P_E)} = 0 \Leftrightarrow$$

$$\begin{aligned} &\tfrac{A^{(1-\gamma)}}{\delta^*}\tfrac{\beta}{(1-\alpha)}\tfrac{\alpha(1-\gamma)}{(\alpha-1)} P_E(t)^{\frac{\alpha(1-\gamma)}{\alpha-1}-1} K^*(t)^{\frac{\beta(1-\gamma)}{1-\alpha}-1} \\ &+B_1'(K^*(t))\nu_1 P_E(t)^{\nu_1-1} = \tfrac{\alpha(-\gamma)}{\alpha-1} A^{(-\gamma)} K^*(t)^{\frac{\beta(-\gamma)}{1-\alpha}} P_E(t)^{\frac{\alpha(-\gamma)}{\alpha-1}-1} \end{aligned} \tag{18}$$

The resolution of this system with two equations and two unknown variables (the value of the option to invest and the desired capital stock) allows us to get:

$$K_d^*(t) = \left[\frac{A}{\delta^*}\frac{\beta}{1-\alpha} P_E(t)^{\frac{\alpha}{\alpha-1}}\left(1 - \frac{\alpha}{(\alpha-1)\nu_1 + \gamma\alpha}\right)\right]^{\frac{1-\alpha}{1-\alpha-\beta}} \tag{19}$$

where $\delta^* = \delta - \frac{1}{2}\frac{\alpha(1-\gamma)(1-\alpha\gamma)}{(\alpha-1)^2} > 0$ and $\nu_1 < 0$. The desired capital existence condition is thus:

$$(1-\gamma)/\nu_1 > (\alpha-1)/\alpha$$

This requires the cash-flow $(AK(t)^{\beta/(1-\alpha)}P_E(t)^{\alpha/(\alpha-1)})$ not to be a too convex function of the energy price. Notice that if $\gamma > 1$ (note that it is largely admitted as far as the relative risk aversion coefficient is concerned but recall that we do not know whether here γ stands for the risk aversion or for the intertemporal elasticity of substitution), this condition is not binding.

Uncertainty affects the desired capital stock through ν_1 and δ^*. Moreover the preferences parameters, that would not appear in the expression of the optimal capital in a determinist world, here affect $K_d^*(t)$. We also get:

$$\begin{aligned} &B_1'(K(t)) = \\ &A^{\frac{(\alpha-1)\nu_1}{\alpha}}\left[\tfrac{\beta}{\delta^*(1-\alpha)}\right]^{\gamma-\frac{(1-\alpha)\nu_1}{\alpha}}\left(1 - \tfrac{\alpha}{(\alpha-1)\nu_1+\gamma\alpha}\right)^{-(1-\gamma)-\frac{(1-\alpha)\nu_1}{\alpha}} \\ &\times\left(\tfrac{\alpha}{(1-\alpha)\nu_1-\gamma\alpha}\right)K(t)^{(-\gamma)+\frac{(1-\alpha-\beta)\nu_1}{\alpha}} \end{aligned} \tag{20}$$

Since $\left(\frac{\alpha}{(1-\alpha)\nu_1-\gamma\alpha}\right) < 0$ whatever the parameters values, one may check that $B_1'(K(t)) < 0$, *i.e.* the option value to invest in the future is a decreasing function of the installed capital stock. Moreover $B_1(K(t))$ is the integral of the expression we got for $B_1'(K(t))$, which converges as soon as:

$$(1-\gamma)/\nu_1 > \frac{\alpha+\beta-1}{\alpha} \tag{21}$$

This is a bit more restrictive than $(1-\gamma)/\nu_1 > (\alpha-1)/\alpha$, that has already been assumed. If the integral of $B_1'(K(t))$ converges, the expression for $B_1K(t))$ is positive, that is the option to invest in the future $(B_1(K(t))P_E(t)^{\nu_1})$ is positive:

$$\begin{aligned} &B_1(K(t)) = \\ &\frac{A^{\frac{(\alpha-1)\nu_1}{\alpha}}}{\frac{(1-\alpha-\beta)\nu_1}{\alpha}+(1-\gamma)}\left[\frac{\beta}{\delta^*(1-\alpha)}\right]^{\gamma-\frac{(1-\alpha)\nu_1}{\alpha}} \\ &\times\left(1-\frac{\alpha}{(\alpha-1)\nu_1+\gamma\alpha}\right)^{-(1-\gamma)-\frac{(1-\alpha)\nu_1}{\alpha}} \\ &\times\left(\frac{\alpha}{(1-\alpha)\nu_1-\alpha\gamma}\right)K(t)^{(1-\gamma)+\frac{(1-\alpha-\beta)\nu_1}{\alpha}} > 0 \end{aligned} \tag{22}$$

The desired capital stock is again a "power" function of the energy price and thus follows a geometric Brownian motion. Since investment is irreversible, the effective capital stock is the same as the desired capital stock only when the energy price falls below its historically lowest level and thus, does not follow a geometric Brownian motion. Nevertheless, one may determine its expected long-term level and its long-term rate of growth.

4.4 Optimal expected long-term capital stock

Using the expression for the desired capital stock, one gets:

$$A\frac{\beta}{1-\alpha}P_E(t)^{\frac{\alpha}{\alpha-1}}K_d^*(t)^{\frac{\beta}{1-\alpha}-1} = c \tag{23}$$

with $c = \delta^*\left(1+\frac{\alpha}{\nu_1(\alpha-1)-\alpha(1-\gamma)}\right)$.

The optimal decisions of the central planner consists in preventing the marginal cash-flow (noted $cf(t)$) from exceeding the value c. Finally, $cf(t)$ follows a geometric Brownian motion regulated by c (which is a reflecting barrier), with a trend $M = \frac{\alpha}{\alpha-1}\left(\frac{\alpha}{\alpha-1}-1\right)\frac{\sigma^2}{2}$ and a standard deviation $\Sigma = \sqrt{\left(\frac{\alpha}{\alpha-1}\right)^2\sigma^2}$. One may deduce that the process $ln(cf(t)) = \epsilon(t)$ follows an arithmetic Brownian motion with a reflecting barrier in $(ln(c))$, with a trend $(M - \Sigma^2/2)$ and a standard deviation Σ. The trend of this process is positive which implies that it exhibits an ergodic distribution (see also Dixit et Pindyck, 1994, p.372). The conditional density of the distribution of the process $\epsilon(t)$ given the observed energy price is thus:

$$f(\epsilon(t)) = \lambda e^{\lambda(\epsilon(t) - ln(c))} \tag{24}$$

with $\lambda = \frac{2M}{\Sigma^2} - 1 = \frac{1-\alpha}{\alpha}$.

Once the density of $\epsilon(t)$ is known, a variable change allows to get the conditional density of the capital distribution (see also Bertola, 1998, and Bentolila et Bertola, 1990):

$$g(K(t)) = \frac{-1}{z'(\epsilon(t))} f(\epsilon(t)) = \frac{-1}{z'(z^{-1}(K(t)))} f(z^{-1}(K(t))) \tag{25}$$

where $K(t) = z(\epsilon(t)) = \left[e^{-\epsilon(t)} A \frac{\beta}{1-\alpha} P_E(t)^{\frac{\alpha}{\alpha-1}}\right]^{\frac{1-\alpha}{1-\alpha-\beta}}$

One may deduce:

$$g(K(t)) = \frac{1-\alpha-\beta}{\alpha} K(t)^{\frac{\beta-1}{\alpha}} K^{*\frac{1-\alpha-\beta}{\alpha}} \tag{26}$$

where K_d^* is the desired capital stock. Assuming $\frac{1-\alpha-\beta}{\alpha} > 1$ (the integral is then converging), the expected long-term capital stock is then:

$$K_{LT} = E_t\left[K(LT)/P_E(t)\right] = \int_{K_d^*}^{+\infty} g(K(t)).K(t) \quad dK$$

$$= \int_{K^*}^{+\infty} \frac{1-\alpha-\beta}{\alpha} K(t)^{\frac{\alpha+\beta-1}{\alpha}} K_d^{*\frac{1-\alpha \ \ \beta}{\alpha}} dK(t)$$

$$= \frac{1-\alpha-\beta}{1-2\alpha-\beta} K_d^* \tag{27}$$

with $\frac{1-\alpha-\beta}{1-2\alpha-\beta} > 0$. Of course, we find $K_{LT} > K_d^*$ (there exists an over accumulation). Uncertainty affects in the same way K_d^* and K_{LT}, but the size of this effect is greater for K_{LT} than for K_d^*.

Moreover, the fluctuations of the expected long-term capital stock are similar to those of the desired capital stock. It could be shown (see Pommeret, 2000) that these fluctuations are also similar to that which would appear if investment were reversible. The evolution of the other economic variables can be found in appendix 2.

4.5 The transversality condition

The transversality condition is:

$$\lim_{t\to\infty} E_0\left[V(K(t), P_E(t))e^{-\delta t}\right] = 0 \tag{28}$$

A sufficient condition for it to be satisfied is:

$$\frac{E_t\left[dV_{LT}(K(t), P_E(t))e^{-\delta t}\right]}{V_{LT}(K(t), P_E(t))} < 0$$

where V_{LT} is the expected long-term value of the program. We show (see appendix 3) that V_{LT} has the form: $V(t) = ZP_E(t)^{\frac{\alpha(1-\gamma)}{\alpha+\beta-1}}$ where Z is a constant, and a sufficient condition for the transversality condition to be satisfied is thus:

$$\delta > \frac{\alpha(1-\gamma)}{(\alpha+\beta-1)}\left(\frac{\alpha(1-\gamma)}{(\alpha+\beta-1)} - 1\right)\frac{\sigma^2}{2}$$

5. The effect of uncertainty on the optimal capital stock

Proposition 2 *If $1 < \gamma < 1/\alpha$, the total effect of uncertainty in a general equilibrium is non ambiguous. The direction of this effect is the same as in partial equilibrium under monopolistic competition: uncertainty reduces the optimal desired stock of capital.*

If $\gamma > 1/\alpha$, the effect of uncertainty remains ambiguous and there may exist plausible parameters values for which the stronger the uncertainty the larger the optimal desired stock of capital. This reverses the result that would have been obtained in partial equilibrium under monopolistic competition.

Uncertainty affects the desired capital stock at two different levels, first through the option value to invest in the future and second through the adjusted discount rate.

First, uncertainty affects δ^*, the time preference rate, which is adjusted to take account of uncertainty. We have already seen that $\delta^* = \delta - \alpha(1-\gamma)/(\alpha-1)EC$ where EC is the certainty equivalent of the energy price rate of growth with:

$$\frac{\partial EC}{\partial \sigma^2} > 0 \quad if \quad \gamma > \frac{1}{\alpha}$$

$$\frac{\partial EC}{\partial \sigma^2} < 0 \quad if \quad \gamma < \frac{1}{\alpha}$$

An increase in this certainty equivalent generates an income effect (which encourages investment) and a substitution effect (which reduces investment). If the agent is not very reluctant to intertemporal substitution ($1/\gamma > 1$), the substitution effect prevails and the desired capital stock is smaller. Finally, the desired capital stock is larger (*resp.* smaller) if uncertainty is stronger as soon as $\gamma < 1$ or $\gamma > 1/\alpha$ (*resp.* $1 < \gamma < 1/\alpha$).

Moreover, we have seen that the option value to invest in the future is also affected by uncertainty. Indeed, a stronger uncertainty increases this option value which in turn reduces the marginal value of capital and generates a smaller desired capital stock.

The total effect depends on the value of the preferences parameters. The different effects of uncertainty are summed up into Table 1 below. We recall that an increase in the option value to invest reduces the desired capital stock.

Table 1. Effects of uncertainty on $K_d^*(t)$

	$\gamma < 1$	$1 < \gamma < 1/\alpha$	$\gamma > 1/\alpha$
Effect on the desired capital through the adjusted time preference rate	+	-	+
Effect on the option value to invest in the future	+	+	+
Total effect on the desired capital stock $K_d^*(t)$	?	-	?

Note: The notation ? indicates that the total effect is ambiguous.

One may notice that it is only possible to identify without ambiguity the total effect of uncertainty on a restricted range for γ ($1 < \gamma < 1/\alpha$). The intuition (which would be confirmed by the use a utility function disentangling between risk aversion and intertemporal elasticity of substitution, see Pommeret, 2000) is the following: if the representative agent is not very reluctant to intertemporal substitution ($1/\gamma > 1$) and has a "reasonable" risk aversion ($\gamma < 1/\alpha$), a stronger uncertainty urges the central planner to install more capital. When $\gamma > 1/\alpha$, even if the effect of uncertainty remains ambiguous for any value for the model parameters, there may be plausible cases for which uncertainty increases then the desired stock of capital, as will be shown in a numerical example below.

Using the plausible parameters values proposed in Table 2 below, Figure 1 illustrates the effect of uncertainty on the desired capital stock. The capital dynamics if the central planner ignores uncertainty (but observes each energy price realization) is depicted in thin line; the capital dynamics if the central planner takes uncertainty into account is depicted in thick line.

Table 2. Parameters values

γ_1	γ_2	α	β	δ	σ
2	8	0.15	0.3	0.02	0.1

The sufficient condition for the transversality condition to be verified is satisfied by these parameters values. Moreover, for these parameters values, the value of the program and the values of the expected long-term variables exist (γ_1 is such that $1 < \gamma < 1/\alpha$, γ_2 is such that $\gamma > 1/\alpha$).

For the parameters values corresponding to combination 1 ($\gamma = \gamma_1$), the optimal capital stock represents 70% of the stock the central planner would have installed if she had ignored uncertainty. In the case of combination 2 ($\gamma = \gamma_2$), the central planner installs 100% more capital if she takes uncertainty into account! Thus, starting from plausible values for the economy parameters, uncertainty may favor or reduce the desired stock of capital depending on the value of a preference parameter with respect to that of a technological parameter.

Analyzing the effect of uncertainty in a partial equilibrium framework, with a firm producing according to the same technology as the one considered in this paper would of course lead to a different result (see Pommeret, 2000): energy price uncertainty always urges the firm to desire less capital. Therefore the extension of the study to a general equilibrium framework allows to exhibit cases for which the reverse relationship between uncertainty and the desired level of capital prevails.

We have already noticed that the effects of uncertainty on the expected long-term cash-flow, on the expected long-term capital and on the desired capital play in the same direction even if they are of different sizes. Thus, the analysis above is still valid for the expected long-term capital and the expected long-term cash-flow.

Figure 1. Desired capital stock under uncertainty

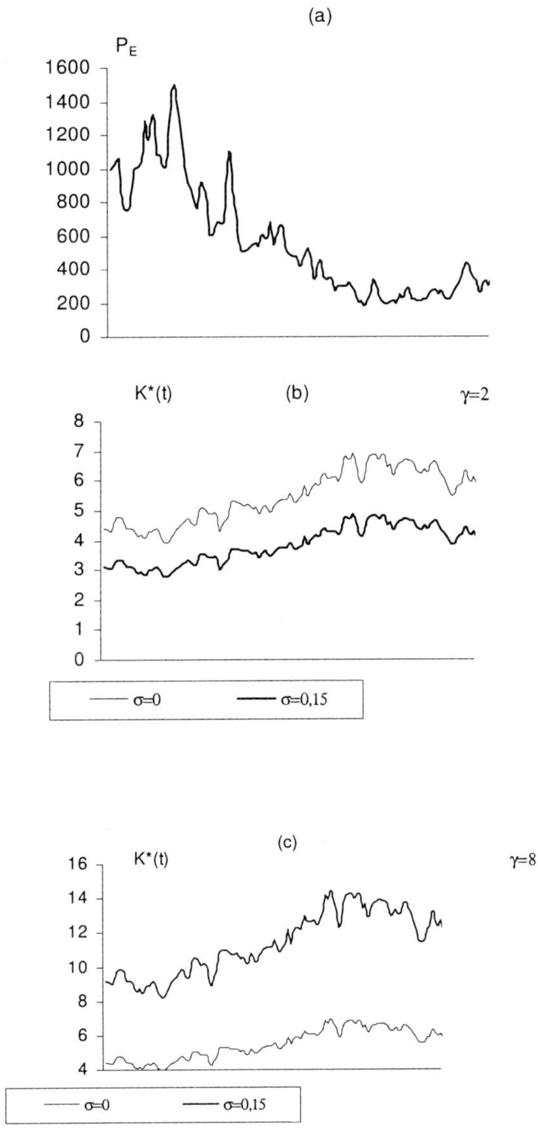

6. Illustration of the economy evolution

The variables of the model are simulated using two different values for γ. We use the parameters values given in Table 2 above.

Figures 2 and 3 illustrate the dynamics of the economic variables respectively under the assumptions $\gamma = \gamma_1$ and $\gamma = \gamma_2$. They show the dynamics of the energy price (part (a) of the figures), of the optimal capital stock (part (b) of the figures) and of the cash-flow (part (c) of the figures). The optimal evolution of the economic variables if the central planner ignores uncertainty (while observing the energy price realization) is depicted by a thin lines and thick lines show these evolutions if the central planner takes uncertainty into account.

One may check that under the assumption of a relative risk aversion greater than unity but less than $1/\alpha$ (Figure 2), the optimal capital stock and the cash-flow are at each time smaller under uncertainty. On the contrary, if the relative risk aversion is greater than $1/\alpha$ (Figure 3), uncertainty may lead to a larger optimal capital stock.

7. Conclusion

This paper has considered uncertainty transmission to the optimal capital stock in a general equilibrium framework. The representative agent preferences are then crucial for the effect of uncertainty on the optimal capital stock.

Since investment is irreversible, uncertainty affects the desired capital stock through two distinct channels. First, uncertainty modifies the option value to invest in the future, and the direction of this effect is always the same: a larger uncertainty increases this option value. Second, uncertainty affects the rate at which the sum of the instantaneous utilities are discounted; the direction of this effect is governed by complex relationships between preferences and technological parameters. Nevertheless, the total effect of uncertainty especially depends on the value of the relative risk aversion coefficient with respect to that of a technological parameter. *If investment is irreversible, uncertainty may increase the optimal capital stock in the economy if the relative risk aversion coefficient is sufficiently large.* Indeed in such a case, the effect of uncertainty through agent's preferences that encourages savings prevails on that of irreversibility which discourages capital acquisition.

Nevertheless intuition suggests that the agent's behaviour with respect to the intertemporal substitution should affect the transmission of uncertainty to optimal decisions. In fact, isolating the effect of the risk aversion from the one arising from the intertemporal substitution seems to be a good idea as soon as stochastic models are considered. It

Figure 2. Uncertainty and dynamics of the energy price, of the optimal capital stock and of the cash-flow: $1 < \gamma < 1/\alpha$

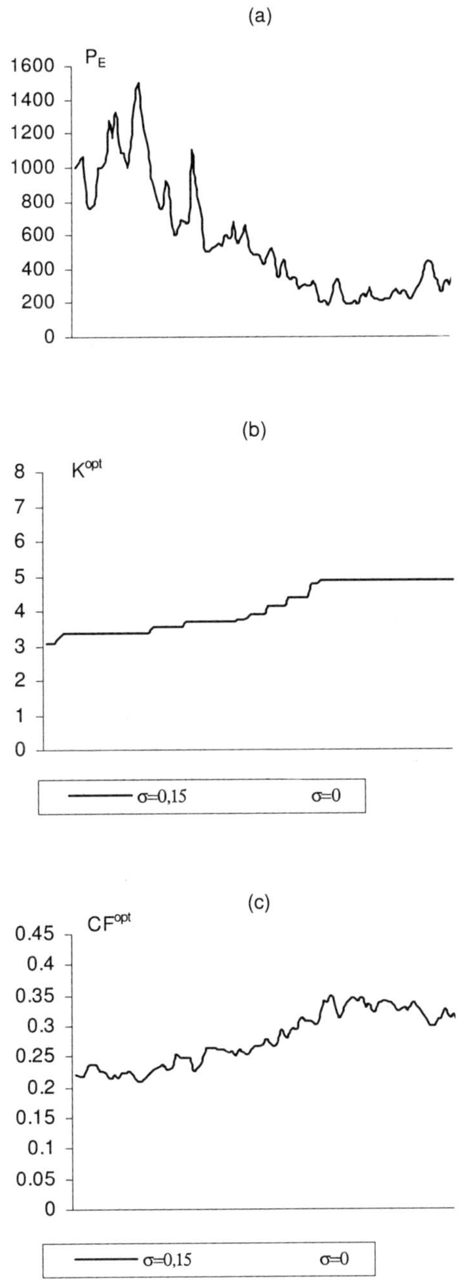

Figure 3. Uncertainty and dynamics of the energy price, of the optimal capital stock and of the cash-flow: $\gamma > 1/\alpha$

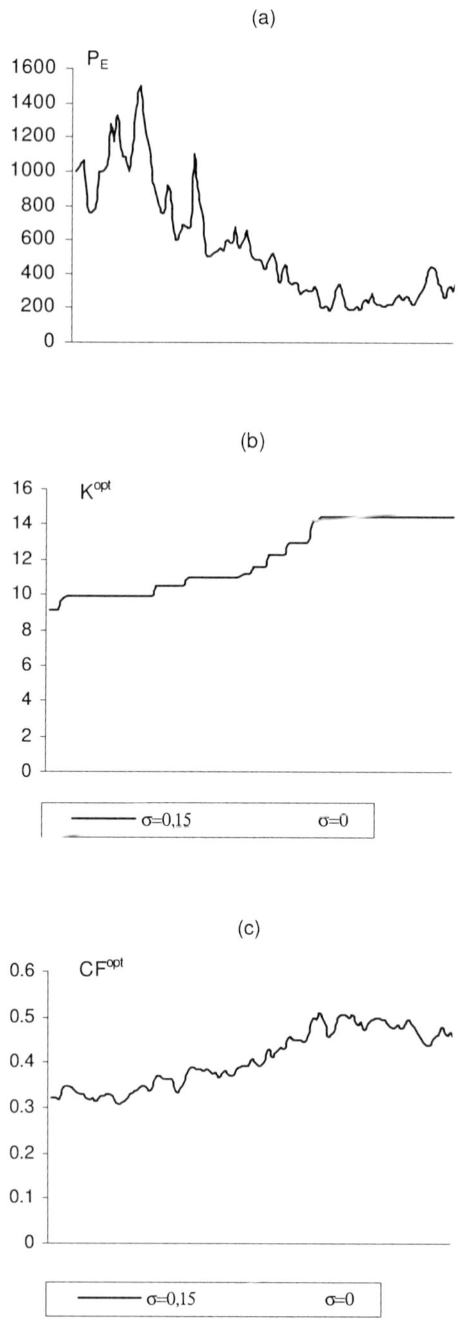

requires the use of a more sophisticated utility function, such as a recursive utility function as proposed by Kreps and Porteus, 1978. Such a utility function would then allow to analyze the role of each preferences parameter in the uncertainty transmission.

Appendix

Determination of the particular solution of the differential equation (7).

This solution is postulated of the form:

$$W(t) = \frac{B}{(1-\gamma)} K(t)^{\frac{(1-\gamma)\beta}{1-\alpha}} P_E(t)^{\frac{\alpha(1-\gamma)}{\alpha-1}}$$

Replacing $V(t)$ by this expression in the differential equation (7), one gets:

$$\begin{aligned} \tfrac{B}{(1-\gamma)} K(t)^{\frac{(1-\gamma)\beta}{1-\alpha}} P_E(t)^{\frac{\alpha(1-\gamma)}{\alpha-1}} &= \tfrac{A^{(1-\gamma)}}{(1-\gamma)} K(t)^{\frac{(1-\gamma)\beta}{1-\alpha}} P_E(t)^{\frac{\alpha(1-\gamma)}{\alpha-1}} dt \\ +e^{-\delta dt} \tfrac{B}{(1-\gamma)} K(t)^{\frac{(1-\gamma)\beta}{1-\alpha}} E_t \left[P_E(t+dt)^{\frac{\alpha(1-\gamma)}{\alpha-1}} \right] \end{aligned} \tag{A.1}$$

with

$$\begin{aligned} E_t \left[P_E(t+dt)^{\frac{\alpha(1-\gamma)}{\alpha-1}} \right] &= E_t \left(dP_E(t)^{\frac{\alpha(1-\gamma)}{\alpha-1}} \right) + P_E(t)^{\frac{\alpha(1-\gamma)}{\alpha-1}} \\ &= P_E(t)^{\frac{\alpha(1-\gamma)}{\alpha-1}} \left[1 + \frac{1}{2} \frac{\alpha(1-\gamma)}{\alpha-1} \left(\frac{\alpha(1-\gamma)}{\alpha-1} - 1 \right) \sigma^2 dt \right] \end{aligned}$$

Replacing this into equation (A.1), and using a limited expansion, we have:

$$\begin{aligned} \tfrac{B}{(1-\gamma)} K(t)^{\frac{(1-\gamma)\beta}{1-\alpha}} P_E(t)^{\frac{\alpha(1-\gamma)}{\alpha-1}} &= \tfrac{A^{(1-\gamma)}}{(1-\gamma)} K(t)^{\frac{(1-\gamma)\beta}{1-\alpha}} P_E(t)^{\frac{\alpha(1-\gamma)}{\alpha-1}} dt \\ +(1-\delta dt) \tfrac{B}{(1-\gamma)} K(t)^{\frac{(1-\gamma)\beta}{1-\alpha}} P_E(t)^{\frac{\alpha(1-\gamma)}{\alpha-1}} &\left[1 + \tfrac{1}{2} \tfrac{\alpha(1-\gamma)}{\alpha-1} \left(\tfrac{\alpha(1-\gamma)}{\alpha-1} - 1 \right) \sigma^2 dt \right] \end{aligned}$$

$$\Leftrightarrow B = A^{(1-\gamma)} dt + B \left[1 + \frac{1}{2} \frac{\alpha(1-\gamma)}{\alpha-1} \left(\frac{\alpha(1-\gamma)}{\alpha-1} - 1 \right) \sigma^2 dt \right] - \delta B dt \tag{A.2}$$

After some simplifications, one deduces the constant B expression:

$$B = \frac{A^{(1-\gamma)}}{\delta - \frac{1}{2} \frac{\alpha(1-\gamma)(1-\alpha\gamma)}{(\alpha-1)^2} \sigma^2} = \frac{A^{(1-\gamma)}}{\delta^*} \tag{A.3}$$

which allows to get the expression of the particular solution of the differential equation.

Evolution of the other economic variables

As soon as the irreversible nature of investment is binding, the cash-flow is not only a function of the observed energy price but also of the installed capital stock; one may then get the expression of the expected long-term cash-flow, using a variable change and following the same reasoning as for the expected long-term capital stock. The conditional density of the cash-flow is:

$$h(CF(t)) = \frac{-1}{w'(\epsilon_t)} f(\epsilon(t)) = \frac{-1}{w'(w^{-1}(CF(t)))} f(w^{-1}(CF(t))) \tag{A.4}$$

with: $CF(t) = w(\epsilon(t)) = \left[e^{-\epsilon(t)} A^{\frac{\alpha-1}{\beta}} \frac{\beta}{1-\alpha} P_E^{\frac{\alpha}{\beta}}\right]^{\frac{\beta}{1-\alpha-\beta}}$. One finally gets:

$$h(CF(t)) = \frac{(1-\alpha-\beta)(1-\alpha)}{\alpha\beta} CF(t)^{\frac{(\alpha+\beta-1)(1-\alpha)}{\alpha\beta}-1} CF_d^{*\frac{(1-\alpha-\beta)(1-\alpha)}{\alpha\beta}} \tag{A.5}$$

where CF_d^* is the cash-flow when the optimal capital is equal to the desired capital. Assuming $(1-\alpha-\beta)/\alpha\beta > (1-\alpha)$ to ensure the integral convergence, the expected long-term cash-flow is thus:

$$CF_{LT} = \int_{CF_d^*}^{\infty} h(CF(t)).CF(t) \quad dCF(t)$$

$$= \int_{CF_d^*}^{\infty} \frac{(1-\alpha-\beta)(1-\alpha)}{\alpha\beta} CF(t)^{\frac{(\alpha+\beta-1)(1-\alpha)}{\alpha\beta}} CF_d^{*\frac{(1-\alpha-\beta)(1-\alpha)}{\alpha\beta}} dCF(t)$$

$$= \frac{(1-\alpha-\beta)(1-\alpha)}{(1-\alpha-\beta)(1-\alpha)-\alpha\beta} CF_d^*(t) \tag{A.6}$$

with $(1-\alpha-\beta)(1-\alpha)-\alpha\beta > 0$. The direction of the effect of uncertainty (on energy price) on the expected long-term cash-flow is the same as the one of its effect on CF_d^*, but the size of this effect is larger. Evolutions of the expected long-term cash-flow, of CF_d^* and of the cash-flow when investment is reversible (for the latter case, see Pommeret, 2000) are the same.

Moreover, the consumption $C(t)$ depends on the realized investment (see program (6)):

$$C(t)dt = AK^{\frac{\beta}{1-\alpha}} P_E(t)^{\frac{\alpha}{\alpha-1}} dt - dK(t) \tag{A.7}$$

Thus, when the effective capital and the desired capital are the same, the expression of consumption during dt is:

$$C_d^*(t)dt = \left[\frac{\delta^*(1-\alpha)}{\beta\left(1-\frac{\alpha}{(\alpha-1)\nu_1+\alpha\gamma}\right)} - \frac{1}{2}\frac{\alpha(1-\beta)}{(\alpha+\beta-1)^2}\sigma^2\right] K_d^*(t)dt - \frac{\alpha}{\alpha+\beta-1} K_d^*(t)\sigma dz_t \tag{A.8}$$

$$\Rightarrow E_t\left[\frac{C_d^*(t)dt}{K_d^*(t)}\right] = \left[\frac{\delta^*(1-\alpha)}{\beta\left(1-\frac{\alpha}{(\alpha-1)\nu_1+\alpha\gamma}\right)} - \frac{1}{2}\frac{\alpha(1-\beta)}{(\alpha+\beta-1)^2}\sigma^2\right] dt \tag{A.9}$$

When irreversibility becomes binding, there is no investment and the consumption is equal to the cash-flow. Moreover, the expected long-term consumption is as follows:

$$C_{LT}dt = CF_{LT}dt - dK_{LT} = \frac{(1-\alpha-\beta)(1-\alpha)}{(1-\alpha-\beta)(1-\alpha)-\alpha\beta} CF_d^* dt - \frac{(1-\alpha-\beta)}{1-2\alpha-\beta} dK_d^* \tag{A.10}$$

Expected long-term value of the program

We recall that the value at each time is:

$$V(t) = O(K(t), P_E(t)) + PVU(K(t), P_E(t))$$

where $O(K(t), P_E(t))$ is the option value to invest in the future and $PVU(K(t), P_E(t))$ is the present value of the sum of the instantaneous utilities and with:

$$O(K(t),P_E(t)) = XK(t)^{(1-\gamma)+\frac{(1-\alpha-\beta)\nu_1}{\alpha}}P_E(t)^{\nu_1}$$

where X is a constant and

$$PVU(K(t),P_E(t)) = \frac{A^{(1-\gamma)}}{\delta^*(1-\gamma)}K(t)^{\frac{(1-\gamma)\beta}{(1-\alpha)}}P_E(t)^{\frac{(1-\gamma)\alpha}{\alpha-1}}$$

In this appendix, we determine O_{LT} and PVU_{LT} from which we will deduce $V_{LT}=O_{LT}+PVU_{LT}$.

Determination of O_{LT}. A variable change allows to get the conditional density function of $O(K(t),P_E(t))$ using that of $\epsilon(t)$ (see equation(24)):

$$l\left(O(K(t),P_E(t))\right) = \frac{1}{y'(\epsilon(t))}f(\epsilon(t)) = \frac{1}{y'\left(y^{-1}\left(O(K(t),P_E(t))\right)\right)}f\left(y^{-1}\left(O(K(t),P_E(t))\right)\right)$$

with $O(K(t),P_E(t)) = y(\epsilon(t)) = \left[e^{-\epsilon(t)}X'P_E^Z\right]^{\frac{(\alpha(1-\gamma)+(1-\alpha-\beta)\nu_1)(\alpha-1)}{\alpha(\alpha+\beta-1)}}$ where X' and Z are constant. One deduces:

$$\begin{aligned} l\left(O(K(t),P_E(t))\right) &= \frac{\alpha+\beta-1}{\alpha(1-\gamma)+(1-\alpha-\beta)\nu_1}O^{*\frac{1-\alpha-\beta}{\alpha(1-\gamma)+(1-\alpha-\beta)\nu_1}} \\ &\times O(K(t),P_E(t))^{\frac{\alpha+\beta-1}{\alpha(1-\gamma)+(1-\alpha-\beta)\nu_1}-1} \end{aligned}$$

where $O^*$is the option value if the optimal capital is equal to the desired capital. We finally get:

$$\begin{aligned} O_{LT} &= \int_0^{O^*} l\left(O(K(t),P_E(t))\right).O(K(t),P_E(t))\,dO \\ &= \frac{\alpha+\beta-1}{(\alpha+\beta-1)+\alpha(1-\gamma)+(1-\alpha-\beta)\nu_1}O^* \end{aligned}$$

Since $\alpha(1-\gamma)+(1-\alpha-\beta)\nu_1<0$, one gets $0<O_{LT}<O^*$.

Determination of PVU_{LT}. In the same way as for O_{LT}, a variable change allows to get the conditional density function of $PVU(K(t),P_E(t))$ depending on the value of the intertemporal elasticity of substitution relative to unity:

$$\begin{aligned} m_1(PVU(K(t),P_E(t))) &= \frac{-1}{u_1'(\epsilon(t))}f(\epsilon(t)) \\ &= \frac{-1}{u_1'\left(u_1^{-1}\left(PVU(K(t),P_E(t))\right)\right)} \\ &\times\ f\left(u_1^{-1}\left(PVU(K(t),P_E(t))\right)\right) \\ \text{with } PVU(K(t),P_E(t)) &= u_1(\epsilon(t)) = \left[e^{-\epsilon(t)}\frac{\beta A}{(1-\alpha)}Z\right]^{\frac{\beta(1-\gamma)}{1-\alpha-\beta}} \quad \text{if}\gamma<1 \end{aligned}$$

$$m_2(-PVU(K(t),P_E(t))) = \frac{1}{u_2'(\epsilon(t))}f(\epsilon(t))$$

$$
\begin{aligned}
& = \frac{1}{u_2'\left(u_2^{-1}\left(-PVU(K(t),P_E(t))\right)\right)} \\
& \times\ f\left(u_2^{-1}\left(-PVU(K(t),P_E(t))\right)\right) \\
\text{with} - PVU(K(t),P_E(t)) & = u_2(\epsilon(t)) = \left[e^{-\epsilon(t)}\frac{\beta A}{(1-\alpha)}Z\right]^{\frac{\beta(1-\gamma)}{1-\alpha-\beta}} \quad \text{if } \gamma > 1
\end{aligned}
$$

We deduce

$$
\begin{aligned}
& m_1(PVU(K(t),P_E(t))) \\
= \ & \frac{(1-\alpha-\beta)(1-\alpha)}{(1-\gamma)\alpha\beta} PVU^{*\frac{(1-\alpha-\beta)(1-\alpha)}{(1-\gamma)\alpha\beta}} PVU(K(t),P_E(t))^{\frac{(\alpha+\beta-1)(1-\alpha)}{(1-\gamma)\alpha\beta}-1} \\
& m_2(-PVU(K(t),P_E(t))) \\
= \ & \frac{(\alpha+\beta-1)(1-\alpha)}{(1-\gamma)\alpha\beta}(-PVU^*)^{\frac{(1-\alpha-\beta)(1-\alpha)}{(1-\gamma)\alpha\beta}} (-PVU(K(t),P_E(t)))^{\frac{(\alpha+\beta-1)(1-\alpha)}{(1-\gamma)\alpha\beta}-1}
\end{aligned}
$$

where PVU^* is the value of the present value of the sum of the instantaneous utilities when the optimal capital is equal to the desired capital. Assuming that $(1-\gamma) < \frac{(1-\alpha)(1-\alpha-\beta)}{\alpha\beta}$ (the integral is thus converging) we finally get: :

$$
\begin{aligned}
PVU_{LT1} & = \int_{PVU^*}^{+\infty} m_1(PVU(K(t),P_E(t))).PVU(K(t),P_E(t))\, dPVU \\
& = \frac{(\alpha+\beta-1)(1-\alpha)}{(1-\alpha)(\alpha+\beta-1)+(1-\gamma)\alpha\beta} PVU^* \\
-PVU_{LT2} & = \int_0^{-PVU^*} m_2(-PVU(K(t),P_E(t))).(-PVU(K(t),P_E(t)))\, d(-PVU) \\
& = \frac{(\alpha+\beta-1)(1-\alpha)}{(1-\alpha)(\alpha+\beta-1)+(1-\gamma)\alpha\beta}(-PVU^*)
\end{aligned}
$$

If $\gamma < 1$, we have $PVU_{LT1} > PVU^*$and if $\gamma > 1$, we have $PVU_{LT2} > PVU^*$.

Determination of V_{LT}. One may easily show that O^* and PVU^* are of the form: $O^* = xP_E^{\frac{\alpha(1-\gamma)}{\alpha+\beta-1}}$ and $PVU^* = x'P_E^{\frac{\alpha(1-\gamma)}{\alpha+\beta-1}}$ where x and x' are constant. One may deduce the form of the expected long-term value function: $V_{LT}=O_{LT} + PVU_{LT} = x'''P_E^{\frac{\alpha(1-\gamma)}{\alpha+\beta-1}}$, whatever γ.

References

Arrow K. and Fisher A. (1974). Environmental preservation, uncertainty and irreversibility. *Quarterly Journal of Economics*, 88:312-319.

Bertola G. (1994). Flexibility, investment, and growth. *Journal of Monetary Economics*, 98(5):103-125.

Bertola G. (1998). Irreversible investment. *Research in Economics*, 52:3-37.

Bertola G. and Bentolila S. (1990). Firing costs and labour demand: how bad is Eurosclerosis ? *The Review of Economic Studies*, 57: 381-402.

Brennan M.J. and Schwartz E.S. (1985). Evaluating natural resource investments. *Journal of Business*, 57:135-157.

Coleman W. (1997). The behavior of interests rates in a general equilibrium multi-sector model with irreversible investment. *Macroeconomic Dynamics*, 1: 206-227.

Dixit A. and Pindyck R. (1994). *Investment Under Uncertainty.* Princeton University Press.

Dow J. and Olson L. (1992). Irreversibility and the behavior of aggregate stochastic growth models. *Journal of Economic Dynamics and Control*, 16:207-224.

Epaulard A. and Pommeret A. (1998). Recursive utility, growth, and the welfare cost of volatility. *Working paper ERASME.*

Gilchrist S. and Williams J. (1998). Putty-clay and investment: a steady-state analysis. *Working Paper*, Boston University and NBER.

Henry C. (1974). Investment decisions under uncertainty: the irreversibility effect. *American Economic Review*, 64:1106-1012.

Kimball M. (1990). Precautionary saving in the small and in the large. *Econometrica*, 58(1):53-73.

Kreps D. and Porteus E. (1978). Temporal resolution of uncertainty and dynamic choice theory. *Econometrica*, 46:185-200.

Lund D. (1992). Petroleum taxation under uncertainty-contingent claim analysis with an application to Norway. *Energy Economics*, 14:23-31.

MacDonald R. and Siegel D. (1986). The value of waiting to invest. *Quarterly Journal of Economics*, 101:707-727.

Merton R. (1969) Lifetime portfolio selection under uncertainty: the continuous-time case. *Review of Economics and Statistics*, 51: 247-257.

Merton R. (1971). Optimum consumption and portfolio rules in a continuous-time model. *Journal of Economic Theory*, 3(4): 373-413.

Olson L. (1989). Stochastic growth with irreversible investment. *Journal of Economic Theory*, 47: 101-129.

Pindyck R. (1981). The optimal production of an exhaustible resource when price is exogenous and stochastic. *Scandinavian Journal of Economics*, 83:277-288.

Pommeret A. (2000). Décisions irréversibles en incertitude et préférences des agents, le cas de l'incertitude sur le prix de l'énergie. Ph.D Thesis, Université Paris I Panthéon–Sorbonne.

Slade M. (1988). Grade selection under uncertainty: least cost last and other anomalies. *Journal Environmental Economics and Management*, 15:189-205.